BASIC DATA COMMUNICATIONS

BASIC DATA COMMUNICATIONS

A Comprehensive Overview

William J. Beyda

University of California Extension, Berkeley
International Business Machines Corporation

PRENTICE HALL, Englewood Cliffs, New Jersey 07632

Library of Congress Cataloging-in-Publication Data

Beyda, William J.
   Basic data communications.

   Bibliography: p.
   Includes index.
   1. Data transmission systems. I. Title.
TK5105.B48   1989   621.398'1   88-32251
ISBN 0-13-058421-5

Editorial/production supervision: *Edith Riker*
Cover design: *Bruce Kenselaar*
Cover illustration: *Jim Kinstrey*
Manufacturing buyer: *Mary Noonan*

To my parents

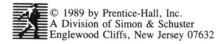 © 1989 by Prentice-Hall, Inc.
A Division of Simon & Schuster
Englewood Cliffs, New Jersey 07632

Printed in the United States of America

10 9 8 7 6 5 4 3 2 1

ISBN   0-13-058421-5

Prentice-Hall International (UK) Limited, *London*
Prentice-Hall of Australia Pty. Limited, *Sydney*
Prentice-Hall Canada Inc., *Toronto*
Prentice-Hall Hispanoamericana, S.A., *Mexico*
Prentice-Hall of India Private Limited, *New Delhi*
Prentice-Hall of Japan, Inc., *Tokyo*
Simon & Schuster Asia Pte. Ltd., *Singapore*
Editora Prentice-Hall do Brasil, Ltda., *Rio de Janeiro*

CONTENTS

PREFACE

After teaching many data communications classes, I was still not satisfied with the scope, clarity, and readability of available textbooks. Some textbooks were aimed at advanced electrical engineering students, while others covered only the business aspects of data communications. I sought to create a text that would be accessible to the novice, and at the same time challenging for the engineer or technical professional. Those desiring a broad overview can simply follow the body of this text, while the more advanced reader can examine concepts in detail inside the special shaded boxes.

Simply stated, I have tried to demystify data communications. I draw on practical examples to explain all technical concepts, as I have found this technique very successful in my teaching experience. This text introduces the language of data communications. It provides a practical understanding of all the relevant terminology, concepts, hardware, software, protocols, architectures, and other information necessary to make the reader literate in data communications. Current and future product offerings are discussed. By the end of the text, the reader should be able to make intelligent decisions on the appropriate design, purchase, integration, and use of data communications equipment and systems.

The text begins with a thorough introduction to telecommunications, which is essential in order to appreciate data communications hardware and software designs. The book then progresses logically, from the basic concepts of data communications, to transmission and interface standards, as well as data integrity and security. At that point, it is appropriate to discuss architectures and protocols to tie the components together, leading to a thorough presentation of different networks. The text concludes with a discussion of current and future trends in data communications, including an in-depth examination of standards currently being developed.

At the end of each chapter, I have provided a summary, as well as a list of newly introduced terms. Exercises are also included to help review the material. A thorough glossary of terms and acronyms, an index, and a topical bibliography, will ensure this book's usefulness as a reference tool long after any courses are completed.

The impact of continuously evolving technologies in this vital industry must not be overlooked. I have therefore focused on both fundamental concepts and practical applications, so that the reader can understand data communications today, and also be prepared to understand future advances in technology, products, and standards.

I believe I have succeeded in providing a clearer, well-balanced, and more practical approach to data communications.

ACKNOWLEDGMENTS

The efforts of a few, and the inspiration of many, have led to the successful completion of this book. Most of all, Barbara M. Beyda applied her considerable editorial skills to ensure the readability of this text. Joseph D. Beyda was a constant source of suggestions, as well as moral support.

Several professors during my academic years had a great impact on my current teaching style, as well as my desire to educate others. In particular, Ralph Gorin, Leonard Ortolano, Peter Rooney, Chuck Williams, Leatrice Yelman, and the late Keith Calkins, all played major roles in leading me to a career in engineering and technical education.

Though I left Stanford University with a strong academic and technical foundation, along with a B.S. in Electrical Engineering and an M.S. in Engineering Management, it was only upon entering the telecommunications industry that I acquired more practical knowledge. My colleagues at IBM/ROLM were especially helpful when I was first exploring data communications; Deborah Dodge, Chuck Drew, Robert Greil, William Schneckloth, and others too numerous to mention, helped spark my interest in this field, and inspired me to continue this specialty.

For several years I have been teaching an introductory class on data communications at University of California Extension, Berkeley. Each student has given me a new perspective on the field, and I am grateful for their insights. Their comments and questions planted the seed for this work. I would like to thank Richard Tsina, chairman of the Engineering Extension program, for his encouragement, and for recommending Prentice Hall to me; otherwise, this text might still be just an idea.

At Prentice Hall, Valerie Ashton and Karen Gettman have been a consistent source of support and Edie Riker's production expertise has been invaluable.

Finally, I would like to thank all of my family and friends, who understood when I said, ''Sorry, I'd love to join you, but I'm too busy writing this book.''

I appreciate the helpful comments from the reviewers: R. Kenneth Walter, Weber State College; Edward H. Nemeth, DeVry Institute of Technology, Decatur, Georgia; Russell C. Hollingworth, Tarrant County Junior College, Texas; Norbert Ludkey, City College of San Francisco; Donna Reese, University of Texas, Austin; Kenneth Yu, US Sprint, Burlingame, California; Ron Teemley, DeVry Institute of Technology, Irving, Texas.

BASIC DATA COMMUNICATIONS

1

OVERVIEW AND INTRODUCTION

In order to understand data communications, we should start with a few basic definitions. Communication is often defined as the exchange of information between two individuals using a common set of symbols, signs, or behavior. More specifically, telecommunications usually involves a significant distance between the individuals, and some electronic equipment for transmission and reception of the information. Finally, data communications requires that the communicating individuals or devices exchange data, or ones and zeroes. Typically, computers and related devices communicate in this manner.

Today, in the so-called "information age," more and more functions in our lives are performed by or with the help of computers. For example, most authors wouldn't even attempt to write a book today with just a typewriter. We have already become adjusted to computerized billings, automated teller machines, and even cars that remember when they're due for their next tune-up. It is only logical that with more and more of society's information stored on computers, we certainly will want to access much of this information and link many of our computers.

The term "data communications" often conjures up images of complex systems; one vendor's perfectly sound equipment is often unable to communicate with equally expensive counterparts from another vendor, because of seemingly insurmountable compatibility problems. Data communications need not be such a mystifying topic. After all, data communications really is nothing more than the transmission of ones and zeroes from one place to another. The complexity arises from the various means we use to transmit and receive those ones and zeroes, and what we do with them at the destination.

This book attempts to demystify data communications. In fact, half the battle in understanding data communications is getting through all of the jargon and acronyms. Therefore, this book introduces the language of data communications; it also provides a basic understanding of all the relevant terminology, concepts, hardware, software, protocols, architectures, and other information necessary to make the reader literate in data communications.

Many of the terms we use throughout this book are generic in nature. For example, there are thousands of terminals on the market, and what is labeled a smart terminal by one manufacturer may be called an automated workstation by another manufacturer. There is a wide variety of terminology in the data communications industry, just as in the auto industry, where there's no clear-cut definition of a "sports car". Throughout this book we will use definitions and examples that represent common industry usage and practice.

The information presented here should help put current and future industry product offerings in context. By providing a comprehensive overview of many topics, the book prepares the reader for further study of any particular subject, such as local area networks. Finally, the reader should be able to make intelligent decisions on the appropriate design, purchase, integration, and use of data communications equipment and systems.

A LOGICAL PROGRESSION

We present topics in a logical order. Our description of the following chapters may include terminology unfamiliar to some readers; all terms are explained in the respective chapters.

Chapter 2, Understanding Telecommunications, includes an overview of telecommunications, which is necessary to put data communications in the appropriate context. A basic understanding of telecommunications should help the reader appreciate the purpose and suitability of the different data communications hardware and software discussed in the rest of the book.

Different network topologies, the public network, signaling, divestiture, regulation, and call routing are all presented. Communications service options are compared, including common carrier services and customer-premises equipment.

Chapter 3, Basic Data Communications Concepts, lays the foundation upon which the rest of the book is built. Host computers and terminals are used to illustrate basic principles.

Common character codes are presented and compared. The differences between parallel and serial transmission, asynchronous and synchronous transmission, and simplex, half duplex, and full duplex transmission, are all analyzed.

Chapter 4, Data Interfaces and Transmission, discusses data transmission and interface standards. It analyzes in detail the methods used to connect terminals to host computers, whether the terminal is located 20 feet or 2000 miles away.

The ANSI, IEEE, EIA, ECSA, NBS, CCITT, and ISO standards organizations are described. The RS-232-C, RS-449, RS-422-A, and RS-423-A standards are compared. The chapter introduces digital and analog bandwidth, and examines different transmission media. Baseband transmission and broadband transmission are discussed, and various modulation methods are illustrated.

Chapter 5, Improving Data Communications Efficiency, explains how special devices can maximize the use of communications circuits and minimize the use of computer resources. While the devices described are not prerequisites for communications, they reduce costs and enhance performance, and are therefore widely used.

Front end processors, port sharing devices, remote intelligent controllers, line splitters, and multiplexers are described. Different multiplexing methods are compared, and data compression devices are explained.

Chapter 6, Data Integrity and Security, discusses means for preventing errors and protecting data. In any data communications network, there is the possibility of errors during transmission. Preventing or correcting such errors is often referred to as maintaining data integrity. Error detection and correction methods, such as echo checking, parity checking, cyclical parity, the Hamming code, various checksums, and the cyclical redundancy check, are all explained.

As computers take on a larger and larger share of business transactions, the need for data security becomes evident. Security goals and measures are explained, including historical and statistical logs, closed user groups, and encryption.

Chapter 7, Architectures and Protocols, explains how communications architectures and protocols enable host computers, terminals, front end processors, and other devices to communicate in an orderly manner by defining precise rules and methods for communications.

The chapter introduces the OSI model, along with examples of widely used protocols and architectures. SNA functions are discussed, and the classification of SNA components is presented. We explain polling and selecting, and compare ARQ methods. BSC and SDLC are presented as examples of byte-oriented and bit-oriented protocols, respectively. The functions of protocol and code converters are also analyzed.

Chapter 8, Data Transport Networks, describes packet switching and local area networks. Data transport networks connect a wide variety of devices located in the same building or across the world, providing the means for transmitting and receiving data.

Packet switching network nodes, IXCs, and PADs are explained. The X.25 standard, along with the related X.3, X.28, and X.29 standards, are presented. PSN routing and services are also described. Local area network topologies are compared, along with the various access methods. Contention and token passing are analyzed in detail, and the IEEE 802 standards are presented. Finally, internetworking applications involving gateways and bridges are described.

Chapter 9, Network Management, describes how harmony in a network can be maintained, ensuring consistent reliability and availability of the network, as well as timely transmission and routing of data.

The chapter introduces network management concepts, as well as specific network management tools. The key functions of network management are presented, and measures of availability, reliability, response time, and throughput are described. Different network management approaches are considered, and diagnostic methods are examined. Finally, the role of specialized test equipment is analyzed.

Chapter 10, The Future of Data Communications, concludes the book with a discussion of the latest data communications technology and the impact of its possible future implementation. As we near the end of the twentieth century, telecommunications and data communications are converging. Digital technology is now being used in almost all types of communications equipment.

Digital PBXs, video transmission, and FAX are discussed. The chapter introduces pulse code modulation and examines the T-1 standard. The ISDN standards are explained, including the differences between European and North American implementations. Equipment classifications and reference points are described, and ISDN services are examined. The chapter concludes with a discussion of the impact of both narrowband and broadband ISDN on the future of data communications.

USING THIS BOOK

This book should be accessible to all readers. Those who have had no prior exposure to computers may need to consult the Appendix on the binary number system.

Readers who have had some exposure to computers, either through regular use, introductory computer science classes, or other technical training, should be able to follow the body of the text. Throughout the book, many specific topics are examined in detail for the advanced or interested reader; these are placed in special shaded boxes.

In addition, there is a summary at the end of each chapter, to help review key ideas and concepts. Terms and acronyms are usually italicized the first time they are introduced or used in a new context, and a list of these terms is provided for review at the end of each chapter. Finally, exercises are provided to review the material further.

For the reader's convenience, a glossary of terms and acronyms can be found at the end of the book. A bibliography of useful reference books and publications is also included.

2

UNDERSTANDING TELECOMMUNICATIONS

THE IMPORTANCE OF TELECOMMUNICATIONS

The invention of the telephone by Alexander Graham Bell in 1876 has forever altered the way we communicate. It is hard to imagine life without telecommunications. *Telecommunications* is defined as the exchange of information, usually over a significant distance and using electronic equipment for transmission. Our businesses and social lives are highly dependent on the telephone.

We now demand that the telephone network carry more than just our voice conversations. The cost of data communications is the fastest-growing segment of most company's telecommunications budgets. Even though most of this book focuses on data communications, we begin with a discussion of today's telecommunications network.

A basic understanding of telecommunications is necessary in order to place data communications in the appropriate context. Since almost all data communications networks include or connect to the public telephone network at one point or another, we start by introducing that aspect of telecommunications.

THE PUBLIC NETWORK

The *public network*, also referred to as the *direct distance dial network*, or *DDD network*, is very familiar to all of us. Each time we pick up our home telephone, we are accessing the public network.

5

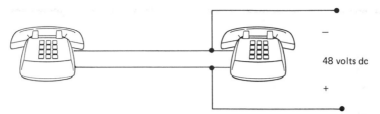

Figure 2-1 Basic telephone connection.

A *network* is simply a group of interconnected devices communicating with each other. These devices may be telephones, as is the case with the public network, or computers, as described in Chapter 3. The word *network* is commonly used today to describe a group of people communicating. In some circles, it is used as a verb: "I networked with a lot of interesting people at that party."

Although the public network allows us to communicate almost anywhere on the globe, simple telephone conversations do not require complex equipment. In fact, when Bell invented the phone, he simply had two makeshift telephone instruments (a microphone and a speaker), two wires, and a power source or battery.

Today's analog telephones require a negative 48 volt DC power source. Think of this as 32 "D" batteries attached end to end. Figure 2-1 shows the connection of two telephones. If we only had phone conversations with our neighbor, we could connect our phone to his with two wires, attach a 48 volt power source, and converse forever.

Eventually, we decide it would be convenient to be able to talk to any of our six neighbors. We start by running wires to each of the other six houses in our neighborhood. They could each run wires to their neighbor's houses. To communicate with a neighbor, the party on each end attaches the correct wires to their phone, and one of them attaches a power source. Figure 2-2 illustrates this network, without any power sources. We call this a *mesh network* because there are wires running from every user to every other user.

If our neighborhood gets any more populated, there will soon be wires everywhere. In fact, with hundreds of millions of telephone customers in the United States alone, it becomes clear that the mesh network is not an effective solution.

Instead, today's telephone network resembles a *star network* as shown in Fig. 2-3. In a star network, each user is connected to the central point. In the telephone network, this central point is responsible for providing the power needed for the telephones, as well as routing the calls to the proper parties.

Central Offices and Local Loops

The *central office* is the term used to describe the hub of our city's telephone network. Each central office is the center of a star network in a particular area. A large city might have several central offices, with each central office handling a portion of the telephone lines. Smaller cities might share a central office with other cities. Our local phone

Understanding Telecommunications

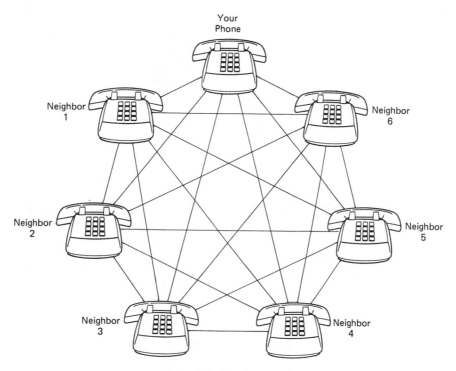

Figure 2-2 Mesh network.

company operates the equipment at our central office. Other names for the central office are the *end office*, or the *local exchange*.

The pair of wires that runs from the central office into our home or business is known as the *local loop*. Many homes actually have two pairs of wires running from the central office, just in case we decide to install a second telephone line. If we have only a single telephone number, the extra pair of wires remains unconnected at the central office.

The central office provides power for our telephones, routes our calls, and bills us accordingly. The piece of equipment that performs all of this work is known as the *central office switch*. The term *switch* is used often in telecommunications when referring to a device that routes communications to different parties. Originally, these devices were made up of a series of mechanical switches. Today, most central office switches are electronic, or even digital, with no moving parts involved. Digital central offices are more reliable than electromechanical switches, and because they are computer-controlled, are able to offer many special features, like call forwarding or three-way calling.

Signaling on a Voice Network

In the process of routing our calls, the central office performs various *signaling* functions. We first signal the central office when we pick up our phone; this is known as the

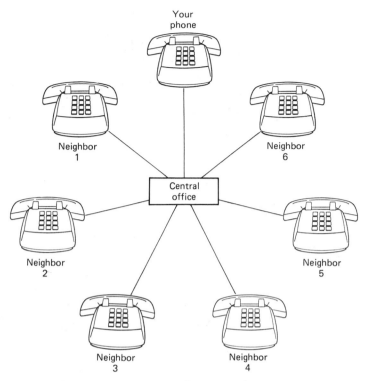

Figure 2-3 Star network.

off-hook signal and tells the central office we would like to dial. The central office then signals us with a *dial tone*, indicating that we may dial a number.

Another example of a signal the central office provides us is the *ringing* of our telephone when we are receiving a call. While ringing our telephone, the central office provides the *ringback signal* to the party calling us. Other signals the central office provides are the *busy signal*, when we call our neighbor and he's already using the phone, and the *howler signal*, that irritating tone that sounds when we leave our phone off the hook. Some common central office/telephone user signals are listed in Fig. 2-4.

When we dial a number on our phone, we are signaling the central office of our desire to be connected to that phone number. Phone numbers are dialed using *rotary dialing*, also known as *pulse dialing*, or by *Touch-tone dialing*, also known as *dual tone multifrequency (DTMF) dialing*.

Rotary, or pulse dialing, requires alternate opening and closing of a switch at the end of the local loop at a fixed rate of speed. When we dial the number 8 on a rotary phone, as we release the dial, the dial mechanism returns at a fixed rate of speed, causing the switch to open and close 8 times, one tenth of a second apart. Special equipment in the central office, often known as a *rotary register*, can detect this switch opening and closing by monitoring the electric current in the local loop. The same closing and opening of the switch can be accomplished by hanging up and picking up our telephone. If we

FIGURE 2-4 CENTRAL OFFICE AND TELEPHONE USER SIGNALS

Signal Name	From:	To:	Function
Off-hook	User	Central office	Informs central office that user wants to place a call
Dial tone	Central office	User	Informs user that central office is ready to accept dialing
Touch-tones or rotary pulses	User	Central office	Informs central office of call destination
Ringback tone	Central office	User	Informs user that the destination phone is ringing
Ringing voltage	Central office	User	Special voltage sent by central office to cause a phone's bell to ring
Busy signal	Cental office	User	Informs user that destination phone is already in use
On-hook	User	Central office	Informs central office that user wishes to disconnect call
Call waiting tone	Central office	User	Informs user that another call is waiting on the line
Flash	User	Central office	A combination of the on-hook and off-hook signals—the user quickly depresses the switch-hook and releases it; often used to pick up a waiting call
Howler tone	Central office	User	Alerts user the phone is off the hook

can briefly depress our switch hook eight times, one tenth of a second apart, without pausing, we will dial the number 8. Most of us aren't this accurate, however, and will pause too long, causing us to dial a 5 and then a 3, for example, instead of an 8.

Touch-tone, or DTMF dialing, works very differently. Each row and column on the DTMF pad has a different tone associated with it. Imagine three different high-pitched tones for the columns, and four different low-pitched tones for the rows. A picture of the DTMF pad is shown in Fig. 2-5, along with the frequencies of the associated tones. We explain frequencies in detail in Chapter 4, but for now, just think of frequency as a measure of how high or low a tone's pitch is; the higher the frequency, the higher the pitch. The number 8 on our DTMF pad is in row 3 and column 2. When we push the number 8 on our DTMF pad, our phone produces two tones simultaneously, the row 3 tone and the column 2 tone. It sounds like one tone to our ear, but two separate tones are actually played together in harmony. At the central office, there is a piece of equipment, often known as a *DTMF register*, that listens to those tones and can determine that we sent a row 3 tone and a column 2 tone, and therefore, that we dialed the number 8.

By now the name *dual tone multifrequency* should make sense; we send two tones at the same time (dual tone), and each can be one of several pitches (multifrequency). Since the name *dual tone multifrequency* is so cumbersome, the name "Touch-tone" has caught on. Interestingly enough, the DTMF standard actually provides for a fourth column, allowing 16 different combinations of row and column tones. This 16-number

Understanding Telecommunications

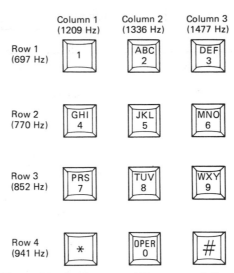

	Column 1 (1209 Hz)	Column 2 (1336 Hz)	Column 3 (1477 Hz)
Row 1 (697 Hz)	1	ABC 2	DEF 3
Row 2 (770 Hz)	GHI 4	JKL 5	MNO 6
Row 3 (852 Hz)	PRS 7	TUV 8	WXY 9
Row 4 (941 Hz)	*	OPER 0	#

Figure 2-5 Dual tone multifrequency dialing.

keypad, however, is used only in special applications, and most applications today use the abbreviated 12-key pad (the numbers 1, 2, 3, 4, 5, 6, 7, 8, 9, 0 and the * and # symbols).

We are so accustomed to hearing the dial tone almost instantly when we pick up the phone that we hardly think of it as a signal to dial; some people don't even listen for it. But if every telephone user attached to our central office picks up the phone at once, most central offices would not be able to provide dial tone to everyone. That's because a dial tone is an indication that there is a piece of equipment in the central office ready to listen to our pulse or DTMF digits. The phone companies don't expect everyone to pick up the phone at once, so they usually don't install enough DTMF and rotary registers to listen to everyone dial at once. If we pick up the phone on Mother's Day and notice a delay in getting a dial tone, that's because so many people are already dialing their phones that there are no rotary or DTMF registers available at the central office to listen to us dial. As soon as a register is available, it is connected electronically to our line and we hear a dial tone.

DIVESTITURE

The methods used for routing calls throughout the telephone network today are largely a result of the United States government's antitrust case against *American Telephone & Telegraph*, or *A.T.&T.* We will briefly examine the results of this case as it relates to telephone call routing.

A local phone company, known as a *local exchange carrier*, or *LEC*, operates the central office. These local phone companies include companies formerly controlled by A.T.&T., known as the *Bell Operating Companies*, or *BOCs*, as well as many *Independent Telephone Companies*, or *ITCs*.

Understanding Telecommunications

In 1974, the U.S. Department of Justice filed an antitrust law suit against A.T.&T. At that time, A.T.&T. owned a controlling share of 22 of the 24 BOCs and carried a large majority of America's long-distance traffic; together, these two components were referred to as the *Bell System*. The domination of both the regulated local and long-distance service by A.T.&T. was deemed an unfair monopoly by the U.S. Department of Justice.

A.T.&T. eventually reached a settlement with the government, described in a document known as the *Modified Final Judgment*, or *MFJ*. The MFJ required A.T.&T. to divest itself of the BOCs on January 1, 1984. This *divestiture* is commonly referred to as the *breakup* of the Bell System. A.T.&T. accomplished the divestiture by exchanging its old stock for shares of stock in the new A.T.&T. and the newly formed holding companies we will discuss later.

The MFJ allowed A.T.&T. to continue to provide long-distance service. A.T.&T. could enter other businesses, but could no longer provide local telephone service. In addition to relinquishing control of the local phone service, A.T.&T. would be forced to compete on an equal basis with other long-distance carriers, known as *interexchange carriers*, or IECs.

The newly divested BOCs would have to provide *equal access* to all long-distance phone companies, and A.T.&T. would have no special priority with its newly divested BOCs. A.T.&T. kept some of the *Bell Labs* research facility, and the *Western Electric* manufacturing facility, which produces central office switches, PBXs, and other telephone equipment. A new company, known as *Bell Communications Research*, or *Bellcore*, was formed to act as a research and administrative services company for the newly formed BOCs.

As a result of divestiture, A.T.&T., often referred to as Ma Bell, was split into many so-called Baby Bells. To allow the newly divested BOCs to remain efficient and achieve economies of scale, they were allowed to group together to form *Regional Holding Companies (RHCs)* or *Regional Bell Operating Companies (RBOCs)*. Figure 2-6 presents a chart of the newly formed BOCs and RBOCs just after divestiture. The RBOCS, in addition to owning their BOCs, could enter other businesses, though they could not manufacture equipment or provide long-distance service. For example, NYNEX has opened a chain of computer stores that is operated separately from the regulated business of its BOCs.

As part of the divestiture settlement, each BOC divided itself into several *local access and transport areas*, or *LATAs*. The BOC is responsible for providing customers access to the public network, as well as for transporting all calls placed inside the LATA. When a call's destination is outside the LATA, the BOC must only transport the call to the *point of presence*, or *POP*, of a long-distance carrier. This POP is located inside the LATA, and it is the long-distance carrier's responsibility to transport the call to its destination in another LATA. Hence, the BOC's two main functions within its LATA are local access and local transport.

A LATA is usually centered around a major metropolitan area. For example, there is a LATA for the entire San Francisco Bay Area, including the cities of San Francisco, Oakland, and San Jose, spanning two different area codes, 415 and 408. Most of this LATA is served by Pacific Bell, a BOC.

FIGURE 2-6 RBOCS AND BOCS AFTER DIVESTITURE

RBOC	BOC	States
Ameritech	Illinois Bell Telephone	Illinois
	Indiana Bell Telephone	Indiana
	Michigan Bell Telephone	Michigan
	Ohio Bell Telephone	Ohio
	Wisconsin Bell	Wisconsin
Bell Atlantic	Bell Telephone of Pennsylvania	Pennsylvania
	Chesapeake & Potomac	Maryland
		Virginia
		Washington, D.C.
		West Virginia
	Diamond State Telephone	Delaware
	New Jersey Bell Telephone	New Jersey
BELLSOUTH	South Central Bell Telephone	Alabama
		Kentucky
		Louisiana
		Mississippi
		Tennessee
	Southern Bell Telephone	Florida
		Georgia
		North Carolina
		South Carolina
NYNEX	New England Telephone	Connecticut
		Maine
		Massachusetts
		New Hampshire
		Rhode Island
		Vermont
	New York Telephone	New York
Pacific Telesis	Nevada Bell	Nevada
	Pacific Bell	California
Southwestern Bell	Southwestern Bell Telephone	Arkansas
		Kansas
		Missouri
		Oklahoma
		Texas
U S WEST	Mountain Bell	Arizona
		Colorado
		Idaho
		Montana
		New Mexico
		Utah
		Wyoming
	Northwestern Bell	Iowa
		Minnesota
		Nebraska
		North Dakota
		South Dakota
	Pacific Northwest Bell	Oregon
		Washington

Understanding Telecommunications

INTRA-LATA CALL ROUTING

If a customer in San Jose places a call within his own central office, the call routing is fairly simple. As shown in Fig. 2-7, parties 1 and 2 are both connected to the same central office. Party 1 picks up the phone, waits for dial tone, and then dials party 2's phone number. The central office looks at the first three digits of the phone number and determines that the called party is in this central office. The central office checks to see if party 2 is already on the phone. If party 2 is already on the phone, the central office sends party 1 a busy signal. If party 2 is not on the phone, the central office sends party 1 a ringing tone and sends a special voltage to party 2's phone, causing it to ring. This call is placed entirely through Pacific Bell lines and offices.

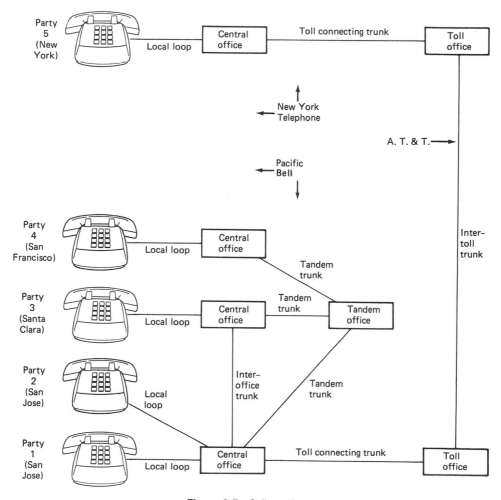

Figure 2-7   Call routing.

The central office knows that party 2 is one of its customers because it knows which *office codes* are in its territory. As an example, in the phone number 555-1234, 555 is the *office code* or *prefix*, and 1234 pinpoints the particular customer in that office code. A central office may have several office codes for its customers.

Suppose that party 1 calls party 3 in Fig. 2-7. Party 3 lives in Santa Clara, another city in the 408 area code and within party 1's LATA, but in a different central office. In this case, the San Jose central office will recognize that the call is destined for the Santa Clara central office by examining the office code. The San Jose central office will route the call to the Santa Clara central office over an *interoffice trunk*, or *IOT*. A *trunk* is another name for a line connecting two switches; an interoffice trunk connects two central offices switches in a local area. In this case, the call is routed over party 1's local loop, through one central office, over an interoffice trunk, to another central office, and finally, to party 3's local loop. This call is placed entirely through Pacific Bell lines and offices.

Area codes, which were in use long before divestiture and the concept of LATAs, have nothing to do with whether a call is local or long distance. They represent a certain geographical area, usually determined by the population in that area. Sometimes an area code covers an entire state, as in Wyoming (307). In the case of a large city, two area codes are sometimes required, as in New York City (212 and 718).

Suppose that party 1 in San Jose, within the 408 area code, calls party 4 in San Francisco, as illustrated in Fig. 2-7. This is a call to the (415) area code, but still within the San Francisco Bay Area LATA. Party 1 dials the number, and the San Jose central office examines the area and office code and determines that the destination is a Pacific Bell central office in San Francisco, in the same LATA. Instead of running trunks from every central office in a LATA to every other central office, the local phone company can run *tandem trunks* from all of the central offices into a *tandem office*, as shown in Fig. 2-7. In this case, party 1's call is routed over his local loop, through the San Jose central office, through a Pacific Bell tandem office, through the San Francisco central office, and over Party 4's local loop. Once again, all of this call routing is done over Pacific Bell equipment and lines in a fraction of a second, and Pacific Bell will bill the customer for the call.

Calls inside a LATA, or intra-LATA calls, are not necessarily what we think of as "local calls." The local phone company may label some intra-LATA calls covering great distances as *toll calls*, but they are not true long-distance calls, because they are still intra-LATA. All intra-LATA calls are routed entirely over the local phone company's equipment, and are billed to the customer by the local phone company, without involving any long-distance carriers.

One constant source of confusion is the fact that not all LATAs are served entirely by one phone company. For example, in the LATA we have been describing, a group of customers in the town of Los Gatos is served by GTE, an independent phone company, while most of the rest of the San Francisco Bay Area LATA is served by Pacific Bell. In cases like these, the different local phone companies cooperate to ensure that customers receive the same service that a single company would provide.

INTER-LATA CALL ROUTING

What happens when party 1 wants to call a number outside his LATA? This is an *inter-LATA*, or *long-distance call*, and a long-distance carrier must enter the call routing process. Before divestiture, the call would have usually been placed over A.T.&T. lines. Since divestiture and the advent of equal access, customers are free to choose their long-distance carriers. Figure 2-8 lists some of the long-distance carriers that entered the market for inter-LATA calls after divestiture.

Telephone customers with equal access choose a particular carrier to be their standard, or *default*, long-distance company, through a process known as *presubscription*. Whenever the customer dials an inter-LATA call, the call will be automatically routed over the presubscribed carrier unless the customer dials a special code.

In some areas, a customer must dial a 1 before placing inter-LATA calls. The presence or absence of this requirement does not affect equal access. Dialing a 1 plus the phone number will still route the call over the presubscribed carrier. Dialing a special code, in the format 10xxx, where xxx is the carrier code, will route the call over an alternative carrier. A list of carrier codes is also provided in Fig. 2-8.

A central office is connected to a long-distance carrier's office, known as a *toll office*, by a *toll connecting trunk*, or *TCT*. A long-distance carrier connects its toll offices all around the country with *intertoll trunks*, in much the same way that the local phone companies connect their central offices with interoffice trunks. Intertoll trunks are also often called *IXCs*, or *interexchange circuits*. Intertoll trunks that can carry many conversations simultaneously are known as *high-usage intertoll trunks*.

We will assume for our example that Party 1 has presubscribed to A.T.&T. for his long-distance service. Referring to Fig. 2-7, party 1, in San Jose, California, is calling party 5 in New York. This call is clearly outside the San Francisco Bay Area LATA. The call is routed over party 1's local loop, to the San Jose Pacific Bell central office, over a toll connecting trunk, to an A.T.&T. toll office in California, across the country on an A.T.&T. intertoll trunk, to an A.T.&T. toll office in New York, over a toll connecting trunk, to a New York Telephone central office, and out over party 5's local loop. It will

Figure 2-8   A SAMPLING OF LONG DISTANCE
CARRIERS AFTER DIVESTITURE

Carrier	Access Code
Allnet	10444
A.T.&T.	10288
I.T.T. Longer Distance	10488
M.C.I.	10222
U.S. Sprint	10777
Western Union	10220

Note: Not all carriers serve all areas.

be the New York central office's responsibility to provide a busy signal or ringing tone, depending on whether party 5 is on the line.

This call routing involves three separate companies: 2 BOCs and one long-distance carrier. This is possible because there are very clear standards for the signaling that must take place between the different offices handling a call. These standards apply to all central offices and all long-distance carriers.

The Pacific Bell central office informs the A.T.&T. toll office of the call originator and the call destination by special signaling. The long-distance company has the choice of billing the customer directly, billing through a third party, such as Pacific Bell, or even billing the customer's credit card. All of this call routing and signaling takes place in a few seconds. Long-distance calls take longer to go through than local calls because these signals have to be passed through many different offices and switches.

Though our example assumes an intertoll trunk between San Jose and New York, this is not necessarily the case. The long distance carrier is free to route the call to New York through whatever cities it wishes, just as an airline may require passengers to change planes in Chicago. The long-distance carrier might run all of its trunks into Chicago, routing all calls through a national switching center there. Typically, this is done regionally, with several switching centers spread out all over the country. There is an entire hierarchy involving regional and area toll offices, but we won't consider them here because they don't directly affect the customer. In our example, Pacific Bell routed the call to A.T.&T. and it becomes A.T.&T.'s responsibility to get the call to New York using any route it wishes.

REGULATION

Companies that provide voice and data communications transmission services to the general public are known as *common carriers*. This includes the local phone companies and the long-distance companies. These common carriers must file *tariffs* for all services they offer with the appropriate regulating bodies. A tariff describes a particular service in detail, along with the rate charged for that service. In some cases, the regulating body may reject a particular tariff, for example, if it feels the rates are too high.

The *FCC*, or *Federal Communications Commission*, is responsible for regulating all interstate communications in the United States. Thus the FCC regulates calls that are inter-LATA and interstate, as well as the few calls that are intra-LATA and interstate (where LATAs cross state lines).

Each state has a *PUC*, or *public utilities commission*, responsible for regulating all intra-state phone service. The PUCs regulate all local phone service, all intra-LATA/intra-state calls, and all inter-LATA/intra-state calls.

Each regulating agency reviews and approves tariffs filed for services in its jurisdiction. Since the local phone companies have a basic monopoly on providing phone service within their communities, PUCs are likely to scrutinize rate increases very carefully. The FCC, on the other hand, may allow the long-distance carriers more leeway in pricing new and innovative services, since consumers have equal access to all carriers and can choose the services they prefer.

National issues affecting all of the RBOCs are typically addressed by the FCC. In the post-divestiture environment, the FCC started to require that the RBOCs implement an *Open Network Architecture*, or *ONA*. With ONA, the public network services are divided into *basic service elements*, or *BSEs*; customers can subscribe to any combination of the BSEs. For example, one BSE might be the ability to forward calls, while another might be conference calling. The customer could select either or both of these BSEs, but would not be forced to take both together as a package. By separating all of the public network's services into BSEs, an *enhanced service provider*, or *ESP*, would be guaranteed access to network services needed to perform special functions. For example, an answering service company is an ESP that would use the call forwarding BSE, combined with its staff of operators or answering machines, to provide a special, or enhanced, service to the customer.

Many countries have their own equivalent of the FCC, often known as a *PTT*, or *postal, telephone, and telegraph administration*. In some countries, the PTT regulates and runs the public network. This would be the equivalent of the FCC owning, operating, and regulating the pre-divestiture A.T.&T., with all of its BOCs.

VOICE COMMUNICATIONS SERVICE OFFERINGS

Many different communications services are available, particularly to the business community, which has large volumes of telephone traffic. One of these is *WATS*, or *wide area telecommunications services*. WATS is a bulk-rate, long-distance service for users with high call volumes. Traditionally, WATS pricing was done in bands; the United States was divided into several bands, or zones, and the customers paid a per hour cost for calls to each zone. A California business that placed a lot of calls on the West Coast but very few to the East could subscribe to WATS only for the West Coast bands. Since divestiture, many long distance carriers are offering services labeled as WATS with different characteristics. Some are simply volume discounts regardless of zone; others are more complex, offering discounts to certain area codes and office codes at certain times. The only safe generalization that can be made about a post-divestiture WATS line is that it offers some discounts for volume long-distance users.

A type of WATS service, *inward-WATS*, is known to most of us as a *toll-free number*, or an *800 number*. The customer agrees to pay for all incoming long-distance calls from certain areas, but at the reduced WATS rates. Another service, known as a *foreign exchange*, is used by a business that wants a phone number in a city other than where its offices are located. The business pays a fixed rate for the service, in addition to a mileage charge to the distant area. Calls to and from its customers in that area can then be made at local call rates.

Another way for businesses to save on communications costs is to use *leased lines* to locations they call frequently. A leased line is a permanent connection from one point to another provided by common carriers. In a sense, it's a phone call that never hangs up. Since the carrier only has to route the call once, after that, all the customer is really renting is a pair of wires from one point to another, along with some amplifying equipment and power. Leased-line services are generally priced by the mile. Whether the line is used frequently or not at all, the monthly price is still the same, because that line has been reserved for the exclusive use of the customer.

For example, a corporation with offices in Santa Clara, California, and Austin, Texas, may discover that it is making many long-distance calls between the two facilities. Rather than continue to pay per minute rates on the dial-up network, or even per hour rates through WATS, the customer can opt to lease lines. Leasing lines becomes economical surprisingly fast, often after a few dozen hours of use per month. If the business has an advanced PBX which ensures that the leased lines are used wherever appropriate, the economic benefit is almost guaranteed.

When we pick up our home phone and dial a number, we are accessing the dial-up network. It's up to the common carriers to route our call to the appropriate destination, but we have no control over what route the call takes. Furthermore, every time we place a call to the same number, it may take a slightly different route, depending on what facilities the carriers have available at that instant. This explains why sometimes we get a ''good'' connection, and sometimes the other party is barely audible.

One of the key attributes of the dial-up network is that the flexible routing of calls allows for a very high reliability of making a connection. For example, a call from San Jose to New York might normally go over a transcontinental intertoll trunk, but if that line is currently out of service, the call could be routed through Chicago. However, with this high reliability of making a connection comes the uncertainty of whether or not our next connection will be of high quality.

Leased lines, however, can assure consistently high-quality connections. When a leased line is installed, it must meet a certain specification, such as *voice grade*, suitable for voice communications and most data communications. The customer can even demand a special leased line, suitable for high-speed data transmission, known as a *conditioned* leased line. There will be an extra charge for the hardware required to meet this improved specification.

A leased-line customer, however, is vulnerable to a service outage on that line's particular wire and hardware. If the line is down, the telephone network will not automatically reroute the call. Either the line must be repaired, another line installed, or a backup call placed on the dial-up network.

The choice boils down to the high reliability and questionable quality of the dial-up network, versus the questionable reliability and high quality of a leased line. Of course, the application and priorities of each customer determine which solution is appropriate.

There are many ways to provide leased-line services in higher volumes and at lower costs. These include T-1 carrier, satellite, microwave, and fiber optics. We consider these high-volume transmission options in Chapter 4.

ECHO SUPPRESSORS AND CANCELLERS

The dial-up telephone network is equipped with a variety of devices to help stop echoes during normal conversation. The nature of telephone transmission causes some signals to ''bounce back'' from the receiving telephone, just as our voices bounce off a canyon's walls and return to our ears.

Understanding Telecommunications

On a local call, we don't even notice the echo. That's because the party we are speaking with is within a few miles of us, and our voice travels at the speed of electricity (almost 300 million meters per second). Our echo will return to our earpiece so quickly that it doesn't even seem to be an echo; it sounds as if the telephone is simply amplifying our voice in the earpiece.

However, long-distance connections can span many thousands of miles. It may take an echo a half second to complete its round trip back to your telephone. An echo a half second after we have said something is very disconcerting. Several different devices are in use today to help eliminate echoes, including *echo suppressors* and *echo cancellers*.

Echo suppressors work by allowing only a one-way communications path. As soon as we start talking, the path from the other person to us is cut off. If our voice echoes back, it will not be transmitted. If the other person begins speaking louder than us, they get control of the line. This works well for normal conversation; when we stop talking, and the other person begins, their voice will take over. If they interrupt us mid-sentence, they will probably be speaking louder than we are so we will hear them. The echo suppressor hears the volume difference and gives them the line. Since echoes are going to be softer than the original voice, an echo on the rebound will never take control of the line. Echo suppressors are shown at work in Fig. 2-9.

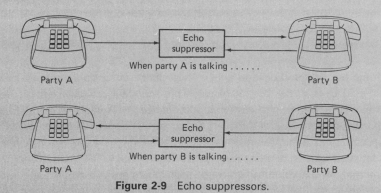

Figure 2-9 Echo suppressors.

Echo cancellers are more sophisticated devices. They allow a continuous two-way conversation, but are able to remove your own echo before it returns to your telephone. Echo cancellers are a sophisticated version of acoustical ceiling tiles used to absorb noise. The difference is that echo cancellers are able to detect the difference between true conversation and an echo, and will selectively absorb only the echo.

Most long-distance carriers install either echo suppressors or cancellers at the end of their equipment. This equipment can be disabled on a particular call by using a special tone. This is useful for certain data communications transmissions we will review later.

TASI vs. VOICE CALL MULTIPLEXING

Long-distance carriers will often combine several calls on the same intertoll trunk using one of two methods. The first method, known as *TASI*, or *time assignment speech interpolation*, allocates a communications path a few milliseconds after the caller begins to speak. This is not noticed during voice transmission, but is often damaging to data transmission, where a few lost milliseconds can result in the loss of precious data. The preferred method, known as *voice call multiplexing*, combines conversations without risking any loss of voice or data. Fortunately, most carriers today use the latter technique.

LEASING SERVICES VS. BUYING
CUSTOMER PREMISES EQUIPMENT

Regardless of the size of a business or the diversity of its telecommunications requirements, there is always the option of leasing services from others or owning them outright. Equipment used at the customer's site is known as *customer-premises equipment*, or *CPE*. Many of us already own our own CPE: our home telephones.

Centrex

Some businesses choose to let the local phone company handle all of their external and internal calls in the central office. This service is called *Centrex*, because the central office is acting as the customer's exchange, or switch. A local loop connects every extension to the central office. The central office will interpret the numbers dialed in a special way for the Centrex customer. For example, if employee A in Fig. 2-10 dials the four-digit extension of employee B, the central office will recognize this call as an internal one and route it back to the appropriate desk. If employee C dials a 9, attempting to call home, the central office will recognize that it is an external call, and grant the employee an outside dial tone, without any operator intervention.

Centrex gives a business the appearance of having its own phone system. Employees dial internal calls just by dialing the last few digits, and don't usually realize that their call is going through the phone company's central office. Centrex is usually very dependable, because central office switches are highly reliable, with a full-time maintenance and troubleshooting staff. However, the customer must pay a fee for each Centrex line each month, in addition to per call charges, just as we do for our home telephone service. With Centrex, the customer usually has the option of purchasing or renting the phone instruments.

Today's Centrex services can be tailored to offer some of the same advanced features previously found only in customer-owned systems. However, Centrex is by

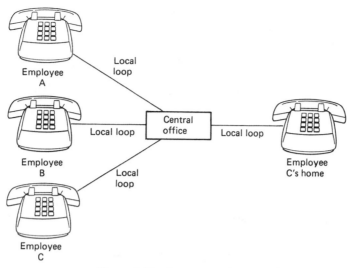

Figure 2-10 Centrex service.

nature inefficient, since a call destined for a colleague's desk only 10 feet away must take a 2-mile round trip to the central office. In addition, the user relies on the phone company to perform most changes, such as moving telephone locations or changing extensions. Some customers, however, prefer Centrex because they don't have to purchase and maintain a phone system. They are willing to pay higher monthly fees to avoid the initial capital outlay required to purchase a phone system.

Key Systems

For some small businesses, *key systems* may provide a suitable telecommunications solution. Early key systems were merely a collection of multiline phones connected with special wiring. These early key systems provided intercom functions, allowing customers to communicate internally over intercom lines. Any external calls were made over local loops.

Early key systems had little or no intelligence, and the user performed all functions manually by pushing the appropriate buttons. To place an external call on early key systems, the user pushed an external line button on the phone. Similarly, internal conversations were initiated by pressing an intercom button. In addition, calls could be placed on hold using a hold button. Early key systems were limited to only a handful of telephone lines.

Today's key systems are more sophisticated, providing special features such as call forwarding and call transfer. Some of today's key systems can handle up to 150 users.

Key systems are usually compact and use standard electrical power. In addition, they can often be repaired by the customer. Key systems, and the phones attached to them, are usually purchased by the customer, though they can be leased.

Key systems eliminate the inefficiency of Centrex, as an internal call does not go to the central office. A key system customer does not need a local loop for each telephone, only one for each outside line.

However, most key systems cannot provide many advanced features, and are severely limited in their ability to grow beyond 150 lines. For these reasons, medium-sized to large businesses usually do not choose key systems. There is another alternative to Centrex for these customers.

Private Branch Exchange

The *PBX*, or *private branch exchange*, is the most advanced customer-premises equipment telecommunications solution. A PBX acts as a mini-central office, dedicated not to an entire community or town, but to the customer that owns it. The lines running from the PBX to employees' phones are known as PBX *station lines*, and are owned by the customer, not the phone company. A PBX can often accommodate thousands of phones, enough to satisfy the needs of even the largest customers.

All internal calls are routed through the PBX and never go to the central office. If an employee places an external call, the PBX will route the call off the premises to the central office. For example, in Fig. 2-11, assume that employee A dials employee B. The PBX connects the two parties, and the entire connection is inside the customer's private network. Hence, there are no charges from the central office for this call; in fact, the local phone company doesn't know, or care, that the call took place, because their facilities were not used.

What about external calls? One advantage of a PBX is that a company does not need a local loop for each employee, because only a small percentage of employees make external calls at any given moment. In typical companies, one outside line for every ten extensions might be sufficient. Special situations require more outside lines. For example, at an airline reservations center, employees spend a majority of their time answering incoming calls from outside lines. Every business will have different requirements; the fewer outside lines needed, the more a PBX saves the customer in local loop costs.

We have already mentioned that two switches are connected together using a special type of line known as a trunk. PBXs, therefore, are connected to the central office using trunks. Several different types of PBX trunks are illustrated in Fig. 2-11. An employee gains access to those trunks by dialing a special code, like 9. The PBX can then select the appropriate trunk, based on the call's destination.

The *central office trunk* is the standard trunk used for all external intra-LATA calls and for calls which the central office will be routing to a long-distance carrier. Incoming calls over a central office trunk must be answered by the customer's *operator*, or *attendant*.

Customers that want incoming calls automatically routed to their employees desks without going through an operator must rent *direct inward dial trunks*, or *DID trunks*, from the central office. On a DID trunk, the central office actually signals the PBX which extension an incoming call is destined for, allowing the PBX to route it properly.

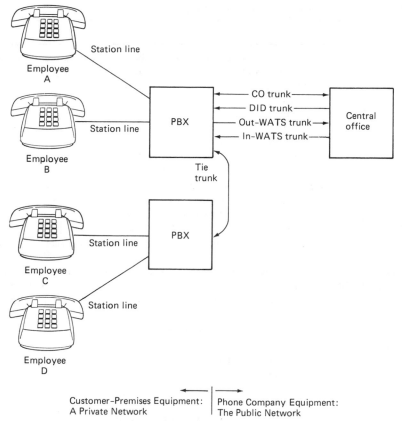

Figure 2-11 PBX call routing.

An *outward-WATS trunk* is a connection to a discounted long-distance service we have already mentioned. An *inward-WATS trunk* is the PBX's connection for a *toll-free number*.

Finally, a *tie trunk* is used to connect two PBXs. These PBXs can be at the same location or at different locations. An employee on one PBX can place a call to an employee on the other PBX, and it can be automatically routed over these tie trunks. Calls over the tie trunks incur no per call cost, since these lines are leased on a monthly basis.

Early PBXs provided a cost savings simply by reducing the number of local loops. Today's advanced PBXs are loaded with features, which are generally divided into two basic categories, system features and station features.

System features are functions performed and controlled for the entire system, like voice messaging. A table of popular PBX system features is presented in Fig. 2-12. *Station features* are functions performed for and controlled by each individual user, like call forwarding. A table of popular PBX station features is shown in Fig. 2-13. Although

FIGURE 2-12 POPULAR PBX SYSTEM FEATURES

Feature Name	Function
Automatic call distribution (ACD)	Allows callers to be routed to a group of agents, with calls distributed evenly among all of them. Statistics are available on each agent, including the number of calls, duration, etc. Often used for customer service departments, airline reservationists, etc.
Call detail recording (CDR)	Provides records on each call placed out of the PBX, including the caller, the called party, the duration, time of day, etc. Allows a company to track its telephone costs by department or even by user. Further enhancements allow special account codes to be entered when placing a call to bill it to a particular client or project.
Class of service distinction (COS)	Allows users to be combined into different groups, each with access to different features, and each with different external calling capabilities.
Data switching	Available only on digital PBXs, it allows for switched digital pathways. This provides for sharing of resources, including host computers or modems, among many different terminal devices. Personal computers can also communicate with each other through data switching.
Direct inward dial (DID)	Callers from outside the company can dial directly to employees' desks, or station lines.
Direct inward system access (DISA)	Allows a user away from the office to dial the PBX, enter a special code, and then use the PBX for placing internal and external calls, exactly as if she were at her desk.
Direct outward dial	Users can dial external calls directly, without going through the PBX operator.
Distinctive ringing	Different ring patterns can be provided for different calls. For example, internal calls may be indicated by a single ring; external calls by two quick rings, etc.
Hunt groups	Allows phones in a department to be assigned to a special group. People calling the departmental number will be routed to the first available person in the department's hunt group.
Intercom lines	Allows abbreviated dialing within a department, making it seem that each department has its own system.
Least-cost routing	Automatically routes all external calls over the cheapest route, including WATS lines, tie trunks, foreign exchanges, etc.
Music on hold	Provides a PBX connection to a music source so that callers placed on hold will know they're still connected.
Paging	Provides a PBX connection to a loudspeaker so that users can page someone by dialing a special code and speaking into the telephone.
Remote polling	The computers of the PBX manufacturer's service organization can telephone the PBX on a regular basis, and check the PBX's diagnostic information for any irregularities. A service technician can then be dispatched if necessary, often before the customer is even aware of any problem. In addition, call detail recording information can be collected from the PBX for further analysis.
Route optimization	Same as least-cost routing.
System speed dial	Allows a set of telephone numbers to be programmed into the system. Any system user can then automatically dial one of these numbers by entering a brief code.
Trunk queuing	Users placing an external call when all trunks are busy will be queued, or put in line, for a trunk. With some systems the user can hang up, and the system will call back when a trunk is available.
Voice messaging	Provides automated call answering for phones left unattended or phones that are busy. Calls are usually answered by an attached voice messaging system that plays a greeting in the call receiver's own voice and then offers several options. The caller can leave a message, which is stored in the system and can be retrieved by the user. Users are usually notified of messages through message waiting lights on their phones, or an interrupted dial tone, known as stutter, or a broken dial tone. Messages can usually be forwarded to other users.

Understanding Telecommunications

FIGURE 2-13 POPULAR PBX STATION FEATURES

Feature Name	Function
Account codes	Allows users to key in a special code for each call, ensuring that each call is billed to a particular acount. Accounts often represent clients or projects.
Buzz	Allows users to buzz each other as they would on an intercom system.
Camp-on	When a user encounters a busy signal on an internal call, he can camp-on. This is an automated version of waiting for the line to be free. With some systems, the user can hang-up and the system will call back when the called party is free.
Conference calls	Allows users to create telephone conferences, adding multiple users to each conversation.
Do not disturb	Allows users to block incoming calls. Callers receive a busy signal.
Executive override	Allows a high-priority user to interrupt the conversations of others in case of emergency or for urgent messages.
Forwarding	Allows users to forward their incoming calls to another user, or to voice messaging systems.
Hold	Allows users to place calls on hold.
Mute	Allows users to listen to callers without callers hearing them.
Park	Allows users to put calls in progress on hold at another person's extension. For example, a call answered at your desk can be parked at your colleague's desk. You can then go to your colleague's office, get some information, and pick up his phone, continuing your conversation.
Pick	Allows users to answer their phone from another person's desk.
Station speed dial	Allows users to program in their own set of frequently dialed phone numbers, which can later be dialed using a short code. This is similar to system speed numbers, but system speed numbers are preprogrammed for the entire system.
Transfer	Allows users to transfer a call to other users.

not all PBXs have all of these features, the system and station features presented in the tables are a representative sample of features provided by most advanced PBXs.

Many advanced PBXs are able to send calls over the least expensive route. This system feature, known as *least-cost routing*, or *route optimization*, has become increasingly sophisticated with the advent of equal access. An advanced PBX can be programmed with the rates of all of the long-distance carriers, and can select the cheapest carrier for each call based on the rate tables and the time of day. This feature can provide considerable cost savings, and is often the main reason for purchasing a PBX instead of using Centrex services.

Almost all of today's advanced PBXs are *digital PBXs*. IBM's ROLM CBX, or Computerized Branch Exchange, first installed in 1975, was the first computer-based digital PBX. Digital PBXs are actually computers that treat the telephones and trunks as specialized input and output devices.

One advantage of digital PBXs is their ability to provide a myriad of sophisticated features. In addition, these digital PBXs can use special digital telephones that allow the transmission of voice and data over a single telephone line. Some digital PBXs even have integrated terminals and telephones in a single unit. Further advantages of digital communications are discussed later in the book.

SUMMARY

Understanding the basics of telecommunications is the first step in studying data communications. There are many different network topologies, including mesh and star. The public network, or direct distance dial network, is a series of interconnected star networks. At the center of each star network is a central office, connected to the users by local loops. Users signal the central office of call destinations using rotary pulses or Touch-tones. The central office provides the user with other signals, including dial tone, ringback tone, and the busy and howler signals.

The divestiture of A.T.&T. resulted in the formation of the Bell Operating Companies and Regional Bell Operating Companies. There are also many long-distance carriers now competing for customers' business, all with equal access to the customer. The BOCs have divided their territory into local access and transport areas. Call routing inside these areas involves only the local exchange carrier; inter-LATA calls involve interexchange carriers. There are many different trunks used to connect the various central offices and toll offices in the public network. The Federal Communications Commission regulates interstate calls, and the PUCs regulate intrastate calls. Internationally, many countries are regulated by PTTs.

Many voice service options are available to businesses, including outward WATS, inward WATS, and leased lines. Some businesses choose to lease basic telephone services by using their phone company's Centrex service. Key systems and private branch exchanges are both examples of customer-premises equipment that can be purchased. Many PBXs can handle thousands of lines and provide a variety of sophisticated features. A PBX can also help reduce a company's telecommunications costs by using the most efficient route. Today's digital PBX's will handle not only voice, but data traffic as well.

TERMS FOR REVIEW

American Telephone &
   Telegraph
Area code
A.T.&T.
Attendant
Basic service element
Bell Communications
   Research
Bell Labs
Bell Operating Company
Bell System
Bellcore
BOC
Breakup
BSE
Busy signal
Central office
Central office switch
Central office trunk
Centrex
Common carrier
Conditioned line
CPE
Customer-premises
   equipment
DDD network
Default
Dial tone
DID trunk
Digital PBX
Direct distance dial network
Direct inward dial trunk
Divestiture
DTMF
DTMF register
Dual tone multifrequency
   dialing
Echo canceller
Echo suppressor
800 number
End office

Enhanced service provider
Equal access
ESP
FCC
Federal Communications
   Commission
Foreign exchange
High-usage intertoll trunk
Howler signal
IEC
Independent Telephone
   Company
Interexchange carrier
Interexchange circuit
Inter-LATA call
Interoffice trunk
Intertoll trunk
Inward-WATS trunk
IOT
ITC
IXC
Key system
LATA
Leased line
Least-cost routing
LEC
Local access and transport
   area
Local exchange
Local exchange carrier
Local loop
Long-distance call
Mesh network
MFJ
Modified Final Judgment
Network
Off-hook signal
Office code
ONA
On-hook signal
Open Network Architecture

Operator
Outward-WATS trunk
PBX
Point of presence
POP
Postal, telephone, and
   telegraph administration
Prefix
Presubscription
Private branch exchange
PTT
Public network
Public utilities commission
PUC
Pulse dialing
RBOC
Regional Bell Operating
   Company
Regional Holding Company
RHC
Ringback signal
Ringing signal
Rotary dialing
Rotary register
Route optimization
Signaling
Star network
Station feature
Station line
Switch
System feature
Tandem office
Tandem trunk
Tariff
TASI
TCT
Telecommunications
Tie trunk
Time assignment speech
   interpolation
Toll call

Toll connecting trunk
Toll-free number
Toll office
Touch-tone dialing

Trunk
Voice call multiplexing
Voice-grade circuit
WATS

Western Electric
Wide area
   telecommunications
   services

EXERCISES

2-1. Why is the public telephone network a star network rather than a mesh network?

2-2. What functions does a central office perform?

2-3. What are the common signals between the central office and the user during a typical telephone call?

2-4. Explain the differences between rotary and DTMF dialing methods.

2-5. What are the roles of the local exchange carriers and the interexchange carriers, respectively, in inter-LATA calls?

2-6. What is a tariff? What is the difference between the FCC and the PUCs? Which agencies review which tariffs?

2-7. Compare WATS service to leased lines. Which is more useful for a customer always calling between the same two locations? What about calling between many different locations but not often to any one location?

2-8. What are some ways for a business to enable an out-of-town customer to reach it at reduced cost or no cost? What about calls from its own out-of-town factory?

2-9. What are the advantages and disadvantages of using the dial-up network versus leased lines?

2-10. Which equipment does the customer provide with Centrex service? What does the local exchange carrier provide?

2-11. What makes Centrex service inherently inefficient?

2-12. How does a PBX's method of handling internal calls differ from Centrex service? How does this affect the customer's central office charges?

2-13. Compare the different types of PBX trunks.

2-14. What is the difference between PBX system features and PBX station features?

2-15. What is the main advantage of the route optimization feature found in advanced PBXs?

3

BASIC DATA COMMUNICATIONS CONCEPTS

DEFINING DATA COMMUNICATIONS

Data communications is usually defined as the exchange of digital information between two devices using an electronic transmission system. *Digital* information is another name for ones and zeroes. Therefore, a less formal definition of data communications is the art of sending ones and zeroes from one point to another.

To help illustrate basic data communications concepts, we will begin by examining two devices that often need to communicate: host computers and terminals.

HOST COMPUTERS AND TERMINALS

A *host computer*, or *central processing unit (CPU)*, is at the heart of any data communications network. The host computer can perform numerical calculations, store and retrieve data, and perform a variety of tasks known as *applications*. Examples of host computer *applications software* include word processing programs, spreadsheets, accounting programs, and payroll programs.

There are many different types of host computers. *Mainframes* are host computers usually serving a large company. *Minicomputers* are host computers usually dedicated to a smaller set of users, perhaps a department or a division. *Microcomputers*, or *personal computers*, usually serve only one user. A *supercomputer* is an extremely fast mainframe dedicated to extensive mathematical calculations.

Many data communications networks allow host computers to exchange information with other locally or remotely located devices. One of these devices is known as a *terminal*. Other names for a terminal include *cathode ray tube (CRT), video display terminal (VDT)*, or *display station*. Regardless of the name used, a terminal's basic function is to allow a user to communicate with a host computer. Terminals include a *keyboard* for entering information to be transmitted to the host computer, and a *screen* for displaying information received from the host computer.

Terminals are often classified in one of three ways: dumb, smart, or intelligent. A *dumb terminal* simply receives data from a host computer and displays it on its screen, and is unable to modify or change the data it receives. Similarly, any data typed into the keyboard is sent directly to the host computer, without any major modifications by the terminal.

A *smart terminal* will usually send extra information to a host computer, in addition to what the user types. This additional information can include the terminal's address, or location, as well as special information to prevent errors from occurring. The host computer will also send similar information to the smart terminal, including specific instructions regarding when the terminal can send data. The smart terminal is smart enough to interpret these instructions and pass on any actual data to the user. We discuss the rules for smart terminal communications in detail in Chapter 7.

The difference between an *intelligent terminal* and a smart terminal is very subtle. Intelligent terminals are just like smart terminals, but their behavior can be modified or programmed. After a smart terminal leaves the factory, it never changes its behavior, and can never learn to perform new functions. An intelligent terminal can be programmed to perform new functions by many means, including special tapes, cartridges, diskettes, or keyboard commands, depending on the manufacturer.

BITS AND BYTES

Almost all computers and terminals, from the $300 terminal to the multimillion-dollar computer, communicate by sending a series of ones and zeroes to each other. We call each one or zero a *bit*, and a group of several (usually eight) ones and zeroes a *byte*. Terminals and computers use the *binary number system* to represent digital information. Readers who have not been exposed to the binary number system before, or who simply need a quick review, should refer to the Appendix.

To help simplify our discussion, we first concentrate on dumb terminals. The dumb terminal in Fig. 3-1 is connected to a host computer. Each time the user hits a key on the keyboard, a series of bits is transmitted to the host computer. The host computer receives those bits, and then determines what *character* they represent. Characters include letters of the alphabet, numbers, all punctuation marks, and special keys used by different terminals, such as Delete.

Basic Data Communications Concepts

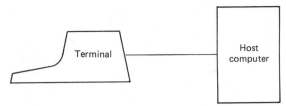

Figure 3-1 Terminal and host computer.

CHARACTER CODES

Each time a user strikes a particular key on the dumb terminal, the terminal must translate it into a series of bits, and the host computer must always recognize that series of bits as representing the same character. There are many ways to represent characters, and these different representations are known as *character codes*.

There are several different character codes in use today. We will examine in detail some of the more popular ones in order of their evolution: Morse, Baudot, EBCDIC, and ASCII.

Morse Code

Morse code is one of the first character codes developed. It is a crude, but effective code for transmitting characters over a telegraph circuit. Morse code was designed with a telegraph operator in mind; the operator sent combinations of a short beep, known as a *dot*, and a long beep, known as a *dash*, to transmit characters. The characters used the most frequently need the fewest dots and dashes for transmission. A table of the Morse code is shown in Fig. 3-2.

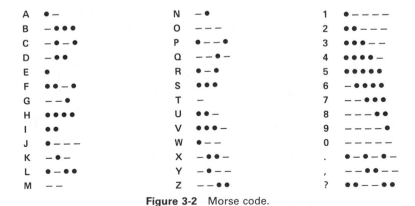

Figure 3-2 Morse code.

Basic Data Communications Concepts

Notice in Fig. 3-2 that the letter "A" consists of a dot and a dash, or a short beep followed by a long beep. Every time a telegraph operator sent "dot-dash," the receiving operator knew that the letter "A" was being transmitted. Notice that the letter "R" starts out just like the letter "A" but then adds an extra dot at the end. How would the operators distinguish between the letter "A" (dot-dash) followed by the letter "E" (dot) and the letter "R" alone (dot-dash-dot)? Morse code handled this problem by requiring the operator to pause for a short time between letters. "AE" became "dot-dash-pause-dot" and the letter "R" was "dot-dash-dot."

One of the features that makes Morse code unsuitable for computer communications is the extra time required between characters. Why waste the time of a multimillion-dollar computer by pausing between characters? The small number of different characters that can be transmitted in Morse code is also severely limiting. Clearly, other character codes needed to be developed for computer communications.

Baudot Code

Baudot code is one of the first character codes developed with machines, and not humans, in mind. Baudot code uses ones and zeroes, rather than dots and dashes, to represent characters.

Baudot code addressed the shortcomings of Morse code by using five bits of information for each character. The Baudot code table is presented in Fig. 3-3. As shown in the table, we number the bits in the Baudot character code with the bit on the far left as bit 5, and the bit on the far right as bit 1.

Let's begin by examining the *Lower Case* column in this table. If a user types the letter "A" on a terminal that communicates using Baudot code, the terminal sends five bits, 00011, as shown on the first line of our chart. Assuming that the host computer receiving 00011 also uses the Baudot code, it will then recognize 00011 as the letter "A." Similarly, if the user types the letter "B," 11001 will be transmitted; if the user types the letter "C," 01110 will be transmitted, and so on, as shown in the Baudot table.

What if the user types the number "3"? Notice that the number "3" is in the *Upper Case* column of our chart. The Baudot terminal must now switch to Upper Case to send the number "3." Much as one would hit the Shift Lock key on a typewriter, the terminal sends a special code to the host computer, 11011, to instruct it to switch to Upper Case. This code, known as the *Figures* code, instructs the host computer that all further transmissions will be from the Upper Case column of the chart. In this instance, Upper Case doesn't mean capital letters, but rather a whole new set of characters. Once the host computer has been alerted that future characters are from the Upper Case column, the terminal can send the number "3" by sending 00001.

When the user later strikes a key from the Lower Case column, the terminal will send the *Letters* code, 11111, which instructs the host computer that future transmissions are from the Lower Case column again. This is equivalent to releasing the Shift Lock key on a typewriter.

In addition to the Letters and Figures characters, there are two additional special characters: the *line feed* and *carriage return* characters. A line feed, when sent to a

Figure 3-3 BAUDOT CODE

Character		Data Bits				
Lower Case	Upper Case	5	4	3	2	1
A	-	0	0	0	1	1
B	?	1	1	0	0	1
C	:	0	1	1	1	0
D	$	0	1	0	0	1
E	3	0	0	0	0	1
F	!	0	1	1	0	1
G	&	1	1	0	1	0
H	#	1	0	1	0	0
I	8	0	0	1	1	0
J	'	0	1	0	1	1
K	(	0	1	1	1	1
L	)	1	0	0	1	0
M	.	1	1	1	0	0
N	,	0	1	1	0	0
O	9	1	1	0	0	0
P	0	1	0	1	1	0
Q	1	1	0	1	1	1
R	4	0	1	0	1	0
S	BELL	0	0	1	0	1
T	5	1	0	0	0	0
U	7	0	0	1	1	1
V	;	1	1	1	1	0
W	2	1	0	0	1	1
X	/	1	1	1	0	1
Y	6	1	0	1	0	1
Z	"	1	0	0	0	1
Letters (shift to Lower Case column)		1	1	1	1	1
Figures (shift to Upper Case column)		1	1	0	1	1
Space		0	0	1	0	0
Carriage Return		0	1	0	0	0
Line Feed		0	0	0	1	0
Blank		0	0	0	0	0

terminal, causes the terminal to advance one line, and a carriage return moves the print head (or cursor) back to the left margin.

Baudot code was used for many years on telex equipment, and some teletype machines still use this code. In fact, the punched tape so familiar to teletype users is a direct representation of Baudot code. There are five positions across the punch tape; a hole in the tape represents a one, and no hole represents a zero.

Occasionally, a bit is changed during data transmission. We call this a *bit error*. In Baudot code, there is no way the receiving device can tell that a bit error occurred during transmission. The need for *error detection* led to an improvement on the Baudot code known as *International Baudot*. International Baudot adds a sixth bit, known as a *parity bit*, to check for errors. We explain in detail how parity bits work in Chapter 6. Simply stated, a parity bit is an extra bit transmitted in addition to the character code bits. It helps ensure that data can be checked for errors at the receiving end.

Basic Data Communications Concepts

The five information bits of Baudot code yield 32 different combinations of ones and zeroes. To represent more than 32 characters, the Letters and Figures characters shift the user into different transmission and reception modes (Upper and Lower Case). Switching back and forth between Upper and Lower Case wastes a computer's time. For this reason, Baudot code is not often used for high-speed data communications. Later character codes remedied this problem.

Extended Binary Coded Decimal Interchange Code

Extended Binary Coded Decimal Interchange Code, known as *EBCDIC*, is an eight-bit character code developed by IBM (International Business Machines Corporation). EBCDIC is a descendant of several older codes, including *Binary Coded Decimal*, or *BCD*, an early code used by computers to represent information internally. BCD led to the development of *Extended Binary Coded Decimal*, or *EBCD*, and finally to EBCDIC.

The eight bits of EBCDIC offer 256 different possible combinations of ones and zeroes. Most EBCDIC implementations, however, do not utilize all of the possible combinations. One EBCDIC implementation is presented in Fig. 3-4. Empty spaces in the chart can be used for other characters and functions needed for other implementations, including foreign language and graphics characters. We number the bits in EBCDIC with the bit on the far left as bit 0, and the bit on the far right as bit 7. To read the EBCDIC chart, simply find a particular character; bits 0, 1, 2, and 3 are found on the left end of the row, and bit 4, 5, 6, and 7 are found at the top of the column.

If a user types the letter "A" on an EBCDIC terminal, the bits 11000001 are transmitted, as shown in Fig. 3-4. Similarly, typing the letter "B" causes 11000010 to be transmitted, typing the letter "C" causes 11000011 to be transmitted, and so on, as shown in the EBCDIC table. There are many special characters in EBCDIC; the abbreviations of those relevant to our discussion are also explained in Fig. 3-4. Certain characters, such as the line feed character, simply control printers and terminals. Others, such as the Start of Header (SOH) character, are used extensively in special communications protocols. These special characters are discussed in detail in Chapter 7.

In most cases, EBCDIC is used without parity bits. Usually, groups of EBCDIC characters are sent together, in blocks, and an entire block of characters is checked for errors at once. This technique is explained in detail in Chapter 6. Some variations of EBCDIC do add a ninth bit for parity checking, though in most cases, this bit is removed before transmission.

American National Standard Code
for Information Interchange

American National Standard Code for Information Interchange, known as *ASCII*, is a seven-bit data code with a single additional parity bit. ASCII (pronounced as-key) was developed by the *American National Standards Institute*, or *ANSI*, as a general-purpose

Figure 3-4 EBCDIC CODE

Bits 4 5 6 7 (columns, top), bits 0 1 2 3 (rows, left side)

Bits 0123 \ 4567	0000	0001	0010	0011	0100	0101	0110	0111	1000	1001	1010	1011	1100	1101	1110	1111
0000	NUL	SOH	STX	ETX	PF	HT	LC	DEL				VT	FF	CR	SO	SI
0001	DLE	DC1	DC2	DC3	RES	NL	BS	IL	CAN	EM			IFS	IGS	IRS	IUS
0010			FS		BYP	LF	EOB	PRE			SM			ENQ	ACK	BEL
0011			SYN		PN	RS	UC	EOT					DC4	NAK		SUB
0100	SP										¢	.	<	(	+	|
0101	&										!	$	*	)	;	¬
0110	-	/									¦	,	%	-	>	?
0111										\	:	#	@	'	=	"
1000		a	b	c	d	e	f	g	h	i						
1001		j	k	l	m	n	o	p	q	r						
1010		~	s	t	u	v	w	x	y	z						
1011																
1100	{	A	B	C	D	E	F	G	H	I						
1101	}	J	K	L	M	N	O	P	Q	R						
1110			S	T	U	V	W	X	Y	Z						
1111	0	1	2	3	4	5	6	7	8	9						□

Note: To read this chart, simply find the character on the chart, then look to the left side of the row for bits 0, 1, 2, and 3, and to the top of the column for bits 4, 5, 6, and 7. This is only one of many possible implementaitons of EBCDIC.

EBCDIC Special Characters

ACK	Acknowledgement
BEL	Bell
BS	Backspace
BYP	Bypass
CAN	Cancel
CR	Carriage Return
DC1	Device Control 1
DC2	Device Control 2
DC3	Device Control 3
DC4	Device Control 4
DEL	Delete
DLE	Data Link Escape
EM	End of Medium
ENQ	Enquiry
EOB	End of Block
EOT	End of Transmission
ETX	End of Text
FF	Form Feed
FS	File Separator
HT	Horizontal Tab
IFS	Information File Separator
IGS	Information Group Separator
IL	Idle
IRS	Information Record Separator
IUS	Information Unit Separator
LC	Lower Case
LF	Line Feed
NAK	Negative Acknowledgement
NL	New Line
NUL	Null
PF	Punch Off
PN	Punch On
PRE	Prefix
RES	Restore
RS	Reader Stop
SI	Shift In
SM	Start Message
SO	Shift Out
SOH	Start of Heading
SP	Space
STX	Start of Text
SUB	Substitute
SYN	Synchronous Idle
UC	Upper Case
VT	Vertical Tab

character code. The ASCII table is presented in Fig. 3-5. The seven data bits of ASCII offer 128 different possible combinations of ones and zeroes. We number the bits in ASCII with the bit on the far left as bit 8 and the bit on the far right as bit 1. Bit 8 is the parity bit, and bits 1 through 7 are the data bits.

If a user types the letter "A" on an ASCII terminal, the seven data bits transmitted are 1000001, as shown in Fig. 3-5. Similarly, typing the letter "B" causes 1000010 to be transmitted, typing the letter "C" causes 1000011 to be transmitted, and so on, as shown in the ASCII table. In addition to these seven data bits, a parity bit will usually be transmitted.

There are several *control characters* in ASCII, similar to those used in EBCDIC, and their abbreviations are also explained in Fig. 3-5. Some of these characters, known as *format effectors (FE)*, perform special display functions on printers and terminals. Other characters, known as *information separators (IS)*, are used by host computers in

FIGURE 3-5 ASCII CODE

Bits 7654321	Character	Bits 7654321	Character	Bits 7654321	Character	Bits 7654321	Character
0000000	NUL	0100000	SP	1000000	@	1100000	'
0000001	SOH	0100001	!	1000001	A	1100001	a
0000010	STX	0100010	"	1000010	B	1100010	b
0000011	ETX	0100011	#	1000011	C	1100011	c
0000100	EOT	0100100	$	1000100	D	1100100	d
0000101	ENQ	0100101	%	1000101	E	1100101	e
0000110	ACK	0100110	&	1000110	F	1100110	f
0000111	BEL	0100111	'	1000111	G	1100111	g
0001000	BS	0101000	(	1001000	H	1101000	h
0001001	HT	0101001	)	1001001	I	1101001	i
0001010	LF	0101010	*	1001010	J	1101010	j
0001011	VT	0101011	+	1001011	K	1101011	k
0001100	FF	0101100	,	1001100	L	1101100	l
0001101	CR	0101101	-	1101101	M	1101101	m
0001110	SO	0101110	.	1001110	N	1101110	n
0001111	SI	0101111	/	1001111	O	1101111	o
0010000	DLE	0110000	0	1010000	P	1110000	p
0010001	DC1	0110001	1	1010001	Q	1110001	q
0010010	DC2	0110010	2	1010010	R	1110010	r
0010011	DC3	0110011	3	1010011	S	1110011	s
0010100	DC4	0110100	4	1010100	T	1110100	t
0010101	NAK	0110101	5	1010101	U	1110101	u
0010110	SYN	0110110	6	1010110	V	1110110	v
0010111	ETB	0110111	7	1010111	W	1110111	w
0011000	CAN	0111000	8	1011000	X	1111000	x
0011001	EM	0111001	9	1011001	Y	1111001	y
0011010	SUB	0111010	:	1011010	Z	1111010	z
0011011	ESC	0111011	;	1011011	[	1111011	{
0011100	FS	0111100	<	1011100	\	1111100	|
0011101	GS	0111101	=	1011101	]	1111101	}
0011110	RS	0111110	>	1011110	^	1111110	~
0011111	US	0111111	?	1011111	__	1111111	DEL

Basic Data Communications Concepts

FIGURE 3-5 ACSII CODE (*continued*)

ASCII Control Characters

BEL	Bell	EM	End of Medium
CAN	Cancel	ESC	Escape
DC1	Device Control 1	NUL	Null
DC2	Device Control 2	SI	Shift In
DC3	Device Control 3	SO	Shift Out
DC4	Device Control 4	SUB	Substitute
DEL	Delete		

Control Codes

ACK	Acknowledge	ETX	End of Text
DLE	Data Link Escape	NAK	Negative Acknowledge
ENQ	Enquiry	SOH	Start of Heading
EOT	End of Transmission	STX	Start of Text
ETB	End of Transmission Block	SYN	Synchronous Idle

Format Effectors

BS	Backspace	HT	Horizontal Tabulation
CR	Carriage Return	LF	Line Feed
FF	Form Feed	VT	Vertical Tabulation

Information Separators

FS	File Separator	RS	Record Separator
GS	Group Separator	US	Unit Separator

storing and retrieving data. Finally, another group of characters, known as *control codes (CC)*, are used in protocols that we examine in detail in Chapter 7.

Some manufacturers of terminals and host computers have chosen to use their own modified versions of ASCII. Such versions, often known as *extended ASCII*, replace the parity bit with an eighth data bit. This allows for 256 combinations of ones and zeroes, doubling the number of characters that can be represented. Such an extension of the character set allows unusual characters, including foreign-language characters and accent marks, and graphic or scientific characters, to be represented in the second 128 characters. These extra characters come at the expense of the parity bit and its error detection capabilities which we consider in Chapter 6.

Equipment Compatibility and Character Code Comparisons

We have introduced several different character codes with different bit lengths. Clearly, terminals using a particular character code are designed to connect to computers using that same code. But what about the user with a terminal that uses ASCII code and a host computer that uses EBCDIC code? *Code conversion* is required to connect devices using dissimilar character codes, and *protocol conversion* may be necessary as well. These functions are reviewed in more detail in Chapter 5.

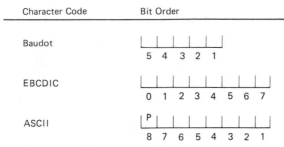

Figure 3-6 Bit position differences among various character codes.

Figure 3-6 shows the bit position differences among the various character codes. In most implementations, the lower-numbered bit (usually 0 or 1) is transmitted first, followed by the other bits. Remember that the bit numbering schemes used in the different codes are simply conventions followed in the industry to ensure that transmitting and receiving devices send and receive the bits in the same order. The "P" shown in bit 8 of the ASCII code represents the parity bit.

Some typical data and parity bit combinations in the different character codes are compared in Fig. 3-7. Notice that there are variations in parity bit implementations even within a single character code. The most common implementation is presented first in each case. Some manufacturers may choose different parity schemes from those shown. Doing so, however, may render their proprietary versions of the character codes incompatible with the rest of the industry.

To the user, it's not really important which character code a terminal is using, as long as the host computer is able to understand the terminal. Character codes merely define exactly which sets of ones and zeroes are transmitted for each character. We will now turn to other important data transmission issues.

FIGURE 3-7 TYPICAL DATA AND PARITY COMBINATIONS FOR VARIOUS CHARACTER CODES

Character Code	Data Bits	Parity Bits	Total Bits
Baudot	5	0	5
International Baudot	5	1	6
ASCII	7	1	8
	8	0	8
EBCDIC	8	0	8
	8	1	9

Note: This chart contains the most commonly used parity/data bit combinations. There are other possible variations.

Basic Data Communications Concepts

CHARACTER CODE DESIGN
AND TERMINAL IMPLEMENTATION

The most advanced character codes we discussed, ASCII and EBCDIC, both include upper- and lowercase letters. In the ASCII code chart in Fig. 3-5, notice that the letter "A" is represented by 1000001, while the letter "a" is represented by 1100001. Similarly, the letter "B" is represented by 1000010, and the letter "b" by 1100010. Throughout the alphabet, the only difference between an ASCII letter in lower case and upper case is in bit number 6. Upper caseletters have a 0 in bit 6, and lowercase letters have a 1 in bit 6.

This simplifies the character code implementation on a terminal. Typically, a terminal user will press the shift key to send an uppercase character. Pressing the shift key on an ASCII terminal simply causes bit 6 to be sent as a 0 when another key is struck; if the shift key is released, the terminal sends a 1 for bit 6 when another key is struck. If the terminal has a Shift Lock or Caps Lock feature, using that feature sets bit 6 to be a 0 all the time.

Similarly, in EBCDIC, as shown in Fig. 3-4, the only difference between the letter "A" and the letter "a" is in bit 1. Uppercase letters in EBCDIC use a 1 in bit 1, and lowercase letters use a 0 in bit 1.

Many ASCII terminal users are familiar with a key known as the *control key*. Users can press the control key, and then hit another key, to perform a special function. Pressing the control key causes bit 7 and bit 6 both to be 0.

One special character on the ASCII chart is the BEL character. Most ASCII terminals will sound a short beep when they receive this character. An ASCII terminal user pressing the control key and the "G" simultaneously will send the BEL character. The "G" is normally 1000111, but the control key changes bits 6 and 7 to 0, resulting in 0000111, or the BEL character. Similarly, pressing the control key and the "g" simultaneously will also send a BEL.

One common function often performed on ASCII terminals with control characters is *XON/XOFF*. In this case, an ASCII terminal can ask the host computer to stop transmitting data by sending the XOFF character, usually the DC3 character. Notice on the ASCII chart that an "S" is usually 1010011. Pressing the control key and an "S" simultaneously results in 0010011, or the DC3 character. Transmission can be resumed by sending the XON character, usually a DC1. The DC1 character can be sent by pressing the control key and a "Q" simultaneously.

From the discussion above we can see how character code designers have allowed keyboards to use each key for several functions. Rather than needing hundreds of different keys, special keys like the shift key and the control key allow the size and cost of terminals to be minimized.

Basic Data Communications Concepts

PARALLEL VS. SERIAL TRANSMISSION

Though a character code determines what bits need to be transmitted to represent a particular character, it does not define how these bits will be sent. There are two common methods of data transmission: parallel and serial.

We will assume we have eight bits of information to send from point A to point B. For our example, assume that the eight bits are 01000001. This happens to be the ASCII representation of the letter "A" with a 0 used for the parity bit. How do we send these ones and zeroes?

One method is to send all eight bits at once. This is known as *parallel transmission*, as illustrated in Fig. 3-8. This method requires at least eight wires for transmission, one wire for each bit sent. It also requires other wires for functions examined in Chapter 4.

An analogy for parallel transmission can be drawn using cars and highways. If we have eight cars that need to travel between point A and point B, the fastest way to get them there is with an eight-lane highway; all eight cars arrive at their destination at the same time.

The main advantage of parallel transmission is that the entire byte is received at once since all eight ones and zeroes are sent at the same time. The main disadvantage is the number of wires (or lanes on the data highway) required for transmission.

Another method is to send the eight bits one after another, requiring only one wire for transmission. This is known as *serial transmission*, as illustrated in Fig. 3-9.

An analogy for serial transmission is a one-lane road, with the eight cars traveling one behind the other. No matter how fast the cars travel, the first car in the line always arrives at the destination before the others. Of course, it is less expensive to build a one-lane highway than an eight-lane highway.

The main advantage of serial transmission lies in minimizing the number of wires (or lanes on the data highway) that are necessary for data transmission. However, some time is wasted, because the byte must be disassembled, sent one bit at a time, and reassembled at the other end.

Both parallel and serial transmission have their places in data communications applications. For example, many personal computers communicate with their printers using parallel transmission. Since printers are usually located within 10 or 20 feet of the personal computer, the extra wires required for parallel transmission are short, and the slight extra cost is more than offset by the added speed.

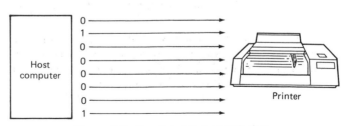

Figure 3-8 Parallel data transmission.

Basic Data Communications Concepts

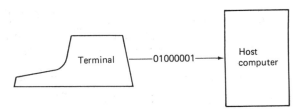

Figure 3-9 Serial data transmission.

A user connecting his terminal to a host computer two buildings away, however, will likely be using serial transmission. In this case, the additional distance involved makes the cost of parallel transmission prohibitive, and speed is sacrificed for the economical advantage of serial transmission. Only one wire, or channel, is needed for sending data in each direction, thereby lowering the transmission cost.

Since manufacturers expect most terminals to be located some distance from host computers, terminals and host computers almost always communicate using serial transmission. In fact, almost all data communications equipment we consider in the next few chapters use serial transmission. Parallel transmission can be thought of as a special case, or an exception, suitable for short-distance transmission.

Now that we've established that most data communications is accomplished with serial transmission, we will examine the timing of the bit transmission.

ASYNCHRONOUS VS. SYNCHRONOUS TRANSMISSION

There are two common methods in use today for timing serial data transmission: asynchronous and synchronous.

Asynchronous transmission is commonly used by the dumb terminals we mentioned earlier. For our discussion, we will assume that our characters are represented by 8 bits, including any parity bit. With asynchronous transmission, each device must be set to transmit and receive data at a given speed, known as the *data rate*. The data rate is often measured in *bits per second*, or *bps*. When an asynchronous device sends a byte, it begins by sending a *start bit*, which is a always 0, followed by each of the eight bits in the byte, and then sends a *stop bit*, which is always a 1. These bits add up to form a ten-bit package for transmission. Some asynchronous devices send more than one stop bit, which simply lengthens the number of bits required to send a character.

The asynchronous transmission of the letter "A," followed by the letter "B," from a dumb terminal to a host computer using ASCII code is shown in Fig. 3-10. The terminal user types the letter "A" on the keyboard, and the terminal converts the letter "A" to the bit sequence 01000001, with a 0 used as the parity bit. If we assume that the terminal is set to transmit at 1 bit per second, the terminal can send each bit 1 second apart. The terminal begins by sending the start bit, a 0, for the first second. It then sends the first data bit, a 1, during the next second; it then sends the next bit, a 0; and so on. This continues until the start bit, seven data bits, one parity bit, and the stop bit have been sent. The host computer, upon receiving the start bit, is thereby notified to expect seven data bits, one parity bit, and one stop bit. Each of these bits will be sent 1 second apart. The start bit actually starts the host computer's internal stopwatch or clock, and the host will then expect to receive the next nine bits 1 second apart. The stop bit is used to halt the host computer's internal stopwatch. It can later be started again by another start bit, sent with the next character. In Fig. 3-10, the next character sent is the letter "B."

To visualize the process of asynchronous transmission, we can pretend we are using a tennis practice machine, which throws balls to us every 5 seconds. We'll use orange balls to represent zeroes and yellow balls to represent ones. A friend loads ten balls into the machine, with the first ball an orange one and the last ball a yellow one. We set the machine to start as soon as it is filled with ten balls; it throws the first ball (an orange ball), or the start ball. After that, we expect a ball (any color) 5 seconds from now, another ball 10 seconds from now, and so on, until we finally receive the tenth ball, or stop ball (a yellow one), 45 seconds from now. If we don't receive one ball every 5 seconds, and a yellow ball (the stop ball) in 45 seconds, we know that either the machine is not functioning, or that one of the balls fell out of the machine.

Similarly, in asynchronous transmission, the only way to know when the next bit will arrive is to time how long it's been since the start bit was received. If fewer than ten bits are received, or the stop bit isn't received when expected, either the transmitter is malfunctioning or one of the bits was lost in transmission.

Asynchronous transmission, often known as *start-stop transmission* because of the start and stop bits, is an excellent means for transmitting characters from terminals to host computers. As soon as the user strikes a key, the terminal decides which byte to send for this character, and adds the start and stop bits; all ten bits can be immediately transmitted. In Fig. 3-10, there is a variable time between when the letter "A" and the letter "B" are transmitted. If the user strikes the keys one after another, the characters will be transmitted one after the other. If the user types only the letter "A," and then takes a coffee break before typing the letter "B," the terminal is idle and does nothing but wait during that coffee break. The user at the keyboard is like our friend loading the tennis ball machine. We never know when our friend will load the machine, but when the machine has its ten balls, it will start firing them at us at a fixed rate of speed. Similarly, we don't know when the user will strike a key, but as soon as the user hits a key on the keyboard, the terminal has the ten bits it needs and will start sending them at a fixed rate.

We've been using data rates of one bit each second, or one every 5 seconds, to

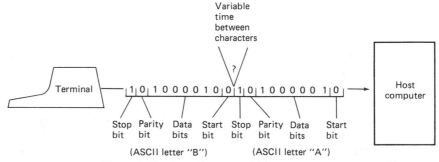

Figure 3-10 Asynchronous data transmission.

make our examples easier to understand. Actual data rates are more likely to be 110 bps, 300 bps, 1200 bps, 2400 bps, 4800 bps, 9600 bps, 19200 bps, all the way up to millions of bits per second. Of course, it is essential that the transmitting and receiving devices both be set at the same speed.

Besides asynchronous transmission, the other commonly used form of data transmission is *synchronous transmission*. Here, start and stop bits are not used. There is no pause between characters in synchronous data transmission, as shown in Fig. 3-11, where the letters "A" and "B" are sent one after the other. Instead of using start and stop bits, timing is supplied in two ways. The two methods, using sync characters or clock signals, can be used independently, though they are often used in conjunction with each other.

First, synchronous data transmission usually involves large blocks of characters, and special *sync characters* can be sent at the beginning of these data blocks. These sync characters are a special series of bits the receiving device can use to adjust to the transmitter's exact rate of speed.

The second method of timing used in synchronous transmission is *transmit clocks* and *receive clocks*. In this case, separate wires or channels are used to send information about the timing of the data being transmitted. The devices transmitting data often send their own timing information on a separate wire from the data. The clock signals are a way of saying "Here comes a bit right now."

We can compare clock signals and sync characters using our tennis ball example. First, to better simulate synchronous data blocks, we'll load the machine not with just ten balls, but a few hundred. Clock signals are the equivalent of setting the tennis ball machine to operate with an audible signal. Just before the machine throws each ball, it will sound a beep. The beep is our clock signal that lets us know when to expect a ball to be thrown. Similarly, in synchronous data transmission, the transmit clock tells a terminal when to send a bit, and the receive clock warns a terminal when to expect to receive a bit.

Sync characters can be simulated in our tennis ball machine if the first eight balls are always the same pattern, for example, yellow-orange-orange-orange-orange-orange-orange-yellow. When we receive this pattern of balls, we "sync up," getting used to the pace. We begin our real practice with the ninth ball. Similarly, a sync character is a known pattern of bits. After receiving a certain number of sync characters, a device expects to receive real data.

There is nothing to prevent us from using both a set pattern of eight tennis balls at the beginning of each session, while at the same time using an audible signal. Similarly, many synchronous devices use sync characters initially to "sync up" to the transmission

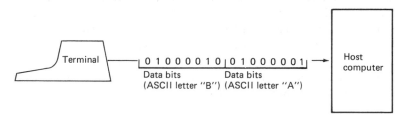

Figure 3-11 Synchronous data transmission.

speed, and use clock signals to keep their internal stopwatch in line with the transmitter's stopwatch.

In addition, synchronous transmission is usually governed by protocols, which we explain in detail in Chapter 7. A major feature of these protocols is that data is usually sent in *blocks*, or groups, of characters, not one byte at a time. Most synchronous terminals are smart or intelligent terminals, and have an ENTER or XMIT key. As the user types information, the terminal holds all of the data until the user hits the ENTER or XMIT key. Then the terminal places special characters at the beginning and end of the data, according to the protocol, and sends the entire block of characters.

Asynchronous vs. Synchronous Transmission Efficiency

Synchronous transmission has an obvious advantage when large blocks of data must be sent. Time is not wasted sending a start and stop bit for each character. For example, as shown in Fig. 3-12, if a block of data contains 1000 characters, and ten special characters need to be used by the synchronous protocol at the beginning and end of the block, 1010 characters need to be sent. If we assume eight-bit characters, 8000 bits out of the 8080 we are sending are actual data bits. This is roughly 99.1% efficient. We consider the special characters, comprising the extra 80 bits, as *overhead* necessary for successful data transmission.

In asynchronous transmission of the same 1000 characters, as shown in Fig. 3-12, we must send 10000 bits, since each character requires eight bits plus one start and one stop bit. Therefore, since 8000 of the 10,000 bits are data bits, and 2000 bits are over-head, asynchronous transmission proves only 80% efficient for eight-bit characters.

Note that no matter how many eight-bit characters are sent, asynchronous transmission remains 80% efficient. Synchronous transmission efficiency, on the other hand, depends on the size of the block of characters being sent. The larger the block, the more efficient synchronous transmission becomes. Synchronous transmission of small blocks of data is relatively inefficient. For example, if the user types only one character before hitting the ENTER key, the same 10 special characters may be needed before and after the one data character, leaving an efficiency of eight data bits in 88 transmitted bits, or only 9.1%.

In our example, we chose one start bit and one stop bit for asynchronous transmission, and assumed that ten special characters were necessary in synchronous transmission. For this example, synchronous transmission becomes more efficient than asynchronous transmission for data blocks larger than 40 characters. This is less than the number of characters in a line of a typewritten page. Synchronous terminals are usually smart or intelligent terminals; they are more expensive to build because they must be able to differentiate between actual data and the special synchronous characters, as well as following special protocols we explain in Chapter 7.

Asynchronous and synchronous transmission are two ways of timing bit transmission once a communications path is available. We must still consider the different types of paths used for communications.

Figure 3-12 SYNCHRONOUS AND ASYNCHRONOUS TRANSMISSION EFFICIENCY

Asynchronous Transmission Efficiency

ABCDEFGHIJKLMNOPQRSTUVWXYZ. .etc. .ABCDEFGHIJKLMNOPQRSTUVWXYZ

Each character = 8 data bits, 1 start bit, 1 stop bit = 10 total bits

If we need to send 1000 characters,
    then 10000 total bits are sent,
    of which 8000 are data bits   ⟶ 80% efficiency

If we need to send 40 characters,
    then 400 total bits are sent,
    of which 320 are data bits   ⟶ 80% efficiency

If we need to send 20 characters,
    then 200 total bits are sent,
    of which 160 are data bits   ⟶ 80% efficiency

Synchronous Transmission Efficiency

*****ABCDEFGHIJKLMNOPQRSTUVWXYZ. .etc. .ABCDEFGHIJKLMNOPQRSTUVWXYZ*****

Assume that each block of data needs 10 special characters (shown as *)

Each character = 8 data bits

If we need to send 1000 characters,
    we add the 10 special characters,
    for a total of 1010 characters,
    so we send 8080 total bits,
    of which 8000 are data bits   ⟶ 99.1% efficiency

If we need to send 40 characters,
    we add the 10 special characters,
    for a total of 50 characters,
    so we send 400 total bits,
    of which 320 are data bits   ⟶ 80% efficiency

If we need to send 20 characters,
    we add the 10 special characters,
    for a total of 30 characters,
    so we send 240 total bits,
    of which 160 are data bits   ⟶ 66.7% efficiency

SIMPLEX, HALF DUPLEX, AND FULL DUPLEX COMMUNICATIONS

There are three different types of communications paths for data transmission: simplex, half duplex, and full duplex.

Simplex communications is a one-way transmission path. One device transmits data, and the other device receives data. A student taught by an old-fashioned professor who does not permit any questions is part of a simplex communications path. The professor is talking to the student, but the student does not have the opportunity to speak and ask questions.

Another example of a simplex path is a one-way street. Cars can only pass in one direction on a one-way street; in simplex data communications, ones and zeroes can be transmitted in only one direction.

An example of simplex data communications can be found at most airports. There is usually a central computer, tracking all of an airline's arrivals and departures. Video monitors are placed throughout the airport to display this arrival and departure information. The host computer sends the information to the video monitor, but the monitors do not send any data back to the host computer. This one-way, or simplex, communications path is illustrated in Fig. 3-13.

Half duplex communications is an alternating transmission path, two ways, but only one direction at a time. For example, a professor typically conducts class in half duplex fashion. First, the professor lectures for a few minutes, pauses for a second, and waits for students to ask questions. A student may ask a question, then the professor answers, another student asks a question, and so on. Only one person, either the professor or a student, is talking at any one time. Most human conversations are conducted in half duplex fashion; first one person speaks, then the other.

Another example of a half duplex path is the reversible commuter lane becoming popular in many metropolitan areas, particularly on bridges or in tunnels. In the morning rush hour, cars are permitted to travel into the city in the reversible commuter lane. At some point in the afternoon, the lane is closed for a few minutes to allow it to be cleared. Then the lane is reversed, and cars are allowed to travel out of the city in this reversible commuter lane. This is a half duplex path: first one direction, a short pause, and then the other direction.

An example of half duplex data communications can be found in certain terminals and host computers. First the user types some information and hits a special key that sends the entire screen to the host computer. The host computer then responds by sending a screen of information back to the terminal. Only one device, either the terminal or the host computer, will transmit data at any given time. Typically, a short pause occurs between completion of one device's transmission and the next device's reply. This half duplex communications path is illustrated in Fig. 3-14.

Half duplex transmission is often called *two-wire communications*, because originally one pair of wires was used for half duplex transmission. Since early equipment was

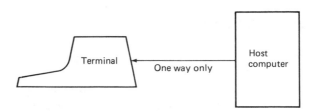

Figure 3-13 Simplex communications path.

Basic Data Communications Concepts

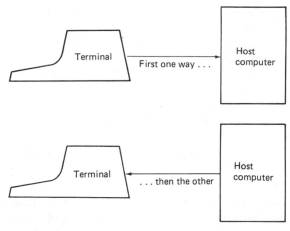

Figure 3-14 Half duplex communications path.

unable to both transmit and receive over one pair of wires at the same time, it was necessary for the devices to share the line by alternating.

Full duplex communications is a two-way communications path. Some professors prefer to be interrupted in mid-sentence if their students have questions. In this case, the professors and students participate in a full duplex communications path. The professor may be talking, and a student may begin speaking at any time. A further example of such a full duplex communications path might be the classic husband/wife argument, where both parties are speaking simultaneously. Each party hears what the other is saying, but both refuse to stop talking.

Another analogy for a full duplex path is a two-way street, with one lane in each direction. Cars can proceed in both directions at the same time, and traffic on one side of the street is unaffected by traffic on the other side of the street.

An example of full duplex data communications can be found in certain terminals and host computers which have the ability to transmit and receive data at the same time. The terminal does not need to wait for the host computer to stop transmitting before the terminal itself transmits. The same is true for the host computer. This full duplex communications path is illustrated in Fig. 3-15.

Full duplex communications is often referred to as *four-wire communications*, because originally, two pairs of wires were needed for full duplex communications. Early equipment transmitted data over one pair of wires in one direction, and received data on the other pair.

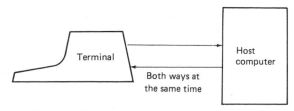

Figure 3-15 Full duplex communications path.

Basic Data Communications Concepts

Today's equipment is more sophisticated than its predecessors, and full duplex communications is now possible over only one pair of wires. Therefore, simply counting the number of wires leaving a device will not help the user determine if the equipment is half duplex or full duplex. Unfortunately, the terminology had already caught on, and the terms "two-wire" and "four-wire" are often used today to refer to half duplex and full duplex communications, respectively, regardless of the number of wires actually used for transmission.

Which method is the best: simplex, half duplex, or full duplex? It depends on the application. In the airport example we used earlier, a simplex communications path is perfect for the job of sending information to a video monitor. However, when a terminal is communicating with a host computer, either half duplex or full duplex is necessary, since a two-way communications path is essential.

Half duplex transmission is by nature slower than full duplex. Only one device can transmit at any one time, and the terminals and computers must often wait to ensure that the other device has finished transmitting. Clearly there is an advantage to having a full duplex connection, since either device is able to transmit data all the time. However, it is sometimes cheaper to provide a half duplex communications path, and in most communications only one party transmits at one time anyway. As a result, many half duplex terminals and host computers are in use today.

SUMMARY

Data communications is the exchange of digital information, or ones and zeroes, between two devices. Host computers and terminals usually communicate using groups of eight bits, or bytes. Character codes are different methods used by devices to represent information. The two most common character codes, ASCII and EBCDIC, use ones and zeroes to represent characters.

Code and protocol conversion are sometimes required to connect different manufacturers' devices. Even within a character code, some manufacturers may vary their use of parity bits, making some equipment incompatible.

A byte of data can be sent with parallel transmission, all at once, with one bit sent on each of eight separate wires. Serial transmission, however, requires only one wire, and the bits are sent one after another. Serial transmission is more widely used in data communications because the single wire is less expensive.

Asynchronous transmission uses start and stop bits to time serial transmission. Synchronous transmission, on the other hand, uses sync characters and clock signals for timing. Synchronous transmission is more efficient then asynchronous transmission for large blocks of data. Asynchronous transmission, however, is usually less expensive to implement.

Simplex communication provides a one-way communications path. Half duplex is an alternating transmission path, two ways but only one direction at a time. Full duplex communications is a two-way communications path. The terms *two-wire* and *four-wire* are often used to describe half and full duplex communications, respectively.

Basic Data Communications Concepts

TERMS FOR REVIEW

American National Standard
  Code for Information
  Interchange
American National
  Standards Institute
ANSI
Applications software
ASCII
Asynchronous transmission
Baudot code
BCD
Binary Coded Decimal
Binary number system
Bit
Bit error
Bits per second
Block
Bps
Byte
Carriage return
Cathode ray tube
CC
Central processing unit
Character
Character code
Code conversion
Control character
Control code
Control key
CPU

CRT
Dash
Data communications
Data rate
Digital
Display station
Dot
Dumb terminal
EBCD
EBCDIC
Error detection
Extended ASCII
Extended Binary Coded
  Decimal
Extended Binary Coded
  Decimal Interchange
  Code
FE
Figures
Format effector
Four-wire communications
Full duplex communications
Half duplex communications
Host computer
Information separator
Intelligent terminal
International Baudot
IS
Keyboard
Letters

Line feed
Lower case
Mainframe
Microcomputer
Minicomputer
Morse code
Overhead
Parallel transmission
Parity bit
Personal computer
Protocol conversion
Receive clock
Screen
Serial transmission
Simplex communications
Smart terminal
Start bit
Start-stop transmission
Stop bit
Supercomputer
Sync character
Synchronous transmission
Terminal
Transmit clock
Two-wire communications
Upper case
VDT
Video display terminal
XON/XOFF

EXERCISES

3-1. What is data communications?

3-2. How do the different types of host computers differ?

3-3. Describe the different types of terminals.

3-4. What is the difference between a bit and a byte?

3-5. What is the major drawback of the Morse code?

3-6. What technique does Baudot code use to practically double the number of characters represented with five bits? What is the disadvantage of using this method?

Basic Data Communications Concepts

3-7. How does the order of bit transmission in ASCII and EBCDIC codes differ?

3-8. What are the functions of the XON/XOFF characters?

3-9. What is the difference between parallel and serial transmission? Which is used more frequently in data communications, and why?

3-10. How do asynchronous and synchronous transmission differ? Which is better suited to large blocks of characters, and why?

3-11. Describe the difference between simplex, half duplex, and full duplex communications.

Basic Data Communications Concepts

4

DATA INTERFACES AND TRANSMISSION

There are many different ways to connect terminals to host computers. We have already discussed basic data communications concepts, such as full and half duplex communications, and asynchronous and synchronous transmission.

We now analyze in detail the methods used to connect terminals to host computers, whether the terminal is located 20 feet or 2000 miles away.

STANDARDS ORGANIZATIONS

Host computer and terminal manufacturers usually conform to certain recognized standards to connect their equipment. Some standards are introduced and promoted by one manufacturer, and they are so successful that they become the industry standard. Other standards are formed by *standards organizations*. These organizations are generally chartered to devise standards for a particular industry within certain countries.

Typically, standards are developed by committees with representatives from leading companies in an industry. Certain standards organizations, particularly those covering military products, also have government representation. We now briefly examine the organizations with the most impact on data communications.

The *American National Standards Institute*, or *ANSI*, is an umbrella organization for all the standards organizations in the United States. ANSI accredits various organizations which can then submit their standards to ANSI for acceptance as a national standard.

The *Institute of Electrical and Electronics Engineers*, or *IEEE*, is a professional organization of engineers. IEEE consists of many specialized societies, whose committees prepare standards in their areas of specialty.

The *Electronic Industries Association*, or *EIA*, is an organization representing many manufacturers in the U.S. electronics industry.

The *Exchange Carriers Standards Association*, or *ECSA*, consists of telephone equipment manufacturing companies. ECSA was formed after the A.T.&T. divestiture, to continue work on standards previously developed by the Bell System.

The *National Bureau of Standards*, or *NBS*, is a federal organization responsible for producing *Federal Information Processing Standards*, or *FIPS*. Meeting these FIPS is a requirement for many government suppliers.

In the United States, most of the standards are only recommendations. With the exception of certain standards regarding interference and safety, the FCC does not regulate the internal workings of equipment, only how it attaches to the public network. Internationally, telecommunications is regulated in most countries by a PTT. PTTs often impose strict requirements on all aspects of communications equipment used in a given country. The PTTs usually represent their countries on international standards organizations. There are two major international standards organizations. The *Consultative Committee on International Telephone and Telegraph*, or *CCITT*, is an international telecommunications standards organization. Its members include the regulating bodies from member countries, and leading companies in the field, as well as representatives from other organizations.

In the *International Standards Organization*, or *ISO*, each member country is represented by its own national standards organization. ISO and CCITT cooperate on certain standards, but often develop their own completely different standards for the same technical areas. Membership in both ISO and CCITT is possible and often occurs.

The domestic and international standards organizations prepare standards on many topics. We now examine those used for data communications.

DIGITAL INTERFACE STANDARDS

The point at which one device connects to another is known as an *interface*. An interface standard defines exactly which electronic signals are required for communication between two devices. Some interface standards also define the physical connector to be used.

The RS-232-C Standard

One of the most common interface standards for data communications in use today is EIA's *Recommended Standard 232C*, or *RS-232-C*. RS-232-C defines exactly how ones and zeros will be electronically transmitted, including voltage levels needed as well as the other electronic signals necessary for computer communication.

The CCITT has standards similar to EIA's RS-232-C, known as *V.24* and *V.28*. The V.24 standard defines all of the signals described in RS-232-C, and the V.28 standard defines the same voltage levels described in RS-232-C.

RS-232-C voltage levels.   What does it mean when we transmit a 1 or a 0? In RS-232-C, ones and zeroes are transmitted using negative and positive voltages. Those readers unfamiliar with the concept of positive and negative voltages should not be concerned; devices can be built that can both send and recognize these different signals.

RS-232-C defines "sending a 1," known as a *mark*, as an electronic signal between -3 and -15 volts. It defines "sending a 0," known as a *space*, as an electronic signal between +3 and +15 volts. Signals outside these ranges are considered undefined, are considered neither a one nor a zero, and are ignored by the receiver. This signal definition is illustrated in Fig. 4-1.

A terminal communicating according to RS-232-C must therefore be able to send and receive voltages in the range of -15 to +15 volts. For example, to send the ASCII letter "A," with a 0 as the parity bit, or 01000001, an asynchronous RS-232-C terminal must first send the start bit, a 0, or +15 volts, followed by a 1, or -15 volts, followed by five 0s, or +15 volt pulses, then another 1, or -15 volt pulse, followed by a 0, or +15 volt pulse, and finally the stop bit, or -15 volts. If we assume a transmission rate of one bit per second, Fig. 4-2 shows the ASCII transmission of the letter "A." If the letter "A" were to be sent at a faster rate, the time periods in Fig. 4-2 would be shorter. For example, at 1200 bits per second, each of the time periods would be 833 microseconds (1/1200 second) long. Remember that these pulses don't have to be exactly 15 volts; all voltages in the range of 3 to 15 are acceptable. After sending the stop bit, the transmitter remains at the negative voltage until the next character, which will begin with a start bit (a positive voltage).

DTEs and DCEs in RS-232-C.   In addition to defining how ones and zeroes are transmitted, RS-232-C also defines other electronic signals useful for communications. RS-232-C assumes that there are two types of interfaces. The first, known as *data terminal equipment*, or *DTE*, is the interface most often found on terminals, host

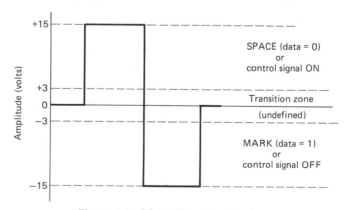

Figure 4-1   RS-232-C voltage levels.

Data Interfaces and Transmission

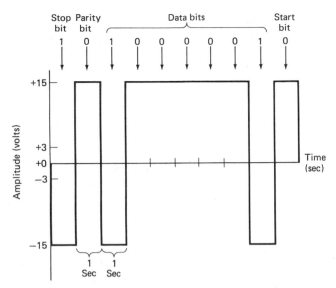

Figure 4-2 RS-232-C transmission of the ASCII character "A."

computers, and printers. The second, known as *data circuit-terminating equipment*, or *DCE*, is the interface usually used on devices known as modems, and some multiplexers. DCE is often also referred to as "data communications equipment." Even though RS-232-C defines only the type of interface, we often describe an entire device by referring to its interface; for example, terminals are often called DTEs, and modems are often called DCEs.

The usual purpose of DCEs is to allow DTEs to be located remotely from each other. The DTEs are the data communications equivalent of the people in a telephone conversation. The DCEs are the equivalent of the phones in the conversation; DCEs are simply instruments used to allow DTEs to communicate. This comparison is presented in Fig. 4-3. Notice that a terminal (DTE) can be connected to a remote host computer (DTE) using a pair of DCEs and the public telephone network. RS-232-C defines how DTEs communicate with DCEs, but not how DCEs communicate with each other. Later in this chapter we examine the methods DCEs use to communicate with each other.

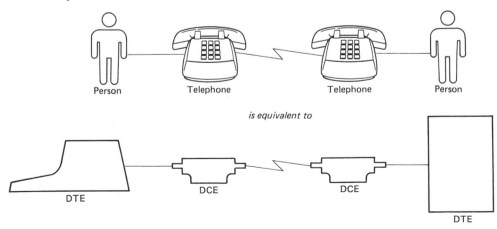

Figure 4-3 DTEs and DCEs.

Data Interfaces and Transmission

RS-232-C specifies the signals exchanged between DTEs and DCEs, but not the exact type of physical connector to be used. For most applications, the *DB25* connector, defined in ISO standard number 2110 and illustrated in Fig. 4-4, has become widely accepted. There are two versions of the DB25 connector, male and female. The male connector contains 25 pins, and the female connector contains 25 small receptacles or sockets for these pins.

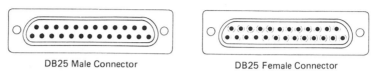

DB25 Male Connector   DB25 Female Connector

Figure 4-4 DB25 connectors.

For an example, consider the standard electrical outlet in our home. These outlets accept two- or three-prong plugs, depending on whether or not the circuit uses the third grounding prong. A DB25 connector takes this concept one step further, with 25 separate pins. In a standard electrical outlet, there is a specific size for each plug, as well as the distance between the prongs. Similarly, the ISO 2110 standard defines the exact size and shape of the DB25 connectors.

Each of the pins, and their corresponding sockets, are numbered from 1 to 25. These connector pin numbers, the commonly used signal names, and the common abbreviations, which we explain in the following sections, are shown in Fig. 4-5. The EIA and CCITT have their own signal abbreviations; although not as commonly used, they are provided in the chart for reference.

There is no technical reason to place certain signals on any particular pin; these conventions are usually followed to allow for compatibility among different vendors' equipment. Figure 4-5 also describes which device, a DTE or DCE, generates each of the signals.

Typically, a cable coming from a DTE device will have a male DB25 connector on its end. DCE devices will usually have a female DB25 connector to accept the cable from the DTE. RS-232-C limits the maximum length of the cable from a DTE to a DCE to 50 feet. In addition, RS-232-C limits data transmission rates to a maximum of 20,000 bits per second (20 kilobits per second or 20 kbps). The distance limitation is often exceeded by users without causing operational difficulties, though doing so violates the RS-232-C standard. Manufacturers will usually refuse to support or service installations that do not comply with the standard.

RS-232-C data signal definitions.   We have already examined how data is transmitted and received, using positive and negative voltages. In RS-232-C, the DTE sends data on the *TD*, or *Transmitted Data* pin. In other words, the DTE can provide a positive (+3 to +15 volt) electronic signal on the TD pin to send a 0 (space), or a negative (-3 to -15 volt) electronic signal on the TD pin to send a 1 (mark). TD is usually found on pin number 2 of the DB25 connector.

Similarly, a DTE receives data on the *RD*, or *Received Data* pin. Notice that the pins are named with respect to the DTE. The DCE will be receiving data from the DTE on the TD pin, and will be sending data to the DTE on the RD pin. Also, regardless of

FIGURE 4-5 RS-232-C SIGNALS

Pin	Abbreviation	Name	Direction	EIA Abbreviation	CCITT Abbreviation
1	GND	Protective Ground	Both ways	AA	101
2	TD	Transmitted Data	DTE to DCE	BA	103
3	RD	Received Data	DCE to DTE	BB	104
4	RTS	Request to Send	DTE to DCE	CA	105
5	CTS	Clear to Send	DCE to DTE	CB	106
6	DSR	Data Set Ready	DCE to DTE	CC	107
7	SG	Signal Ground	Both ways	AB	102
8	DCD	Data Carrier Detect	DCE to DTE	CF	109
9		Positive Test Voltage	DCE to DTE		
10		Negative Test Voltage	DCE to DTE		
11		Unassigned			
12	SDCD	Secondary Data Carrier Detect	DCE to DTE	SCF	122
13	SCTS	Secondary Clear to Send	DCE to DTE	SCB	121
14	STD	Secondary Transmitted Data	DTE to DCE	SBA	118
15	TC	Transmit Clock	DCE to DTE	DB	14
16	SRD	Secondary Received Data	DCE to DTE	SBB	119
17	RC	Receive Clock	DCE to DTE	DD	115
18		Unassigned			
19	SRTS	Secondary Request to Send	DTE to DCE	SCA	120
20	DTR	Data Terminal Ready	DTE to DCE	CD	108.2
21	SQ	Signal Quality Detect	DCE to DTE	CG	110
22	RI	Ring Indicator	DCE to DTE	CE	125
23	DRS	Data Rate Select	Either way	CH/CI	111/112
24	XTC	External Transmit Clock	DTE to DCE	DA	113
25		Unassigned			

whether a device is a DCE or DTE, we almost always refer to pin numbers, rather than sockets, since the signal is named with respect to the DTE and the DTE usually uses the male connector with pins. Therefore, even though RD is a signal produced by the DCE, we state that RD is usually found on pin number 3 of the DB25 connector, because that's the corresponding pin number on the DTE's male connector.

RS-232-C ground signal definitions. Another function needed to ensure proper data transmission is fulfilled by the *Signal Ground*, or *SG* pin. This signal acts as a zero volt reference for all the other signals. An analogy of a reference voltage can be drawn by looking at the sky on a clear day. A philosophy professor asks, ''Is the sky light blue or dark blue today?'' Half of the class thinks it's light blue, and the other half think it's dark blue. That's because every class member has a different idea of what light and dark really means. If the professor is wearing a navy blazer jacket and asks the class, ''Is the sky a darker blue or lighter blue than my jacket?'', the entire class will reply ''The sky is a lighter blue.'' That's because the entire class was using the same reference: the professor's jacket.

The Signal Ground in RS-232-C is a zero volt reference. Signals can be compared to the SG pin; those with higher voltages than the SG pin are positive voltages, and those

Data Interfaces and Transmission

with lower voltages than the SG pin are negative voltages. When a DTE sends a signal on the TD pin, the DCE will compare this voltage to the SG pin to determine whether the data sent was a 1 or a 0. SG is usually found on pin number 7 of the DB25 connector.

There is another ground signal, known as *chassis ground, protective ground, frame ground*, or simply abbreviated as *GND*. This signal is not necessary for data transmission, but can be used to prevent certain errors. Special shielded cable, designed to reduce interference and electronic noise, can attach its shield to the GND pin. Interference and electronic noise can be generated by large electrical motors, such as those found in elevators or factories, or by ordinary fluorescent lights. With shielded cable, the noise never makes it to the data wires because it runs on the shield, through the GND pin, and through the DTE's or DCE's own electrical ground. This shield should be connected to the GND pin only on one side of the cable, or it could pose a potential electrical hazard (if the attached equipment is faulty) and violate the *National Electrical Code*. GND is usually found on pin number 1 of the DB25 connector.

RS-232-C timing signal definitions.   In asynchronous transmission, no timing signals are needed. For synchronous transmission, however, there are clock signals provided in RS-232-C. These clock signals are a series of positive and negative pulses, from +15 to -15 volts, that repeat indefinitely, and are known as a *square wave*. If the data is being transmitted at 1200 bits per second, there will be 1200 complete square waves each second. This allows the device receiving the clock signal to "sync up" to the data rate of the other device. It is a process of continuous calibration, where the device receiving the clock signal is constantly adjusting its speed, if necessary, to match that of the other device. An example of using a square wave as a clock signal to time data transmission is shown in Fig. 4-6.

The *TC* signal, or *Transmit Clock*, is used by the DCE to time the data sent by the DTE on the TD pin in synchronous data transmission. Some DTEs allow the DCE to provide this clock signal. TC is usually found on pin number 15 of the DB25 connector.

The *XTC* signal, or *External Transmit Clock*, is used by the DTE to time the data it sends on the TD pin in synchronous data transmission. Some DTEs insist on providing this clock signal themselves. XTC is usually found on pin number 24 of the DB25 connector.

The *RC* signal, or *Receive Clock*, is used by the DCE to time the data it sends to the DTE on the RD pin in synchronous data transmission. RC is usually found on pin number 17 of the DB25 connector.

RS-232-C control signal definitions.   Using the TD, RD, and SG pins, data could be transmitted asynchronously between DTEs and DCEs. Synchronous transmission would also require use of the TC, RC, and XTC pins. However, there are other functions that are usually performed before data is transmitted.

The *control signals* of RS-232-C are used to indicate the status of a given connection. A control signal is said to be *ON*, or *raised*, or *asserted*, or *true* when it is set to between +3 and +15 volts. Similarly, a control signal is said to be *OFF*, or *low*, or *false* when it is set to between -3 and -15 volts. By raising and lowering the control signal

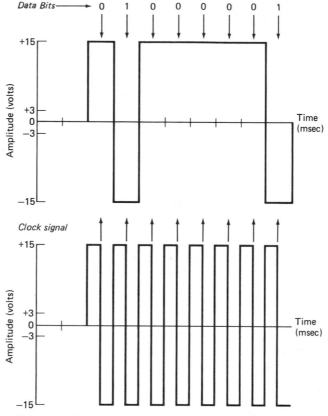

Figure 4-6 Using clock signals to time data transmission.

voltages, the DTE and DCE can communicate information about the status of a given call, and about both devices' readiness to communicate. We will begin by describing the most common control signals used in RS-232-C.

When a DTE device is powered on and placed on-line, it asserts the *DTR* signal, or *Data Terminal Ready*. This is an announcement to the DCE that a DTE is attached and ready to begin communications. DTR is usually found on pin number 20 of the DB25 connector.

The *DSR* signal, or *Data Set Ready*, is asserted by the DCE, and indicates that the DCE is powered on and is ready to begin communications. DSR is usually found on pin number 6 of the DB 25 connector.

The *RTS* signal, or *Request to Send*, is asserted by the DTE to ask permission to send data. In full duplex, the DTE will assert this signal immediately, because a full duplex device wants a continuous two-way communications path. In half duplex devices, the DTE will only assert this signal when it actually has data to send (for instance, when the Enter key has been hit on a terminal). RTS is usually found on pin number 4 of the DB25 connector.

The *CTS* signal, or *Clear to Send*, is asserted by the DCE in response to RTS when the DCE is able to accept data from the DTE. CTS is usually found on pin number 5 of the DB25 connector.

The *DCD* signal, or *Data Carrier Detect*, is asserted by the DCE to alert the DTE to expect to receive data at any time. In full duplex, DCD will remain continuously asserted, since it is a continuous two-way path and data might arrive at any time. In half duplex, DCD will be asserted only when data is being sent to the DTE. This signal is often abbreviated *CD* or *CX*. DCD is usually found on pin number 8 of the DB25 connector.

The *RI* signal, or *Ring Indicator*, is asserted by the DCE to alert the DTE that a remote device wants to initiate communications. RI is usually found on pin number 22 of the DB25 connector.

The control signals we have just analyzed are the most commonly used. There are several other signals used less frequently in RS-232-C.

The *SQ* signal, or *Signal Quality Detect*, is asserted by the DCE when it believes transmissions are of high quality and there are no errors occurring. The DCE drops this signal when it determines that the transmission quality has degraded and an error may have occurred. SQ is usually found on pin number 21 of the DB25 connector.

The *DRS* signal, or *Data Rate Select*, can be asserted by either the DTE or the DCE to change the other device's speed under special conditions. Data Rate Select is usually found on pin number 23 of the DB25 connector.

RS-232-C secondary signals.   There are also several secondary signals. There are *Secondary Transmitted Data* (STD-pin 14), *Secondary Received Data* (SRD-pin 16), *Secondary Request to Send* (SRTS-pin 19), *Secondary Clear to Send* (SCTS-pin 13), and *Secondary Data Carrier Detect* (SDCD-pin 12). These signals are equivalent to their primary counterparts we have already considered, but are rarely used by most DTEs and DCEs. Together, these signals provide a second data channel on which data can be transmitted and received independent of the primary channel.

Other RS-232-C signals.   Two other signals described in RS-232-C as "Reserved for Data Set Testing," pins 9 and 10, are usually defined as positive and negative test voltages, respectively. These signals are often useful for troubleshooting.

The remaining three pins, numbered 11, 18, and 25, were left unassigned by the RS-232-C standard. Many manufacturers have used these pins for their own purposes.

In most cases, when signals are not being used by a manufacturer, such as the clocking pins in asynchronous transmission, these pins are simply omitted from the connector to cut manufacturing costs. Some manufacturers who need only a few of the signals described here actually use a smaller connector than the DB25 to economize and save space (though this is a special case). Still other manufacturers have invented their own functions for the unassigned pins. These variations can make it difficult to connect two different vendors' equipment.

RS-232-C HANDSHAKING

Now that we are familiar with the basic RS-232-C signals, let's see how they're used in asynchronous communications. The interaction of the RS-232-C signals we have already described is known as RS-232-C *handshaking*.

Assume that we have a terminal (DTE) connected to a DCE, which we will refer to as the local DCE, as illustrated in Fig. 4-7. This DCE communicates with another DCE, known as the remote DCE, which is in turn connected to a host computer (DTE).

The terminal is powered up and immediately asserts the DTR signal. The local DCE responds by asserting the DSR signal, and establishes communications with the remote DCE. The remote DCE temporarily asserts the RI signal to alert the host computer that another party would like to communicate with it. The host computer, if powered on and ready, will then assert the DTR signal. The remote DCE responds by dropping the RI signal and asserting the DSR signal, and the connection is complete between the terminal and the host computer.

If the terminal and host computer are communicating using full-duplex, they would have asserted the RTS signals almost immediately after receiving the DSR signal from the DCE. The purpose of the RTS signal is to request a transmission path. The DCEs would then respond with the CTS and DCD signals as soon as communications were established (between the DCEs). The CTS signal confirms that a transmission path is available for the DTE to send data to the DCE. The DCD signal confirms that a transmission path is established in the other direction, from the DCE to the DTE. For devices using full duplex, whenever a transmission path is available, it is available in both directions; therefore, the CTS and DCD signals are asserted by both DCEs. Data transmission can now occur between the terminal and host computer, in both directions simultaneously, through the DCEs.

To summarize, in a full duplex connection, the DTEs assert the DTR and RTS signals, and the DCEs assert the DSR, CTS, and DCD signals. Once the connection is established, these signals do not change. Typically, a DTE will end the connection by dropping its DTR and RTS signals.

An interesting function is performed by the DCEs during the connection. The terminal transmits data on the TD pin to the local DCE, which sends the data to the remote DCE using methods we introduce later in this chapter. The remote DCE sends this data to the host computer on the RD pin. Notice that the DCEs have performed a *crossover* of the data signal, much as telephones do for us. When we talk into our telephone mouthpiece (the equivalent of TD) our voice is received in the other party's earpiece (the equivalent of RD). Similarly, the host computer transmits data on TD to the remote DCE, but this data will be sent to the terminal by the local DCE on the RD pin.

Half duplex communications differs slightly from full duplex. Although the DTR and DSR signaling is the same, half duplex communications require an alternating transmission path (first one direction and then the other). This is accomplished by the use of the RTS, CTS, and DCD signals.

After the DTR/DSR signal interchange at both the terminal and host computer, one of the DTEs will want to transmit data (we'll assume it's the terminal). The terminal asserts its RTS signal, and the local DCE informs the remote DCE that data will be arriving shortly. The remote DCE then asserts DCD to the host computer, to inform it that data will be arriving shortly. Meanwhile, the local DCE has asserted the CTS signal, indicating that the terminal can now send data. A one-way transmission path has now been established from the terminal to the computer. The computer will not try to send data because it is receiving the DCD signal, implying that data is already on its way. When the terminal finishes sending data, it drops the RTS signal; the local DCE then drops the CTS signal and informs the remote DCE the transmission is complete. The remote DCE then drops DCD to the host computer. The host computer is now free to assert its RTS signal and start the process all over again in the other direction. This process will repeat indefinitely, first in one direction, then the other, as long as there is still data to transmit.

We have been discussing asynchronous transmission here. Synchronous transmission functions identically, with the addition of the clock signals (TC, RC, XTC) mentioned previously.

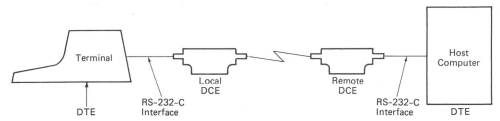

Figure 4-7 Connecting DTEs and DCEs with RS-232-C.

RS-449, RS-422-A, and RS-423-A

The main complaints from the user community about RS-232-C were its speed limitation (20 kbps), its distance limitation (50 feet), and the lack of standardization on both a particular connector type and pin locations. Realizing the deficiencies of RS-232-C, the EIA later introduced a set of three new standards, known as RS-449, RS-422-A, and RS-423-A.

These new standards share the same basic goal as RS-232-C or any other interface standard. All define a standard method for connecting two devices, one known as a DTE and the other as a DCE. Regardless of the shape of the connector, the number of pins used, or the speed of transmission, a similar set of functions must be provided by all interface standards. For example, ''Data Terminal Ready,'' or the equivalent function with a slightly different name, will be found in almost any interface standard.

RS-449 can be thought of as the parent standard, describing the mechanical and functional characteristics of the DTE/DCE interface. *RS-422-A* and *RS-423-A* address the specific details of two different electrical signal characteristics. Together, these three standards were intended as replacements for RS-232-C. However, they are still only in limited use, and RS-232-C devices far outnumber RS-449 devices today.

The RS-449 standard, unlike RS-232-C, defines the exact connector to be used, the *DB37* connector, as presented in Fig. 4-8. The DB37 connector is similar to the DB25, though it is somewhat larger and has 37 pins. In addition, the RS-449 standard develop-

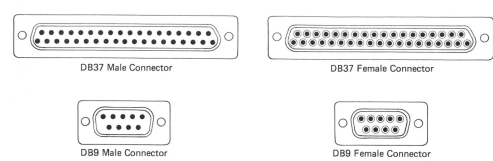

DB37 Male Connector   DB37 Female Connector

DB9 Male Connector   DB9 Female Connector

Figure 4-8 DB37 and DB9 connectors.

ers realized that the secondary channel of RS-232-C was seldom used, so they opted to place those signals on a separate connector, known as a *DB9* connector, also shown in Fig. 4-8. This 9-pin connector is optional, and if the secondary channel is not needed, can be completely omitted. RS-449 therefore defines a total of 46 pins, many more than those in RS-232-C; the extra pins allow for added functions and higher data rates, which we will explain soon. The 37-pin and 9-pin connectors are also defined in the *ISO Standard 4902*.

The functions performed by the RS-449 signals are similar to those used in RS-232-C. The RS-449 signals and their RS-232-C equivalents are compared in Fig. 4-9. Notice that some of the RS-232-C functions are also found in RS-449, with slightly different names. For example, Transmitted Data in RS-232-C is the equivalent of Send Data in RS-449. RS-449 also includes additional signals that were not present in RS-232-C. Most of these new signals are used for testing and diagnostic purposes; others are necessary for RS-422-A and RS-423-A transmission.

Notice that some of the signals in RS-449 use two pins. These signals are known as *Category I* signals, and the second pin allows for RS-422-A transmission, which we will soon present. The other signals on the RS-449 interface, which use only one pin, are known as *Category II* signals.

The real technical advantage of the RS-449 standard is found in its methods of electrical transmission of signals, as described in the RS-422-A and RS-423-A standards. These standards can surpass the RS-232-C speed and distance limits, while allowing for compatibility with older RS-232-C devices.

RS-422-A describes a method of *balanced transmission* that can be used for the RS-449 Category I signals. Balanced transmission requires two wires to send data or a control signal, allowing for high data rates and high reliability. Therefore, each of the Category I signals requires two pins. RS-422-A allows a variable transmission rate, according to the distance involved, as shown in Fig. 4-10. The maximum distance varies from 40 feet to 4000 feet, and the maximum speed can reach 10 million bits per second, or 10 *Mbps*.

RS-423-A describes a method of *unbalanced transmission* used for all of the RS-449 Category II signals. Unbalanced transmission sends the signal over one wire, and all signals share a *common return*. There are two of these returns, *Send Common* and *Receive Common*, one for each direction. RS-423-A also allows a variable transmission rate,

FIGURE 4-9 RS-232-C AND RS-449 SIGNAL EQUIVALENTS

DB9 Connector Pin No.	DB37 Connector Pin Nos.	RS-449 Circuit	RS-449 Description	Category	RS-232-C Equivalent
1	1		Shield		GND
5	19	SG	Signal Ground		SG
9	37	SC	Send Common	II	
6	20	RC	Receive Common	II	
	4,22	SD	Send Data	I	TD
	6,24	RD	Receive Data	I	RD
	7,25	RS	Request to Send	I	RTS
	9,27	CS	Clear to Send	I	CTS
	11,29	DM	Data Mode	I	DSR
	12,30	TR	Terminal Ready	I	DTR
	15	IC	Incoming Call	II	RI
	13,31	RR	Receiver Ready	I	DCD
	33	SQ	Signal Quality	II	SQ
	16	SR	Signaling Rate Selector	II	DRS (DTE)
	2	SI	Signaling Rate Indicator	II	DRS (DCE)
	17,35	TT	Terminal Timing	I	XTC
	5,23	ST	Send Timing	I	TC
	8,26	RT	Receive Timing	I	RC
3		SSD	Secondary Send Data	II	STD
4		SRD	Secondary Receive Data	II	SRD
7		SRS	Secondary Request to Send	II	SRTS
8		SCS	Secondary Clear to Send	II	SCTS
2		SRR	Secondary Receiver Ready	II	SDCD
	10	LL	Local Loopback	II	None
	14	RL	Remote Loopback	II	None
	18	TM	Test Mode	II	None
	32	SS	Select Standby	II	None
	36	SB	Standby Indicator	II	None
	16	SF	Select Frequency	II	None
	28	IS	Terminal in Service	II	None
	34	NS	New Signal	II	None
	3		Undefined		
	21		Undefined		

according to the distance involved, as illustrated in Fig. 4-10. The maximum distance varies from 40 feet to 4000 feet, and the maximum speed can reach 100 kbps.

RS-449 devices can use RS-422-A for their Category I circuits if the added performance is needed. Of course, the extra wires and circuitry costs required for balanced transmission make RS-422-A more expensive than RS-423-A. Therefore, many applications of RS-449 use RS-423-A for their Category I circuits. The balanced transmission has the additional advantage of being less susceptible to noise and interference errors than unbalanced transmission.

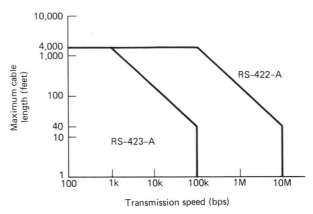

Figure 4-10 RS-422-A and RS-423-A speed and distance limitations.

Category II circuits, where performance is generally not an issue, always use RS-423-A. In addition, RS-423-A devices can be attached to RS-232-C devices using a special wiring adapter, since the unbalanced transmission is similar. Of course, then both devices are confined to the RS-232-C distance and speed limitations. RS-449 handshaking is so similar to that used in RS-232-C that we will we will not elaborate further on the specific RS-449 signals here.

CCITT has a set of equivalent standards for RS-449/RS-422-A/RS-423-A. The functional signals that are shared by RS-232-C and RS-449 are described by the CCITT *V.24* standard already mentioned. The RS-422-A and RS-423-A transmission standards are similar to the CCITT *V.11* and *V.10* standards, respectively.

With the added speed, enhanced distance range, and the other functions of RS-449/RS-422-A/RS-423-A, why are RS-232-C devices still dominant as the general-purpose data communications interfaces? Many of the terminals and host computers themselves can't operate at speeds greater than 19.2 kbps, so any higher transmission speed would be wasted. The distance limitation of RS-232-C can be overcome using inexpensive devices we consider later. In addition, RS-232-C interfaces are inexpensive to implement, as the components are already in mass production. Finally, RS-232-C devices are already installed in large numbers, and connecting to these devices requires conforming to the RS-232-C standard. Although RS-423-A can connect to RS-232-C, it is more expensive to use a 37-pin connector, and then a converter, than to use a standard RS-232-C interface in the first place. For all these reasons, RS-449 is generally used today only where added speed and longer distances are an absolute necessity.

Although there are many other general-purpose data communications interface standards in use today, RS-232-C is certainly the most common, with all the others trailing far behind.

REMOTE DIGITAL TRANSMISSION

All of the interface standards we have mentioned so far in this chapter are intended for

Data Interfaces and Transmission

transmission on a user's premises, over a relatively short distance. The user generally owns all of the wiring or cabling between the devices.

But what about terminals accessing host computers across town, across the country, or across the ocean? Our public telephone network's standard voice communications circuits are not well suited to the *digital transmission* we have been discussing. These square waves, however, can be sent over special *digital circuits* provided by the common carriers.

Typically, the terminal, or host computer, communicates using one of the standard DTE interfaces we have already examined, like RS-232-C. The DTE is then connected to a special device known as a *digital service unit*, or *DSU*. This DSU uses a DCE interface to communicate with the terminal or host computer, and then transmits the data in a special format over the common carrier's digital circuits. Typical use of a DSU is depicted in Fig. 4-11.

Usually the voltage levels required for transmission of data between the DSUs are different from those used by a short-distance interface, like RS-232-C. The DSU is able to convert the signals from the voltage levels used by the terminal to those needed by the digital circuit. Even if RS-232-C is used to connect the terminal to the DSU, the 50-foot limitation applies only to the distance between the DSU and the terminal, not that between the local DSU and the remote DSU.

A *channel service unit*, or *CSU*, is sometimes required at the end of the common carrier's circuit. The trend today, however, is to incorporate the functions of the CSU into the DSU. Since a separate CSU is not always used, it is shown with dashed lines in Fig. 4-11.

The "digital circuit" portion of Fig. 4-11 can span several miles, or several thousand miles, depending on the locations of the host computer and terminal. Special equipment, known as *repeaters*, will be placed at regular intervals in the digital circuits to keep the data signal strong over these long distances (and understandable by the receiving DSU/CSU).

An analogy for the repeater function can be found in the classic firefighter's bucket line. Rather than have one firefighter take the bucket of water up a hill, he hands the bucket to another firefighter, she hands it to the next one, etc. Eventually, the bucket reaches the top of the hill, but the work of sending the water was shared by each firefighter.

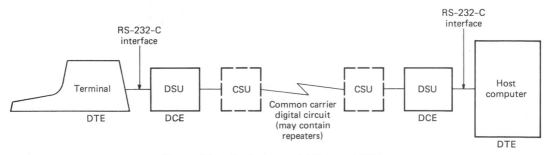

Figure 4-11 Typical use of DSUs and CSUs.

Data Interfaces and Transmission

A digital repeater simply receives a digital signal (a square wave) and sends it on to the next repeater. In the firefighter's bucket line, some water may spill as the bucket is passed from one firefighter to the next. Similarly, as data is transmitted, it becomes weaker the farther it gets from the repeater. It is the function of the repeater to rejuvenate, or regenerate the signal, before sending it on. This is the equivalent of the firefighters keeping a spare glass of water at their side, so they could "top off" the bucket, if necessary, before passing it on.

If we consider a square wave between -10 and +10 volts as our digital signal, Fig. 4-12 illustrates a repeater's function. The signal deteriorates as it gets farther from the DSU. Before entering the repeater, the highest portion of the signal is barely +9 volts, and is far from square. The repeater regenerates the signal, and sends out a clean square wave at the full 10 volts. The key to using repeaters is that they must be placed close enough to each other so that the signal is still recognizable when it enters the repeater. Without repeaters, the signal would simply fade out, much as a person's voice becomes unintelligible as we walk farther and farther away. These digital repeaters can be separate devices or can be incorporated into the common carrier's switching equipment.

We have already considered the general functions of digital transmission. There are several specific digital transmission options available from common carriers for digital circuits.

Dataphone Digital Service

A.T.&T.'s *Dataphone Digital Service*, or *DDS*, provides digital circuits for data transmission speeds of 2400 bps, 4800 bps, 9600 bps, 56 kbps, and 64 kbps. The cost of the

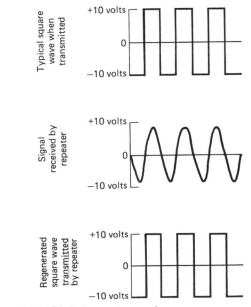

Figure 4-12 Digital repeaters and square-wave regeneration.

Data Interfaces and Transmission

service varies according to the data speed used. The service can be provided over four wires, and the customer can either lease or own the DSU/CSU, depending on the common carrier. DDS is currently marketed under many different names by other common carriers, and describes one method of communicating digitally between DSUs.

T-1 Carrier

T-1 carrier service, available from almost all of the common carriers, is a 1.544 Mbps digital path. For users with lower data rates, but many devices at each location, the T-1 carrier can be divided into 24 separate channels. Since some of the 1.544 Mbps is used for signaling information, the 24 channels can each carry either roughly 64 kbps digitized voice or 56 kbps data. T-1 is nothing more than a high-speed method of communicating digitally between DSUs. We discuss the use of T-1 carrier more extensively in Chapter 10.

Integrated Services Digital Network

The *Integrated Services Digital Network*, or *ISDN*, is an evolving standard for digital voice and data communications. The data circuit portion of ISDN includes data rates of from 16 kbps to 64 kbps for the individual user, and up to 1.544 Mbps for high-volume transmission. We present ISDN more extensively in Chapter 10.

Packet Switching Networks

Another method of long-distance data transmission is through the use of *packet switching networks*. These networks allow terminals and host computers to connect to other host computers anywhere on the network, which can span thousands of miles. The user has the option of connecting to the same host computer all the time, or choosing a different computer with each call, much as we do on the public telephone network. We examine packet switching networks in detail in Chapter 8.

Digital and Analog Bandwidth

A common measure of a communications circuit's usefulness is its *bandwidth*, or carrying capacity. In the digital circuits we have been discussing, bandwidth is simply the capacity in bits per second that can be transmitted. For example, we could say that T-1 is a higher-bandwidth circuit than DDS, because T-1 offers a 1.544 Mbps bandwidth, while DDS offers 64 kbps or less.

However, not all communications circuits are digital. In digital transmission, only ones and zeroes are sent and received. Normal telephone lines, like those found in our homes, are designed to carry the wide range of pitches that make up human speech, not ones and zeroes. We call these different pitches *frequencies*. A high-pitched tone is therefore also a high-frequency tone, and a low-pitched tone is a low-frequency tone. Human speech, music, and the noise made by a car's engine are all a series of unpredictable sounds, each with its own constantly varying pitch and volume; this type of signal is called an *analog* signal. Whereas digital information is a predictable 0 or 1 (and nothing in between), analog information can vary infinitely over a given range. A comparison between a digital and an analog signal can be found in Fig. 4-13.

There is no way to predict what a person will say on the telephone. We can, however, predict what the average human voice sounds like, and what type of equipment will be needed to transmit and receive that voice, whatever it's saying. The analog bandwidth of a communications circuit is the range of frequencies that it can transmit.

How do we determine the frequency of a signal? A perfect tone that maintains its pitch and volume indefinitely looks like a *sine wave* when converted to electrical energy. Notice that a sine wave, as illustrated in Fig. 4-14, repeats itself again and again, and each repetition is known as a *cycle*. Each cycle contains a peak, and a valley, and the height of each peak (and depth of each valley) doesn't vary in a perfect sine wave. The height of each peak is known as the *amplitude* of the sine wave; this amplitude is also equal to the depth of each valley. In addition, the time for each complete cycle is also constant, and is known as the *period* of the sine wave. The number of cycles of a sine wave in a second is known as its *frequency*. The frequency of a sine wave is therefore measured in *cycles per second*; the term *hertz*, abbreviated *Hz*, is equivalent to cycles per second and is commonly used today.

For convenience, each cycle of a sine wave can be divided into 360 degrees, just like a circle, as shown in Fig. 4-14. Regardless of the frequency or amplitude of a sine wave, it crosses the axis at 0, 180, and 360 degrees (360 is the same as 0, since the sine wave repeats forever).The peak is always at 90 degrees, and the valley is always at 270 degrees. For example, a sine wave of one cycle per second would reach its peak a quarter of a second into its cycle, or at 90 degrees; a sine wave of two cycles per second would reach its peak an eighth of a second into its cycle, but still at 90 degrees.

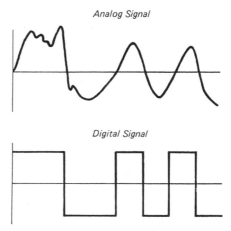

Figure 4-13 Digital and analog signals.

Data Interfaces and Transmission

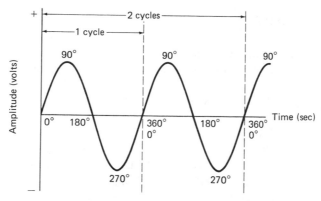

Figure 4-14 Sine wave.

A standard telephone line will adequately transmit tones between 300 Hz and 3300 Hz. As illustrated in Fig. 4-15, the tones near the center of these frequencies are transmitted the best. Most human speech is made up of tones that fall in this range, though a very small percentage of speech falls outside this range. This explains why some people have a "telephone voice," a voice that sounds different on the phone than in person. Another example of the bandwidth limitations of the telephone network can be heard by listening to a radio call-in talk show. The caller always sounds less audible than the host, because only part of the caller's voice reached the radio station: the portion between 300 Hz and 3300 Hz. The telephone lines could support higher frequencies, but economics dictated that the frequencies between 300 Hz and 3300 Hz were sufficient for adequate conversation at a reasonable price. Since the highest frequency passed is 3300 Hz and the lowest is 300 Hz, the bandwidth is the difference, or 3000 Hz.

Why all this concern about telephone line bandwidth when we are studying data communications? In order to transmit ones and zeroes over standard telephone lines, we must first translate them to audible tones. By understanding the bandwidth limitations of the standard telephone line, we can ensure that the tones used can be transmitted reliably.

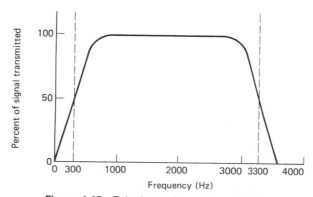

Figure 4-15 Telephone channel bandwidth.

Data Interfaces and Transmission

TRANSMISSION MEDIA

There are many different types of *transmission media* in use in data communications today. Transmission media are the physical paths for carrying information, like a pair of wires.

A typical local loop between the central office and our home is made up of *twisted pair* wire. Each local loop consists of a pair of wires, continuously twisted throughout its entire length. Typically, the wires are made of copper and coated with an insulating material, and information is transmitted by sending electrical current through the wires. The twisting of the wire helps minimize the effects of certain types of noise on the voice or data transmission. The effects of twisting wire can be illustrated with most modern clock radios. A clock radio's power cord often acts as the antenna for FM reception; if we straighten the power cord, we get the best radio signal reception, and twisting it minimizes the signal received from the surroundings. When transmitting voice or data over wire, we want to minimize the interference received.Therefore, we twist the telephone wire to reduce the amount of signals received from the surroundings; not only does this reduce interference from radio stations, it minimizes other forms of electromagnetic interference as well.

Twisted pair wire is often used at customer facilities, and also over long distances, to carry voice as well as data communications. Though its bandwidth is limited to 300 Hz to 3300 Hz in the telephone network, this is partly due to the equipment on each end. Higher frequencies can be achieved using special equipment, but twisted pair is generally considered a low-frequency transmission medium. Shielding can be used on twisted pair wire to reduce further the effects of interference and noise, though this increases the cost. Data rates of 20 Mbps are possible for short distances on customer-owned networks, though 19.2 kbps is the more accepted maximum over the standard telephone network, which is limited by its 300 Hz to 3300 Hz bandwidth.

The main advantages of twisted pair are that it is relatively inexpensive (pennies per foot) and easy to install. The wire is flexible enough to be routed through conduit and on cable trays in office buildings, and each pair of wires is usually less than a sixteenth of an inch in diameter. In many older buildings found in downtown areas of cities, this space requirement is critical, because cables must be run between floors in the narrow space left over in existing elevator shafts. Many pairs of wires are often combined inside a larger cable. In addition, installing twisted pair requires little training, and readily available and inexpensive (less than $2) modular phone jacks can be used to make connections. Finally, many buildings are already wired with several twisted wire pairs in each office to allow for phone lines. Separate twisted wire pairs can be used for voice and data communications, or the two can be combined on a single twisted pair, as found in advanced digital PBXs.

Another type of cabling often used for data communications, video transmission, and some voice communication is *coaxial cable*, or *coax*. Most cable television systems use coax to connect subscribers. A coax cable usually consists of a single wire in the center, surrounded by a core of insulating material, with an outer conductive wrapping, usually a copper cylinder, covered by a final insulating sheath. A cross section of a coax cable is presented in Fig. 4-16, along with a standard coaxial male and female connector.

Data Interfaces and Transmission

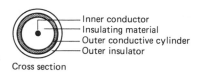

Cross section

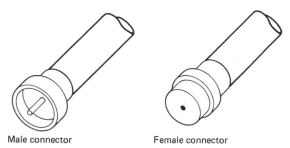

Male connector   Female connector

Figure 4-16 Coaxial cable.

The outer copper cylinder acts as a shield from any external interference; data can be transmitted electronically on the inner wire. Any noise or interference from the surroundings will be absorbed by the copper cylinder and sent to the ground. Coax transmits high frequencies, allowing for high data rates, often up to 150 Mbps, and is less susceptible to noise than is twisted pair.

Coax is slightly more expensive than twisted pair wiring, though the connectors are inexpensive and easy to use with little training. The insulating core does add bulk, making the coax cables a quarter inch or more in diameter and far less flexible than twisted pair.

Another type of cable, known as *twinaxial cable*, or *twinax*, is almost identical to coax, except that there are two inner conducting wires. Twinax is used in a few special-purpose applications.

Many manufacturers combine different cables to provide an all-purpose wiring scheme for customer premises. The *IBM Cabling System* and the *A.T.&T. Premises Distribution System* are two such schemes; each includes different types of cable with special shielding to meet particular customer applications.

Fiber optic cable is a popular high-bandwidth transmission medium. Data is transmitted by shining a light through a special type of glass fiber. Fiber optic transmission is a modern-day form of the signal lights used to transmit information between ships at sea. The only difference is that in fiber optics, the light travels not through the air, but through glass fiber, and the data rates can exceed 1500 Mbps. One method used to send data through fiber optic cables is simply turning the light on and off. For example, when the light is on, a 1 is transmitted, and when the light is off, a 0 is transmitted.

Fiber optic cable is far more expensive per foot than coax or twisted pair, but the high bandwidth can still make fiber optics economical for high-volume applications. The cost of installing fiber optic cable is also high, with connections costing far more than coax or twisted pair; special equipment and training are required.

Fiber optic cable is no bulkier than coax and is about as flexible. It is not affected at all by electrical and radio noise and interference, since the fiber optic transmission uses light, not electricity, to send data. This noise immunity makes fiber optics popular with long-distance carriers seeking to provide high-quality voice and data connections. Some local carriers are already choosing this medium, since the added bandwidth of a fiber optic local loop allows them to provide additional services. On the other hand, existing twisted pair local loops are certainly adequate for most voice and data transmission.

Satellite transmission uses radio waves to transmit data. A *satellite dish*, or antenna, known as the *uplink* station, transmits data to the satellite, which orbits the earth. *Transponders* on the satellite then repeat the signal, which is received by another satellite dish, known as the *downlink* station. Satellite transmission is depicted in Fig. 4-17. Satellites typically orbit approximately 22,500 miles above the earth's surface; any satellite dish pointed at the satellite can receive the signal provided that it is tuned to the proper frequency, much the way we tune in a radio station.

To help understand satellites, picture a strange mirror orbiting above the earth. Standing in Florida, we shine a very powerful flashlight pointed right at this mirror. This special mirror then reflects the light over the entire country. Our friend in Oregon can then read outside in the light provided by this mirror. We could not light up the whole country with our powerful flashlight without the help of the mirror to reflect the light everywhere. Similarly, the satellite takes our data and repeats it so that everyone within reach of the satellite can receive the signal. We simply point our dish at the satellite and begin transmitting. Since the satellite is so high, the same satellite can transmit data to almost a third of the world; going further requires simply relaying the signal to another satellite. A major advantage of satellites is their ability to communicate from almost anywhere to almost anywhere else.

The bandwidth of satellite transmission depends on the equipment used in the uplink and downlink stations and the number of satellite channels used; each satellite is

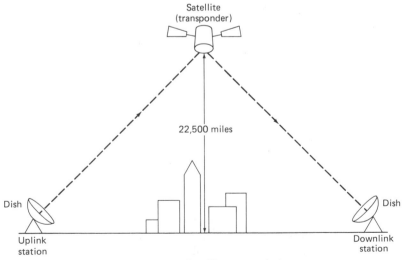

Figure 4-17 Satellite transmission.

Data Interfaces and Transmission

capable of handling many channels at one time, each of different transmission frequencies. Satellite bandwidth can extend from 64 kbps to many Mbps, and is almost unlimited if enough channels are used. Satellite transmission is usually cheaper over long distances than fiber optics or twisted pair, because there is no cabling cost between the two locations. The satellite dishes are a one-time purchase and do not have to be leased monthly from telephone carriers, though the satellite channels must be leased.

However, satellite transmissions are subject to noise and long delays. Since every transmission must go from the ground to the satellite and back to the ground, each transmission takes a 45,000-mile trip. This transmission occurs at roughly the speed of light, so the trip takes a quarter of a second. Sending a message and receiving a response will cause at least a half-second delay for the round trip. A half second wait may seem trivial to us, but a computer might be able to transmit 4800 bits during that time.

The long delays of satellite transmission can produce the so-called ''tunnel effect,'' where annoying echoes are heard during long-distance calls. Though these echoes can be prevented by using echo cancellers, nothing can be done about the delay between transmission and reception. A transcontinental call over twisted pair wire will probably go no farther than 5000 miles, no matter how convoluted the call routing; the same call using a satellite travels nine times farther, and therefore can markedly slow down host computers waiting to transmit data.

Satellites are susceptible to noise and interference caused by a variety of sources. Finally, satellite transmission can be heard by anyone with a dish tuning to the right frequency, causing a potential security risk. We discuss methods for minimizing this risk in Chapter 6.

Terrestrial microwave transmission uses radio frequencies similar to those found in satellite transmission. Instead of bouncing radio waves off a satellite, the users build tall towers and point the dishes at each other, as illustrated in Fig. 4-18. Alternatively, the dishes can be put on top of buildings, as long as there is a clear *line of sight* between the two dishes. If there is an obstruction, like a mountain or building, in between the receiver and the destination, another tower can be placed on top of the obstruction and used as a repeater. This additional tower simply receives a signal on one side and transmits it to the other side.

The signals used for microwave transmission can be sent only 20 to 30 miles. Longer distances require using multiple *hops*, with additional towers in between. These intermediary towers act as repeaters, receiving the signal and passing it on. Microwave transmission bandwidth can exceed 250 Mbps.

The key difference between microwave transmission and satellite transmission is that microwave transmission requires a line of sight between the two dish antennas. There can be no obstructions between the two antennas; if we climbed one of the towers, on a clear night, we should be able to shine our powerful flashlight at the second tower, and our friend at the top of the second tower would see the light. If the other tower was not the final destination but only a repeater station, our friend would see our flashlight and then point his own flashlight at the next tower.

The cost advantages of microwave lie in relatively short-haul, high-bandwidth applications. The towers and dishes are a one-time purchase cost, there are no satellite channels to lease, and there is currently no shortage of microwave frequencies. Like

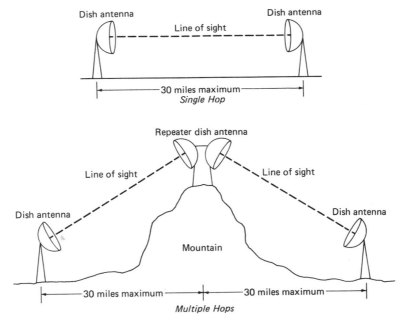

Figure 4-18 Terrestial microwave transmission.

satellite transmission, there is no cabling cost between the locations, because the signal travels through the air. However, each added hop significantly increases the cost, since every repeater requires a separate tower and two dish antennas, one pointed in each direction. Microwave transmission is subjected to the same noise and interference as satellite transmission, though it is less likely that we will be encountering interference on a 30-mile route than on a 45,000-mile transmission.

A chart summarizing the different transmission media, and their advantages and disadvantages, is presented in Fig. 4-19.

BASEBAND VS. BROADBAND

There clearly are many different types of transmission media, each suited to certain applications. In addition, there are two methods used to transmit data, baseband and broadband.

In *baseband transmission*, a single data signal is transmitted directly on a wire. The RS-232-C interface, where a separate wire is used for each signal, is an example of baseband transmission; TD and RD each occupy a separate wire, and the data is transmitted directly on the wires using positive and negative voltages.

Broadband transmission is a technique where the data to be transmitted is sent using a *carrier signal*, such as a sine wave. Since many different frequency carrier signals can be transmitted simultaneously, more than one signal can be sent on the same wire. This technique is found in cable television, where only a single cable enters our house, but there are many separate signals on that cable; we view the desired station by

　　　　　　　　　　　　　　　　　Data Interfaces and Transmission

FIGURE 4-19 A COMPARISON OF TRANSMISSION MEDIA

Type	Advantages	Disadvantages
Twisted pair wire	Very inexpensive Easy to install Already installed in many locations	Doesn't pass high frequencies well Relatively low bandwidth
Coaxial cable	Shielded Fairly inexpensive Moderately high bandwidth	Bulky and somewhat inflexible
Fiber optic cable	Transmission unaffected by noise Very high bandwidth	Expensive to install Repeaters often required
Satellite	No line of sight needed No cabling needed between sites High bandwidth	Channels must be leased High initial equipment cost Long delays
Terrestrial microwave	No cabling needed between sites High bandwidth	Line of sight needed Towers and repeaters can be expensive High initial equipment cost

tuning the particular channel's frequency on our television set. In data communications, broadband transmission always uses analog signals to send data. We will now explain the most common use of broadband transmission in data communications.

MODULATION

The conversion of digital signals to analog form for transmission is called *modulation*, and converting these analog signals back to digital form is called *demodulation*. A device that performs modulation and demodulation is a modulator/demodulator, or a *modem*.

Why is the conversion of the signals necessary? Typically, modems are used when the host computer and terminal are in different locations. Most interface standards, like RS-232-C, transmit data using positive and negative voltages, which form square waves. The square waves used in digital transmission cannot be sent over standard telephone lines without first converting them to analog form, because the public telephone network was designed to carry analog signals like speech. Typical placement of a modem in a data communications circuit is shown in Fig. 4-20. We depict the communications circuit, using common industry practice, as a "lightning bolt." The lightning bolt represents the local loops, the central office(s), and any toll offices present in the connection between the two modems.

In some cases, the telephone line between the two modems is permanent, or *leased*. In other cases, the terminal is contacting a different host computer each time, or only needs to contact the host computer occasionally. These situations are suitable for a *dial-up*, or *switched circuit*, where a new telephone call is placed for each connection.

In every dial-up connection there are two modems; the modem that places the call is known as the *originate modem*, and the modem that answers the call is known as the

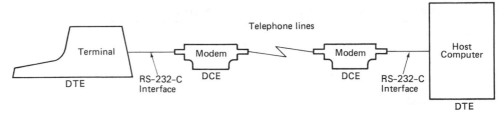

Figure 4-20 Using modems in data communications circuits.

answer modem. Some early modems were *originate only* (could only place calls) or *answer only* (could only answer calls). Most of today's modems can both place and receive calls, and are known as *originate/answer modems*.

Dial-up modem calls can be placed in two ways. Early modems, known as *dumb modems*, performed only modulation and demodulation. In addition to a modem, a telephone instrument had to be attached to the phone line to place calls. The terminal user picked up the telephone and dialed the number of the answer (remote) modem; after reaching the answer modem, the user could then hang up the phone and hit a ''data'' button on the originate (local) modem. This put the originate modem in ''data mode'' and caused it to begin communicating with the answer modem. Some customers used PBXs to automate the dialing process; after dialing the call, instead of hitting a ''data'' button, a PBX would close a switch connecting a pair of wires coming from the originate modem known as the *mode indicator leads*, or *MI/MIC leads*. The originate modem would recognize this as a signal to enter the ''data mode'' and begin communicating with the answer modem.

A newer generation of modems, known as *smart modems*, can accept dialing instructions directly from the user of the terminal, dial the call, and perform the necessary modulation and demodulation when the connection is established. Most modems used with personal computers today are smart modems, since the software can instruct the smart modem to dial and disconnect calls. Since the smart modem is able to dial the call itself, using rotary or Touch-tone dialing, a separate telephone instrument is not needed for a smart modem.

Typically, modems convert the square waves that represent ones and zeroes to sine waves for analog transmission. There are many different methods for performing this conversion, each with its own advantages and disadvantages. Both the originate and answer modem must use the same modulation methods for successful data communications. We now explain several popular types of modulation.

Amplitude Modulation

In one modulation technique, known as *amplitude modulation*, or *AM*, the amplitude, or height, of the sine wave varies to transmit the ones and zeroes. Another name for amplitude modulation is *amplitude shift keying*, or *ASK*, since data is transmitted by shifting amplitudes. The bit pattern 00101001 is being transmitted using amplitude modulation in Fig. 4-21. Notice that the sine wave's amplitude is high when transmitting a 1,

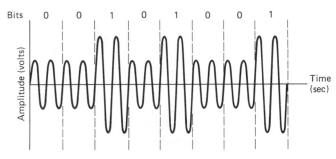

Figure 4-21 Amplitude modulation.

and low when transmitting a 0. The duration (or width) of each cycle of the sine wave does not change throughout the transmission; in other words, the frequency doesn't vary. In Fig. 4-21 there are two complete cycles of the sine wave (two peaks and two valleys) for each bit transmitted. The number of complete cycles used to send a bit with amplitude modulation is an arbitrary choice and will vary depending on the type and speed of the modem.

If we attached a telephone to a modem using amplitude modulation, and listened to it transmit the bit pattern 00101001, we would hear a single tone that never varies in pitch (frequency), but gets louder when transmitting a 1, and softer for a 0. Of course, we would need very sensitive ears, since most modems transmit several hundred bits per second.

One major disadvantage of amplitude modulation is that telephone lines are very susceptible to variations in transmission quality that effect amplitude. Particularly on long-distance calls, we are accustomed to hearing the volume of a person's voice vary during the course of a conversation. If a modem using amplitude modulation is transmitting a 1 when the telephone connection volume fades, the receiving modem will hear a low-amplitude sine wave, and may interpret it as a 0.

We have considered only the transmission of data in one direction at a time. If this is a full duplex communications circuit, another frequency sine wave can be used to simultaneously send data in the other direction. The amplitude of this second sine wave will also vary, to send ones and zeroes in this direction.

Frequency Modulation

Another technique, known as *frequency modulation*, or *FM*, varies the frequency of the sine wave to transmit data while the amplitude remains constant. Another name for frequency modulation is *frequency shift keying*, or *FSK*, since data is transmitted by shifting frequencies. The same bit pattern 00101001 is being transmitted using frequency modulation in Fig. 4-22. Notice that the amplitude of the sine wave doesn't vary, but the length of each cycle, and hence the frequency, varies. A low frequency (1070 Hz) is used to send a 0, and a higher frequency (1270 Hz) is used to send a 1. If we attached a telephone to a modem using frequency modulation, and listened to it transmit the bit

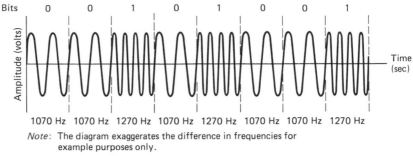

Bits   0   0   1   0   1   0   0   1

1070 Hz   1070 Hz   1270 Hz   1070 Hz   1270 Hz   1070 Hz   1070 Hz   1270 Hz

Note: The diagram exaggerates the difference in frequencies for example purposes only.

Figure 4-22 Frequency modulation.

pattern 00101001, we would hear a low-pitched tone for each 0 and a higher-pitched tone for each 1. The volumes, or amplitudes, of both tones would be the same.

Since the receiving modem recognizes only differences in frequency and is not concerned with the amplitude of the signal, small variations in phone line volume will not cause demodulation errors when using frequency modulation.

If we need to send data in both directions at once, we will need two frequencies (one for a 1 and one for a 0) for each direction, for a total of four frequencies. Frequency modulation is often used for 300 bps transmission according to the *Bell 103/113* specification (also known as A.T.&T.103/113). The originating modem sends a one using a 1270 Hz tone or a zero using a 1070 Hz tone. The answering modem sends a one using a 2225 Hz tone or a zero using a 2025 Hz tone. The CCITT *V.21* standard describes a 300 bps modem used internationally with a similar modulation scheme.

Phase Modulation

A more sophisticated technique is known as *phase modulation*, or *PM*, because data is transmitted by changing the phase of the sine wave. Another name for phase modulation is *phase shift keying*, or *PSK*, since data is transmitted by shifting phase. A sine wave normally repeats itself indefinitely, with one peak and valley after another. Shifting phase breaks the sine wave abruptly and starts it again a few degrees forward or backward.

We'll assume 180 degree forward phase shifts for our example, shown in Fig. 4-23. The sine wave continues uninterrupted for two time periods as we transmit zeroes. Then the sine wave stops abruptly at the axis, and we skip forward 180 degrees; in a sine wave, skipping forward 180 degrees moves us halfway across the sine wave, bringing us to the point where the sine wave starts back up to the next peak. In our example, the 180 degree phase shift is used to send ones, and a continuous sine wave is used to send zeroes; this is only one possible way to use phase modulation to transmit data. Notice that the amplitude and frequency of the sine waves stay constant throughout transmission. We simply shift phase during a time period to send a one, or continue the sine wave uninterrupted to send a zero. The receiving modem can monitor the incoming sine wave and determine if the phase shifted during a particular time period.

Data Interfaces and Transmission

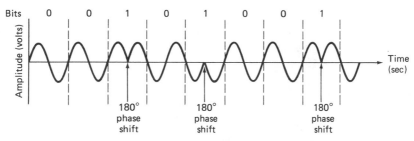

Figure 4-23 Phase modulation.

A forward phase shift is nothing more than skipping ahead in our sine wave. For example, normally a record player will play an entire album. However, we could lift up the needle and skip a song we don't enjoy. If we wanted to send data using this method, we could arbitrarily say, "If I skip a song, I'm sending a 1. If I leave the record alone, I'm sending a 0." The receiver must know what song normally comes next on the album, in order to determine if a song was skipped. With phase modulation, the receiver knows exactly what the sine wave should look like. If part of the sine wave is skipped, the receiver can recognize this, just like we would recognize that a song was skipped. In our record player example, we skip an entire song; in Fig. 4-23, we skip 180 degrees of the sine wave.

If we need to send data in two directions at once, we will use one frequency for each direction. The phases will shift on each of these sine waves as necessary to send data. Like frequency modulation, phase modulation is not affected by slight variations in amplitude normally occurring on the telephone network. The main advantage of phase modulation is that only a single-frequency sine wave is used to send both ones and zeroes in each direction. In frequency modulation, separate frequencies are required for sending a one and sending a zero in each direction.

BITS PER SECOND VS. BAUD

So far we have considered the modulation of only one bit at a time. We have varied amplitude, frequency, or phase to send a one or a zero. In each case, there were two alternatives: a high or low amplitude, a high or low frequency, or a phase shift or no phase shift. We've already discussed the Bell 103/113 standard for 300 bps transmission; for each bit, the transmitting modem needed to decide which frequency to send. The number of these decisions, or possible signal changes in a second, is known as the *baud rate* of a modem. The 300 bps modem described by our example is also a 300 baud modem, because the signal could potentially change 300 times in a second, once for each bit.

Some terminals communicate at much higher speeds, like 9600 bps. However, a telephone circuit's bandwidth will not transmit frequencies higher than 3300 Hz. If we perform only one amplitude, frequency, or phase change in a given cycle, and a single bit is transmitted with each change, we would be limited to

3300 bps. We could build a more sophisticated modem that would recognize an amplitude, frequency, or phase change after half a cycle, but this would still limit us to 6600 bits per second. Clearly there is a need for faster modulation methods to handle higher-speed devices.

What if we could send more than one bit with each shift of amplitude, frequency, or phase? If we wanted to send two bits, that would provide us with four possible combinations: 00, 01, 10, and 11. Therefore, if we were using amplitude modulation, we would need four possible amplitudes; frequency modulation would require four frequencies, and phase modulation would require four phases. When we send two bits in this way, it is known as *dibit modulation*.

One of the most commonly used forms of modulation today is the dibit phase shift keying described by the *Bell 212A* (A.T.&T. 212A) specification. In this specification, the originate modem transmits data using a 1200 Hz sine wave, and the answer modem transmits data using a 2400 Hz sine wave. Phase shifts of 90, 0, 180, and 270 degrees represent the bits 00, 01, 10, and 11, respectively. The bit pattern 01001110 is being transmitted according to the Bell 212A standard in Fig. 4-24. A similar 1200 bps modem standard used internationally is the CCITT *V.22*.

With this dibit transmission, the modem could change the signal only every two bits, when it may shift the signal's phase. In this case, Bell 212A described 1200 bps transmission; if 1200 bits are sent in a second, and two bits are sent with each possible signal change, this is a 600 baud modem. The terminal and host computer require a certain bit per second rate and are not affected by the baud rate. A terminal transmitting 1200 bits per second will function equally well with a 1200 bps/1200 baud modem or a 1200 bps/600 baud modem.

Though we have just described dibit modulation, some modems use tribit (three bits at once) or even quabit (four bits at once) modulation. For example, to use tribit phase shift keying, we need to use 45 degree phase shifts, to give us the eight possible combinations of three bits: 000, 001, 010, 011, 100, 101, 110, and 111. Quabit phase shift keying would require 22.5 degree phase shifts. Though quabit phase shift keying is technically possible, in practice, the required 22.5 degree phase shift changes required are difficult to produce and detect reliably at a reasonable cost.

Since most older modems (300 bps and slower) sent only one bit with each signal change, *bps* and *baud* were equivalent terms and were therefore used interchangeably for many years. Even though today most modems use dibits, tribit, or even quabit modulation, the term *baud* is often mistakenly used instead of *bps*, even by modem vendor sales personnel. For example, the Bell 212A modem, though a 1200 bps/600 baud modem, is often mistakenly referred to as a 1200 baud modem.The easiest way to avoid any misunderstanding when purchasing modems is to specify the bps rate of the host computer or terminal, and request a modem that can handle that transmission speed.

MULTISPEED MODEMS

One interesting feature of certain modem specifications is their *multispeed* capability. For example, when a Bell 212A modem begins communications with another modem, it tries to communicate using the 1200 Hz and 2400 Hz tones already mentioned. If the other modem does not provide the appropriate tone, the Bell 212A modem assumes that it has reached a slower modem and tries to communicate using the Bell 103/113 tones we already presented. In other words, the Bell 212A modem will attempt to communicate at 1200 bps, and if unsuccessful, will fall back to 300 bps. This capability allowed early users of the Bell 212A modem to continue to communicate with older 300 bps modems, yet achieve the increased performance 1200 bps affords when communicating with other Bell 212A modems. This multispeed capability has become an accepted practice in the industry.

HIGH-SPEED MODEMS

The first widely accepted dial-up 2400 bps modem, described by the *CCITT V.22 Bis* standard, also included a fallback to the older 1200 bps speed of Bell 212A. The V.22 Bis specification is widely used both in this country and internationally for 2400 bps transmission.

High-speed modems often combine two modulation methods to allow for faster transmission rates. The V.22 Bis standard achieves 2400 bps by combining changes in phase and amplitude at the same time in a technique known as *quadrature amplitude modulation*. Four bits are sent at once, at 600 baud, for a 2400 bps transmission rate. There are four different phases and four amplitudes, for a total of 16 possible combinations; this allows for all the different possibilities of four bits: 0000, 0001, 0010, 0011, 0100, 0101, 0110, 0111, 1000, 1001, 1010, 1011, 1100, 1101, 1110, and 1111.

Trellis coded modulation is a sophisticated and advanced technique used for high-speed transmission, often at 9600 bps and above. Trellis coded modulation relies on a special error-correcting process, which allows the use of techniques that would normally prove unreliable on standard modems. The receiving modem has sufficient intelligence to correct many transmission errors, allowing the modems to communicate at high speeds without fear of data loss.

Some modem vendors create their own proprietary modulation schemes, and do not follow any established standards. The disadvantage is that these modems will communicate only with their counterparts manufactured by the same vendor. However, a standard modem, like a Bell 212A modem, will communicate with any Bell 212A modem, regardless of the manufacturer.

Short-Haul Modems

All of the modems presented thus far have been designed for use over the public telephone network. Occasionally, users may have a large building, or campus environment, where they need to locate devices a few hundred or even a few thousand feet from each

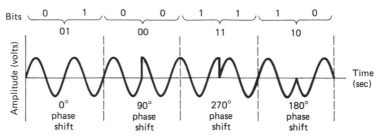

Figure 4-24 Dibit phase shift keying using the Bell 212A specification.

other. If these are RS-232-C devices, the user is limited to 50 feet; any greater distance requires the use of modems. If the user can own or lease wires between these devices, *short-haul modems*, also called *limited-distance modems*, can be utilized.

Short-haul modems transmit data over twisted pair wire, but not through telephone company central offices. They modulate data using frequencies greater than the normal telephone channel bandwidth limit of 3300 Hz. By using these high frequencies, higher transmission rates can be achieved using less expensive hardware. However, the resulting sine waves can be passed over twisted pair wire for only a few miles and cannot be passed through the central office switch. For example, a 9600 bps short-haul modem can be purchased for a little less than the cost of a 1200 bps dial-up modem. The short-haul modem can transmit for a few miles, and the dial-up modem can transmit around the world, with the help of central offices and toll offices in between. Therefore, a user with a terminal in the basement and a host computer on the fifth floor could connect the two with a pair of short-haul modems and twisted pair wire. This user would have high data rates and no monthly phone line costs.

SUMMARY

There are numerous ways to connect terminals to host computers. Many standards organizations, including ANSI, IEEE, EIA, ECSA, NBS, CCITT, and ISO, develop specifications for both domestic and international use.

The most commonly used digital interface standard today is EIA's RS-232-C. RS-232-C defines the voltage levels and necessary signals for computer communication between data terminal equipment (DTE) and data circuit-terminating equipment (DCE) interfaces. There are data, ground, timing, and control signals in RS-232-C. Many of these functions are replicated in the seldom-used secondary channel of RS-232-C. The interaction of RS-232-C control signals between the DTE and the DCE is referred to as handshaking. RS-232-C is limited to a distance of 50 feet and a maximum speed of 20 kbps.

RS-449 is a more recent standard describing DTE-to-DCE communications; it specifies the interface connector, the necessary signals, and two possible transmission methods. RS-422-A is a method of balanced transmission, with a maximum distance of

Data Interfaces and Transmission

up to 4000 feet and a maximum speed of 10 Mbps. RS-423-A uses unbalanced transmission, with a maximum distance of 4000 feet and a maximum speed of 100 kbps.

Remote digital transmission over special digital communications circuits requires DSUs and sometimes CSUs at the end of the circuits. Dataphone Digital Service provides digital circuits up to 64 kbps. T-1 carrier provides a 1.544 Mbps digital path, which can be broken into 24 separate channels. Integrated Services Digital Network is an evolving standard for digital voice and data communications that could provide an all-digital communications network. Packet switching networks provide a means for digital transmission to different locations with each new connection.

A circuit's bandwidth is its carrying capacity. For digital circuits, bandwidth is the number of bits that can be transmitted each second. The bandwidth of an analog circuit is the range of frequencies it will transmit. The bandwidths of different transmission media vary dramatically. Twisted pair, coaxial cable, twinaxial cable, and fiber optic cable are some of the different cabling options. Microwave and satellite transmission media do not require cabling between locations.

In baseband transmission, the data signal is transmitted directly on the wire. Broadband transmission sends data using a carrier signal. Modulation is a common example of broadband transmission, where digital signals are converted to analog form for transmission over telephone circuits. Modems perform modulation and demodulation and can be used with leased lines or dial-up circuits. Both dumb and smart modems can be used with dial-up lines, and modems can originate calls, answer calls, or both originate and answer calls.

There are many different modulation techniques in use today. In amplitude modulation, a sine wave's amplitude varies to send ones and zeroes. Frequency modulation uses different frequencies to send ones and zeroes. Phase modulation uses shifts in a sine wave's phase to send ones and zeroes. A signal's baud rate is the number of possible changes in a second. If one bit is sent for each signal change, the bit per second rate is the same as the baud rate. Often, the bps rate is faster than the baud rate, because more than one bit is sent with each signal change. Most high-speed modems use dibit, tribit, or quabit techniques. Short-haul modems are special modems used for short-distance transmission over customer-owned lines, using frequencies outside the bandwidth of the telephone network.

TERMS FOR REVIEW

AM	*Amplitude shift keying*	*Asserted state*
American National	*Analog*	*A.T.&T. Premises*
Standards Institute	*ANSI*	*Distribution System*
Amplitude	*Answer-only modem*	*Balanced transmission*
Amplitude modulation	*ASK*	*Bandwidth*

Baseband transmission
Baud rate
Bell 103/113
Bell 212A
Broadband transmission
Carrier signal
Category I
Category II
CCITT
CD
Channel service unit
Chassis ground
Clear to Send
Coax
Coaxial cable
Common return
Consultative Committee on
 International Telephone
 and Telegraph
Control signal
Crossover
CSU
CTS
CX
Cycle
Cycles per second
Data Carrier Detect
Data circuit-terminating
 equipment
Data Rate Select
Data Set Ready
Data terminal equipment
Data Terminal Ready
Dataphone Digital Service
DB9
DB25
DB37
DCD
DCE
DDS
Demodulation
Dial-up
Dibit modulation
Digital circuit

Digital service unit
Digital transmission
Downlink
DRS
DSR
DSU
DTE
DTR
Dumb modem
ECSA
EIA
Electronic Industries
 Association
Exchange Carriers
 Standards Association
External Transmit Clock
Federal Information
 Processing Standards
Fiber optic cable
FIPS
FM
Frame ground
Frequency
Frequency modulation
Frequency shift keying
FSK
GND
Handshaking
Hertz
Hop
Hz
IBM Cabling System
IEEE
Institute of Electrical and
 Electronics Engineers
Integrated Services Digital
 Network
Interface
International Standards
 Organization
ISDN
ISO
ISO Standard 4902
Leased

Limited-distance modem
Line of sight
Mark
Mbps
MI/MIC lead
Mode indicator lead
Modem
Modulation
Multispeed
National Bureau of
 Standards
National Electrical Code
NBS
Originate-only modem
Originate/answer modem
Packet switching network
Period
Phase modulation
Phase shift keying
PM
Protective ground
PSK
Quadrature amplitude
 modulation
Raised
RC
RD
Receive Clock
Receive Common
Received Data
Recommended Standard
 232C
Repeater
Request to Send
RI
Ring Indicator
RS-232-C
RS-422-A
RS-423-A
RS-449
RTS
Satellite
Satellite dish
SCTS

Data Interfaces and Transmission

SDCD
Secondary Clear to Send
Secondary Data Carrier
  Detect
Secondary Received Data
Secondary Request to Send
Secondary Transmitted Data
Send Common
SG
Short-haul modem
Signal Ground
Signal Quality Detect
Sine wave
Smart modem
Space

SQ
Square wave
SRD
SRTS
Standards organization
STD
Switched
T-1 carrier
TC
TD
Terrestrial microwave
Transmission medium
Transmit Clock
Transmitted Data
Transponder

Trellis coded modulation
Twinax
Twinaxial cable
Twisted pair
Unbalanced transmission
Uplink
V.10
V.11
V.21
V.22
V.22 Bis
V.24
V.28
XTC

EXERCISES

4-1. How does the role of standards in the United States differ from that in the rest of the world?

4-2. In the RS-232-C standard, how are ones and zeroes transmitted? How are control signals represented?

4-3. What are the two types of RS-232-C interfaces? Which devices typically fit into each category?

4-4. What is the purpose of the signal ground in RS-232-C? Why is it important?

4-5. Which RS-232-C signals are used only in synchronous transmission? Which of these signals are generated by the DTE, and which by the DCE? What is the purpose of these signals?

4-6. What is the purpose of the control signals in RS-232-C?

4-7. What does RS-449 define that RS-232-C leaves undefined?

4-8. What are the main differences between the RS-422-A and RS-423-A standards?

4-9. What is the purpose of the DSU/CSU?

4-10. What is the function of a repeater in a digital circuit?

4-11. What are some common digital transmission methods?

4-12. What is bandwidth? How is analog bandwidth measured? How is digital bandwidth measured?

4-13. Compare twisted pair wire with coaxial cable. Which is a higher bandwidth medium? Which is already installed in many offices?

4-14. What is the highest bandwidth cable available today? What is its greatest drawback?

4-15. Explain the differences between satellite and terrestrial microwave transmission. Which is best suited to shorter distances? Longer distances?

4-16. What is the difference between baseband and broadband transmission?

4-17. What is modulation?

4-18. What are the different types of dial-up modems? How do they originate calls?

4-19. How does amplitude modulation transmit ones and zeroes? Frequency modulation? Phase modulation?

4-20. What is the purpose of a short-haul modem? How does it compare with dial-up modems, both technically and economically?

Data interfaces and Transmission

5

IMPROVING DATA COMMUNICATIONS EFFICIENCY

We have already described the minimum hardware components required for data communications. These include terminals and host computers, and sometimes modems and telephone circuits. We will now turn to other components that improve the efficiency of data communications, thereby reducing costs and increasing performance.

FRONT END PROCESSORS

Host computers are well suited to performing numerical calculations, storing and retrieving documents, and accomplishing other tasks in a few millionths of a second. Human terminal operators, however, may only type a few characters in a second. It would be a waste of valuable computer time if the host computer had to spend all of its time monitoring the attached terminals. One of the terminal operators might go on a coffee break, and the host computer would be tied up with unnecessary monitoring.

A *front end processor*, or *FEP*, is a communications assistant for the host computer. The front end processor handles all the host computer's communications with the outside world, while the host computer concentrates on other things, like calculating this week's payroll deductions. The front end processor is actually a small, special-purpose computer, which is dedicated to a single mission. It communicates with the host computer at a very high speed (often several Mbps), while the terminals usually operate at a much lower speed (several kbps). Front end processors are often referred to as *front ends*.

As an example, consider a brilliant, aloof professor who thinks so fast she considers speaking with students a waste of time. Rather than ask the class, ''Do you have any questions?'' and then waiting to see if students raise their hands, she hires a teaching assistant. Anyone with questions must write them down and hand them to the teaching assistant as he walks around the room. The assistant writes them all on one page, and he waits patiently for the professor. The professor then grabs the whole page from the assistant, quickly reads it and writes down all the answers on another piece of paper, which she then hands back to the assistant. It's up to the assistant to walk around the room again, separating each of the answers, and handing them to the correct students. The professor is pleased because she didn't even have to deal with the slow-speaking students, and while they digest her answers she can continue to think great thoughts. The teaching assistant has acted as a front end processor for the professor; like the host computer, this brilliant professor has better things to do with her time.

In this example, the communication between the students and the teaching assistant occurred at a slow speed, and the communication between the professor and the assistant at a much faster speed. This is exactly analogous to the front end processor communications. The front end processor is made up of different logical components, as shown in

Figure 5-1 Using a front end processor.

Improving Data Communications Efficiency

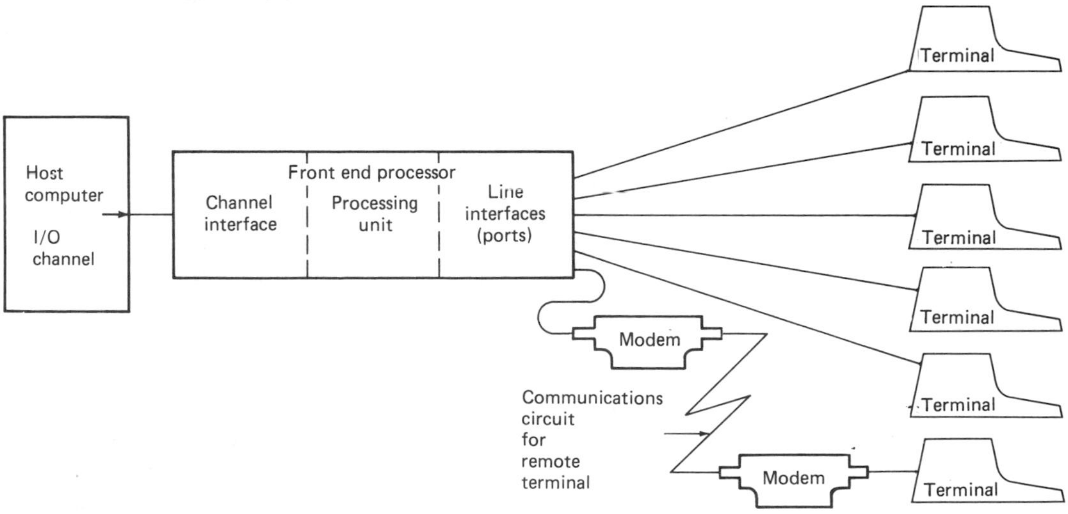

Fig. 5-1. The *channel interface* connects the front end processor to the high-speed *input/output channel* of the host computer. The *processing unit* contains the front end processor's intelligence; it is a special-purpose computer programmed for communications functions. Often the network control programs are loaded into the processing unit on disk or tape, allowing for future modifications to the software, and hence the front end processor's features. Finally, the *line interfaces*, or *front end ports*, are the relatively low-speed interfaces that usually connect to terminals. If the terminal is located remotely, a pair of modems and a communications circuit can be inserted between the line interface and the front end processor.

Since the number of computer ports is often limited by the host computer architecture, front end processors can greatly increase the number of terminals that can be attached to a host computer. A front end processor allows many low-speed devices to share a single high-speed host computer port or channel. Since the channel interface operates at a relatively high speed compared to the line interfaces, the front end processor may need to hold data destined for the terminals, until it can transmit it to the terminals at a slower speed. Holding data in this matter is known as *buffering*.

Some front end processors schedule terminal communications using special rules, known as *protocols*, which we discuss in detail in Chapter 7. The process by which the flow of communications between a host computer and smart or intelligent terminals is controlled by a front end processor is known as *polling and selecting*. *Polling* occurs when the front end processor asks a terminal, "Do you have any data to send to the host computer?" At this point, a smart terminal might send data, or simply answer "No." *Selecting* occurs when the front end processor asks the terminal, "Can you accept data now?" A smart terminal might then answer "Go ahead" or "Not now, I'm busy." Only smart or intelligent terminals can respond to these messages; dumb terminals cannot be controlled using polling and selecting. The host computer could do the polling and selecting, but it is not necessary to waste a host computer's time on such a tedious, repetitive task when a front end processor can accomplish it easily and cost effectively.

Returning to the previous analogy, polling is performed by the teaching assistant when he walks around the classroom, collecting papers from students with questions. Selecting would be the approximate equivalent of the teaching assistant distributing the answers. Technically, selecting would require the teaching assistant to ask each student, "Are you ready to receive your answer now?", and then handing the student the answer.

Many front end processors can perform special functions, varying with each manufacturer and model. One popular function is error detection and correction. Front end processors with this feature can detect, and sometimes correct, any bit transmission errors that occur. This function is explained in detail in Chapter 6.

Another function that some front end processors can perform is *data conversion*. This can include *code conversion*, where the host computer and the terminal device each use a different character code. For example, an ASCII terminal could connect to an EBCDIC host computer using a front end processor with a code conversion feature. Sometimes *protocol conversion* is also needed; connecting a dumb asynchronous terminal, which doesn't understand protocols, to a host computer that uses synchronous protocols requires protocol conversion. Finally, *parallel/serial conversion* can be performed by some front end processors. All of these conversion functions can be performed by separate devices, such as *protocol converters* or *parallel/serial converters*, but it is often less expensive to build these functions directly into the front end processor. Front end processors can be configured differently for each port, allowing different types of terminals to communicate with the same host computer.

Front end processors can often perform *historical logging* or *statistical logging*. Logging provides a record of the users of the front end processor, including various information about the users' actions. These two functions are explained in detail in Chapter 6.

Front end processors are available with many different combinations of the features noted above. The number of line interfaces a front end processor can support varies by manufacturer and host computer model.

PORT SHARING DEVICES

Though front end processors allow terminals to share a high-speed host computer channel, sometimes the front end ports can operate at faster speeds than the attached terminals. Other times, there may be more terminals than front end ports. A *port sharing device*, often called a *concentrator*, allows many terminals to share one front end port, as shown in Fig. 5-2. For example, the front end port might be operating at 9600 bps, while the four terminals attached to the port sharing device might each be operating at 2400 bps. In other configurations, all of the terminals might be at 9600 bps, but only one could transmit at any one time. A user with an eight-port front end and 10 terminals might opt for a front end and a port sharing device, rather than purchasing a second front end.

Port sharing devices are located near the front end processor and usually require special intelligence in the front end that allows many terminals to communicate through a single front end port. For example, if polling and selecting were being used, the front end processor would need to know there were several terminals attached through a port

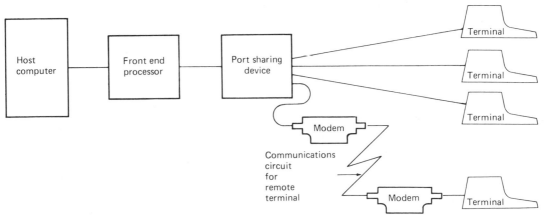

Figure 5-2 Using a port sharing device.

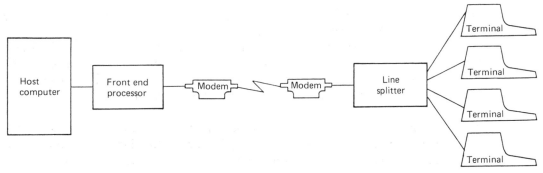

Figure 5-3 Using a line splitter.

sharing device on a particular port; this information allows the front end processor to send the polling/selecting messages for all of these terminals over a single front end processor port. This polling/selecting intelligence is usually found in the front end processor's software. If a terminal is located remotely, the required pair of modems and a communications circuit would be inserted between the port sharing device and the terminal.

LINE SPLITTERS AND REMOTE
INTELLIGENT CONTROLLERS

A *line splitter* performs the same function as a port sharing device, though line splitters are located remotely from the front end processor and host computer. The major advantage offered by line splitters is that only one pair of modems, and one communications circuit, is needed for many remote terminals in the same location. Typically, terminal users in a given area of a building might all be attached to a line splitter, which is then connected to a remote front end processor using a telephone circuit and modems, as shown in Fig. 5-3.

A line splitter's cost can be justified because it reduces the number of modems and telephone circuits needed. Line splitters also require a front end port that can accept more than one terminal. Just as with port sharing devices, the front end processor needs to know there are several terminals accessing the host through that single front end port, so the proper polling/selecting messages can be transmitted to that port.

A *remote intelligent controller* is just like a line splitter, except that it can also perform some front end processor functions. For example, part of the front end processor's task when communicating to smart or intelligent terminals through a line splitter is to poll the terminals constantly. Since humans type slowly compared to the speed at which a front end processor can poll, most of the time the poll will be answered with "No, I have nothing to send now." Normally, a front end processor sends these polling questions and receives the answers over the single pair of modems to the line splitter (which routes the messages to each of the terminals). If one of the terminals has data to transmit, it still must share time on the modems with all the other terminals that are simply sending back negative answers to the polling. Remote intelligent controllers, however, can usually perform the terminal polling themselves, so that only real data is passed over the modems to the front end processor. This frees up the modems for real data transmission and gives the front end processor more time to concentrate on some of its other ports. The appropriate placement of a remote intelligent controller is shown in Fig. 5-4.

Some manufacturers use names other than "port sharing device," "line splitter," and "remote intelligent controller" for equipment performing the functions just described. These generic terms, however, serve to describe functions that are common and universal throughout the industry.

All of these methods for improving data communications efficiency, whether with front end processors, port sharing devices, line splitters, or remote intelligent controllers, require a special compatibility with the attached host computer or terminals. For example, a front end processor can only be attached to a host computer that is designed with special high-speed data channels for that purpose. Port sharing devices, line splitters, and remote intelligent controllers usually require smart or intelligent terminals that can be controlled using polling and selecting. We now turn to other means of improving data communications efficiency that do not require any special features or action on the part of the host computer, front end processor (if present), or terminal.

MULTIPLEXERS

One of the most widely used devices for improving data communications efficiency is the *multiplexer*, often called a *mux*. A multiplexer allows several devices to share the same communications circuit. This can be accomplished in several ways; for instance, faster modems can be used on the communications circuit, or the communications circuit can be split into several separate channels.

Multiplexing is useful when there are parallel communications paths between two locations. The main advantage of multiplexing, as shown in Fig. 5-5, is that fewer telephone lines and modems are needed. The one-time purchase cost of multiplexers is

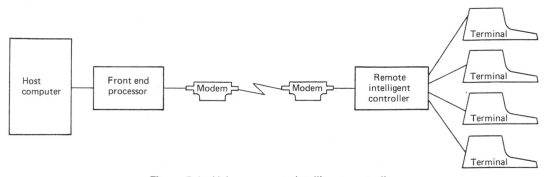

Figure 5-4 Using a remote intelligent controller.

Improving Data Communications Efficiency

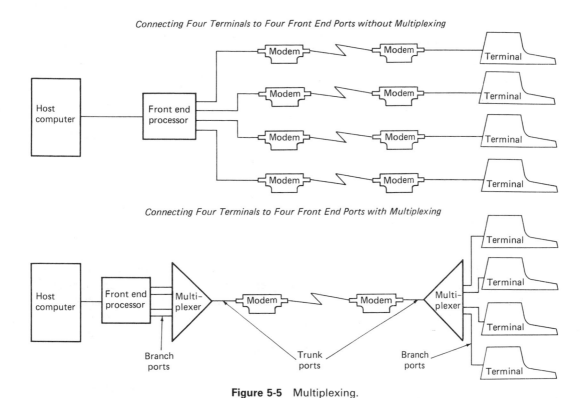

Connecting Four Terminals to Four Front End Ports without Multiplexing

Connecting Four Terminals to Four Front End Ports with Multiplexing

Figure 5-5 Multiplexing.

usually justified over time by the savings of monthly costs for telephone lines. The main purpose of multiplexers, therefore, is to minimize communications circuit costs.

Multiplexers are normally used in pairs, with one multiplexer at each end of the communications circuit. The data from several terminals can be sent over a single communications circuit by one multiplexer. At the receiving multiplexer, the data is separated and sent to the appropriate destinations.

We often refer to the low-speed ports of a multiplexer as *branch ports* and to the high-speed port as the *trunk port*. Just like a tree, there are many branches (terminals or front end ports) and only one trunk (connected to the modems). The branch and trunk ports are labeled in Fig. 5-5.

Time Division Multiplexing

Multiplexers that share the time on a fast communications circuit among slower devices use a technique known as *time division multiplexing*, or *TDM*. In our first example of TDM, shown in Fig. 5-6, the four terminals and front end ports each operate at 2400 bps. The pair of modems between the multiplexers operates at 9600 bps. The four terminals and front end ports actually share the modem's 9600 bps bandwidth. For convenience, we discuss the transmission of data from the terminals to the front end ports, though the same principles apply in both directions.

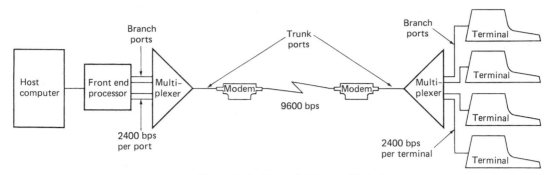

Figure 5-6 Time division multiplexing.

Each of the terminals can transmit and receive at 2400 bps, so if all four are constantly transmitting and receiving data, there will be a total of 9600 bps transmitted and received by the modems. Even though all of the terminals will probably not be transmitting all of the time, there is enough bandwidth between the modems to handle this activity. This technique is known as *pure time division multiplexing* because there is always enough bandwidth to handle the terminals' maximum transmission.

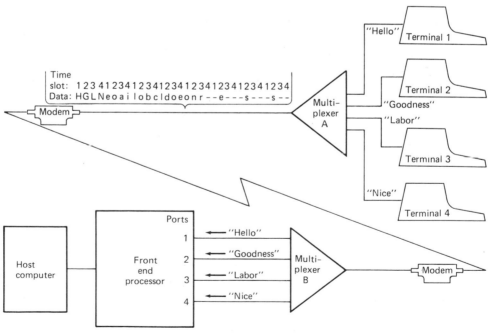

Figure 5-7 Character interleaving.

Improving Data Communications Efficiency

CHARACTER AND BIT INTERLEAVING

How does TDM work? There are two popular methods, known as character interleaving and bit interleaving. The former is the easiest to visualize.

In *character interleaving* (or *byte interleaving*), multiplexing is performed one character at a time. Of course, each character may be made up of eight bits. In Fig. 5-7, each of the terminals is sending a message we have chosen at random. Terminal 1 sends "Hello," terminal 2 sends "Goodness," terminal 3 sends "Labor," and terminal 4 sends "Nice"; the terminals send these words one character at a time. For convenience, we'll refer to the multiplexer attached to the terminals as multiplexer A, and the multiplexer attached to the front end as multiplexer B.

Multiplexer A, using character interleaving, checks each of its branch ports for characters transmitted by terminals. These characters can be sent, one at a time, over the high-speed trunk port. For example, multiplexer A scans its ports, discovering the characters H, G, L, and N. Multiplexer A sends HGLN over its trunk port to multiplexer B. Multiplexer B then sends the characters to each front end port at 2400 bps; the H to port 1, the G to port 2, the L to port 3, and the N to port 4. Next, multiplexer A sends *eoai* over its trunk port. Multiplexer B sends the e to port 1, the o to port 2, the a to port 3, and the i to port 4. This continues until all of the characters are sent.

We call this character interleaving because every fourth character transmitted over the multiplexer's trunk ports is destined for the same branch port. It's the equivalent of four lanes on a highway alternately merging into one lane, taking one car from lane 1, one from lane 2, one from lane 3, one from lane 4, one from lane 1 again, and so on. At the end of the road, the one lane splits off into four again, and the first car feeds into lane 1 again, the next to lane 2, the next to lane 3, the next to lane 4, the next to lane 1, and so on. In character interleaving, characters are merged instead of cars. Remember that each character may be made up of eight bits, but the characters are merged in their entirety.

Each of the terminals is allocated one fourth of the time on the modems in each direction; each time a particular terminal/front end port pair is communicating is called *a time slot*. In our example, terminal 1 had the first time slot, terminal 2 the second, and so on. At multiplexer B, the character in time slot 1 is sent to front end port 1, the character in time slot 2 is sent to front end port 2, and so on. If we used TDM with ten devices instead of four on each end, there would be ten time slots instead of four in each direction.

Notice in our example that terminal 4, with the shortest message ("Nice"), does not use its time slot after it has sent the four characters. We could think of this as wasting a time slot, but the vacant time slot does have a purpose. If terminal 4 had a longer word to transmit, it was guaranteed enough time slots to do so, because the speed of the trunk port is as large as the sum of the speeds of the branch ports (2400 + 2400 + 2400 + 2400 = 9600). Each terminal/front end pair is guaranteed enough bandwidth to carry on its communications. If they don't use all of their bandwidth, some time slots will go unused, even though the full bandwidth capability is there.

Bit interleaving is another way to accomplish TDM. This method takes one bit from each terminal and sends it on the trunk port. For our example, as shown in Fig. 5-8, we'll assume there are still four terminals, and terminal 1 sends the ASCII character A (01000001), terminal 2 sends a B (01000010), terminal 3 sends a C (01000011), and terminal 4 sends a D (01000100). We'll ignore any start and stop bits for simplicity in our example. Since we transmit the bit on the right first in ASCII code, the first bit received from terminal 1 is a 1, from terminal 2 a 0, terminal 3 a 1, and terminal 4 a 0. Multiplexer A then sends 1010 on the trunk port. Multiplexer B receives these four bits and sends the 1 to front end port 1, the 0 to front end port 2, the 1 to front end port 3, and the 0 to front end port 4. Rather than sending four characters at a time, as in character interleaving, the multiplexer sends four bits at a time. Each time slot is shorter, containing only one bit instead of an entire character, but there are eight times the number of time slots in a second. The speed of the trunk port still needs to be as great as the sum of the speeds of the branch ports (2400 + 2400 + 2400 + 2400 = 9600). Bit interleaving functions identically to character interleaving, accept there is a bit in each time slot instead of a full character (or byte).

Whether bit interleaving or character interleaving is used, an important feature of pure TDM is that the terminals and front end ports are unaware that their data is being multiplexed over a single communications line. The 2400 bps of data sent by the terminal always arrive at the front end at the rate of 2400 bps. Neither the terminal nor the front end processor know that the data was combined with other terminals' data, sped up, then separated and slowed down. The data is still transmitted to the front end at 2400 bps, because a full 2400 bps of bandwidth out of the modem's 9600 bps has been reserved for this connection.

Statistical Time Division Multiplexing

In practice, typical terminal users do not use all of their terminals' bandwidth. Humans take coffee breaks, lunch hours, and long weekends. In addition, terminal users often type at slower speeds than their terminals can transmit, so a few characters may be transmitted, then no characters for a while, then a few more characters, and so on. If we use pure TDM with terminals, some of the time slots are left empty when transmission is not occurring from or to one of the terminals.

Statistical time division multiplexing, or *STDM*, takes advantage of the sporadic nature of terminal users and allocates bandwidth to each terminal on the basis of demands and needs. For example, a multiplexer using STDM (often called a *stat mux*), shown in Fig. 5-9, can have a transmission speed in the trunk ports that is lower than the sum of the branch port speeds. In our example, six terminals, each at speeds of 2400 bps, are using a trunk port transmitting at 9600 bps. STDM assumes that not all of the devices will be transmitting all the time, which is a very reasonable assumption when terminals are being used.

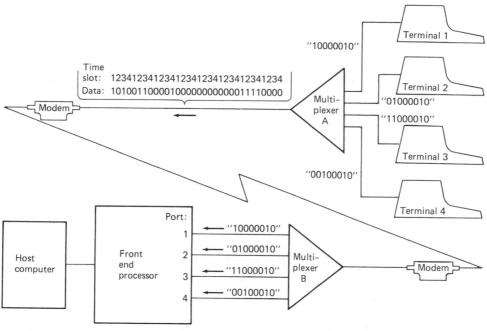

Time
slot: 1234123412341234123412341 2341234
Data: 10100110000100000000000011110000

"10000010"   Terminal 1

"01000010"   Terminal 2

"11000010"   Terminal 3

"00100010"   Terminal 4

Modem

Multi-
plexer
A

Host
computer

Front
end
processor

Port:

1   "10000010"

2   "01000010"

3   "11000010"

4   "00100010"

Multi-
plexer
B

Modem

Figure 5-8 Bit interleaving.

With pure TDM, the time slots are allocated on a constant basis; one terminal always gets time slot 1, the next, time slot 2, and so on. In STDM, terminals only use time slots when they are actually transmitting data. How does multiplexer B in Fig. 5-9 know which data goes to which front end port? Typically, a statistical multiplexer sends not only the data, but also an *address*, which indicates which of the ports the data is destined for. In our example, a 3-bit address is used, which would allow for a maximum of eight ports (000, 001, 010, 011, 100, 101, 110, and 111). In STDM, when a terminal is not sending data, no time slots are allocated to it, and other terminals that are sending data can use these time slots.

The term "statistical" refers to the method by which time slots are allocated. A statistical multiplexer decides how many time slots to allocate in the next second based on the amount of data sent by a given device in the last second. Complicated formulas are calculated constantly, so the time-slot utilization is forever changing based on the user's most recent demands and probable future needs.

What happens when all users try to transmit at the same time? Clearly the 9600 bps port cannot handle all 14,400 bps (6 × 2400 bps). Some statistical multiplexers will buffer, or hold the data, until some of the users stop transmitting and there are extra time slots on the trunk port. Other statistical multiplexers are able to stop a terminal from transmitting when there is a shortage of time slots.

STDM can be more efficient than pure TDM when there is intermittent transmission from the terminals, because it makes better use of the bandwidth on the trunk port. However, if all of the terminals are constantly trying to transmit, STDM will not provide

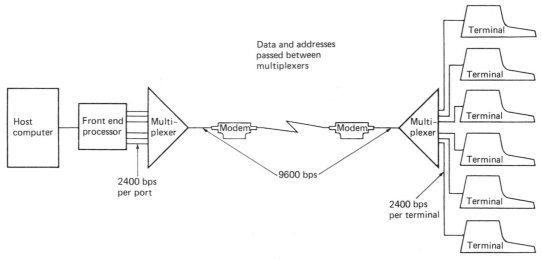

Data and addresses
passed between
multiplexers

2400 bps
per port

9600 bps

2400 bps
per terminal

Figure 5-9 Statistical time division multiplexing.

acceptable transmission time. Not only will there not be enough time slots for the terminals' data, but some of the time slots are used up in sending the terminal addresses.

Pure TDM is often described as *transparent* to the users, meaning that an immediately available transmission path is guaranteed. STDM is not transparent to users, since their data transmission may be delayed.

Clearly, when a guaranteed transmission path is necessary, pure TDM is the only acceptable form of time division multiplexing. STDM offers a more economical solution through more efficient use of the trunk ports, but with the possibility of transmission delays.

Frequency Division Multiplexing

Another common type of multiplexing is *frequency division multiplexing*, or *FDM*. Whereas in time division multiplexing, many terminals share time on a high-bandwidth link, in frequency division multiplexing, the terminals continually share the bandwidth by dividing the link into many separate frequencies or channels.

An example of frequency division multiplexing can be found in cable television: a single coaxial cable carries all of the television channels simultaneously. Each channel is assigned a separate frequency, which the viewer selects by using the television's tuner. The signals from all of the television stations are multiplexed onto a single link, and each is assigned a different frequency.

In data communications, frequency division multiplexing transmits the data from each terminal on a different frequency. As shown in Fig. 5-10, the four terminals can communicate with four remote front end ports by dividing the telephone circuit into four channels. For our example, terminal A will communicate with front end port A over multiplexer channel A, and so on. We'll choose 1000-1300 Hz for channel A, 1500-1800

Improving Data Communications Effic

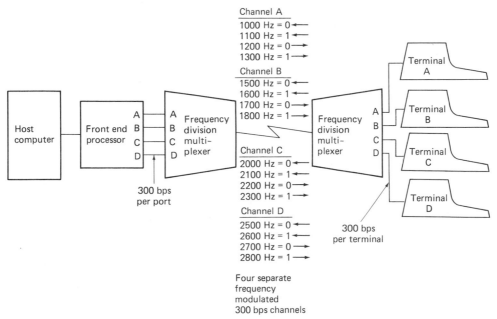

Figure 5-10 Frequency division multiplexing.

Hz for channel B, 2000-2300 Hz for channel C, and 2500-2800 Hz for channel D. As shown in Fig. 5-10, a 0 transmitted from terminal A to front end port A is sent between the multiplexers on channel A with a 1000 Hz tone; a 1 is sent with an 1100 Hz tone. For data sent in the other direction, from front end port A to terminal A using multiplexer channel A, a 0 is sent with a 1200 Hz tone, and a 1 with a 1300 Hz tone. The other three channels use a similar modulation scheme, as shown in the Fig. 5-10. Transmission occurs simultaneously, in full duplex, on all four channels at once, because data is sent using different frequencies for each channel. Though we have chosen four channels for our example, frequency division multiplexing can be performed with any number of channels; using too many channels makes the cost of the multiplexer prohibitive.

Notice that the multiplexer using FDM is not only sharing the communications path among many users (multiplexing), it is also converting the digital data to analog form (modulating). A separate pair of modems is not necessary when using FDM, because FDM combines multiplexing and modulation. Having modulation and multiplexing built into the same device may be convenient, but may be more restrictive in the long run. For example, if advances are made in modem technology, a TDM user could simply purchase a new pair of modems and use the existing TDM multiplexers. An FDM user could only take advantage of new technology by replacing both multiplexers.

Frequency division multiplexing, like pure TDM, is transparent to the end user. Each user has a full bandwidth connection at all times. If a particular terminal does not transmit data, time on its channel is wasted. This is the data communications equivalent of a television station when it is off the air; no one else uses that channel.

Frequency division multiplexing can be more expensive to implement than time division multiplexing because each channel requires separate frequencies. The more

Improving Data Communications Efficiency 99

channels used over a communications circuit, the closer the frequencies will be to each other. If the frequencies are too close together, it becomes extremely expensive to build devices that can separate the different frequencies. In our example, each channel used four frequencies; if we combined phase shift keying techniques with frequency division multiplexing, we would need only two frequencies per channel (one frequency in each direction). However, FDM will always require more frequencies than with a standard single-channel modem, thereby increasing the hardware complexity and costs.

Statistical frequency division multiplexing, or *SFDM*, is sometimes used to make more efficient use of the channels. However, the complexity and cost for sharing channels usually outweigh the benefits. Unlike STDM, which is a practical and economical alternative to TDM, SFDM is rarely used.

DATA COMPRESSION DEVICES

Data compression is another method commonly used to improve data communications efficiency. The philosophy behind data compression is "Why send 9600 bps when 4800 bps will do the job?" The typical arrangement of *data compression devices* is shown in Fig. 5-11. The terminal, front end, and modem are usually unaware that compression is taking place. However, some data patterns occur that cannot be compressed. When this happens, the data compression device must be able to buffer incoming data, or ask the terminal/front end to stop transmitting, while it sends data in an uncompressed fashion. Like multiplexers, data compression devices are used in order to reduce communications circuit costs. Rather than sharing the communications path, a data compression device manages to send the same information using fewer bits. The net result is a higher effective bandwidth for the user.

Data compression devices can be combined with multiplexers for an even greater communications cost savings. For example, eight 2400 bps terminals connected to a multiplexer using TDM would normally require a pair of 19.2 kbps modems. However, a pair of 2-to-1 data compression devices and 9600 bps modems could be used instead. Alternatively, we could increase to as many as 16 terminals with 19.2 kbps modems and 2-to-1 data compression devices.

Data compression can be achieved in many different ways. One common method is

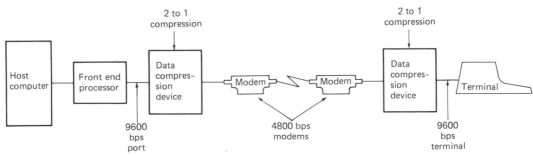

Figure 5-11 Data compression devices.

to use a special shorthand notation for transmitting data. If a certain character is sent frequently, the data compression devices may send an abbreviated form of the character. Just as we use "kbps" instead of "kilobits per second" in this book, a data compression device seeks the same efficiency. Another method used is to send only changes to the data. There are many other methods used to compress data, most of which are proprietary. Therefore, the same vendor's data compression devices must be used at each end of the circuit.

INVERSE MULTIPLEXERS

Not all data communications applications require minimization of communications circuit costs. In some instances, transmission speed is far more important. For example, as shown in Fig. 5-12, a host computer is located in a nuclear power plant control room. A terminal is located 50 miles away, in a remote control center, and is connected to the host computer through modems and phone lines. It is determined that phone lines in that area can support 9600 bps modems, but any higher speed causes low reliability. Safety considerations dictate that the remote user must be able to receive a screen full of information almost instantly, requiring a 19.2 kbps transmission. We can use two telephone lines and an *inverse multiplexer* to combine the bandwidth of the two telephone lines. Rather than sharing one phone line's bandwidth among many terminals, as in the multiplexers discussed earlier, we will combine the bandwidth of two phone lines for use by a single terminal.

Using the arrangement shown in Fig. 5-12, the host computer could send the word "Warning!" to the inverse multiplexer at 19.2 kbps. The inverse multiplexer would send alternating letters over modems attached to each phone line at 9600 bps. At the other end, the receiving inverse multiplexer recombines the letters, resulting in a 19.2 kbps transmission of the word 'Warning!'. An inverse multiplexer acts just like a regular multiplexer, except that the high-speed trunk port is attached to the terminals or front ends, and the low-speed branch ports are attached to the modems and phone lines.

In this example, the inverse multiplexer's high-speed transmission requires twice as many modems, twice as many phone lines, and a pair of inverse multiplexers. However, in some cases, like the example cited, high-speed transmission is vital and well worth the extra cost.

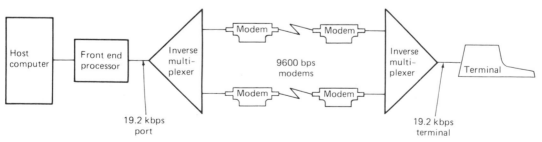

Figure 5-12 Inverse multiplexers.

Improving Data Communications Efficiency

MULTIDROP CONFIGURATIONS

One type of configuration, known as *multidrop*, is unlike any we have discussed so far in this book. We have considered only a host computer or front end port, attached to a single terminal or to a single device, like a line splitter, which could accommodate several terminals. Some host computer architectures, however, will directly accommodate several terminals on the same line. When used locally, these multidrop configurations typically have a single computer or front end port, with a cable running into the first terminal, then from the first terminal to the second, and so on, as shown in Fig. 5-13. Local multidrop configurations are most advantageous when terminals are located near each other, and the front end processor is located in another room. Rather than running long cables from each terminal to the front end processor, only one long cable and several short ones are needed.

The key to multidrop operation is that the host computer must "address" each message to a particular terminal, and each terminal must be able to determine which messages are destined for it. Similarly, terminals must mark their messages with their "return address" so the host computer can determine the sender. Polling and selecting will be necessary to prevent two terminals from trying to use the line at once. In addition, a host computer can send a *broadcast message* to all terminals on the line, by using a special address recognized by all the terminals.

Remote multidrop configurations can also be cost-effective. As shown in Fig. 5-14, a company with locations in San Francisco, New York, and Connecticut needs a communications circuit between the West Coast and each of the East Coast locations. If we used two phone lines and two pairs of modems, the company would pay for two-long distance telephone lines, each about 2500 miles long. However, if we use a multidrop configuration, one 2500 mile line is needed, and the second line is only 40 miles.

A message from San Francisco bound for Connecticut will be routed through New York. The message will not be displayed on the terminal in New York because it is addressed for Connecticut; we could say that the terminal in New York simply ignored the message. There is a potential security risk with multidrop configurations, since a

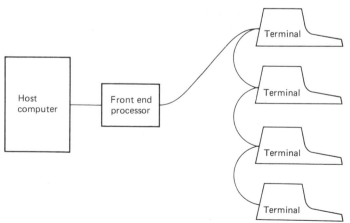

Figure 5-13 Local multidrop configuration.

Improving Data Communications Efficiency

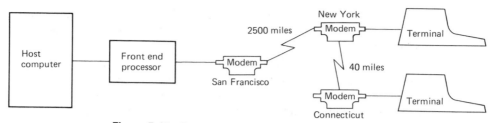

Figure 5-14 Remote multidrop configuration.

determined New Yorker could use special monitoring devices to eavesdrop on all of the communications to and from Connecticut.

Clearly, the long-distance communications costs are reduced; however, the multidrop capability must be present in the host computer or front end processor, and in the terminals used. The economic benefits of this configuration will vary for each user, depending on the geographic layout of their network.

SUMMARY

There are many different types of components for improving data communications efficiency. Front end processors assist the host computer in handling input and output tasks. These tasks may include polling and selecting, error detection, error correction, code conversion, protocol conversion, historical logging, and statistical logging.

Port sharing devices allow many terminals to share a single front end port. Line splitters perform the same function as port sharing devices but are located remotely from the front end port. A remote intelligent controller performs the same functions as a line splitter, but in addition, performs some tasks normally reserved for a front end processor. Port sharing devices, line splitters, and remote intelligent controllers require compatibility with the attached host computers, front end processors, and terminals.

Multiplexers improve communications efficiency without any special features or actions on the part of the host computer, front end processor, or terminal. Multiplexers allow many devices to share one communications circuit, thereby minimizing communications circuit costs. Time division multiplexing splits the communications circuit by allocating time slots to each device. In pure TDM, each terminal has an equal share of the communications circuit and is guaranteed an immediately available transmission path. This is possible as long as the speed of the communications circuit is equal to or greater than the sum of the speeds of the attached devices. TDM can be accomplished using character (byte) interleaving or bit interleaving. In character interleaving, a character occupies each time slot, where in bit interleaving, only a single bit is in each time slot. In statistical time division multiplexing, devices are allocated time slots based on the amount of data recently transmitted. This is more efficient than pure TDM when the data transmission is sporadic. However, STDM does not guarantee an immediately available transmission path. In contrast to TDM, frequency division multiplexing divides the communications circuit into several channels, with data being transmitted on all channels simultaneously but on different frequencies. FDM combines modulation and multiplexing, so modems are no longer needed, though the FDM technique can be fairly expensive to implement.

Data compression devices improve communications efficiency by minimizing the number of bits transmitted. Data is often compressed through various abbreviation techniques. Another device, known as an inverse multiplexer, combines the bandwidth of two or more communications circuits to allow for high-speed transmission. Finally, multidrop configurations can be used to minimize communications circuit distances, and thereby minimize communications costs.

TERMS FOR REVIEW

Address
Bit interleaving
Branch port
Broadcast message
Buffering
Byte interleaving
Channel interface
Character interleaving
Code conversion
Concentrator
Data compression
Data compression device
Data conversion
FDM
FEP
Frequency division multiplexing
Front end

Front end port
Front end processor
Historical logging
Input/output channel
Inverse multiplexer
Line interface
Line splitter
Multidrop
Multiplexer
Mux
Parallel/serial conversion
Parallel/serial converter
Polling
Port sharing device
Processing unit
Protocol
Protocol conversion
Protocol converter

Pure time division multiplexing
Remote intelligent controller
Selecting
SFDM
Stat mux
Statistical frequency division multiplexing
Statistical logging
Statistical time division multiplexing
STDM
TDM
Time division multiplexing
Time slot
Transparent
Trunk port

EXERCISES

5-1. What is the main function of a front end processor?

5-2. Explain the difference between a front end processor's channel interface and line interface.

5-3. Compare a port sharing device with a line splitter.

5-4. What is the difference between a line splitter and a remote intelligent controller?

5-5. What is multiplexing? What is its main purpose?

5-6. Explain the difference between TDM and FDM.

5-7. Compare pure TDM with statistical TDM.

5-8. What is the purpose of a data compression device?

5-9. When is an inverse multiplexer used?

5-10. How can a remote multidrop configuration reduce leased-line costs?

Improving Data Communications Efficiency

6

DATA INTEGRITY AND SECURITY

DATA INTEGRITY

In any data communications network, there is the possibility of errors in data transmission. Preventing or correcting these errors is often referred to as maintaining data integrity.

Sources of Errors

Errors in data transmission can occur for many reasons, including electrical interference from thunderstorms or from other transmission lines. In addition, power surges or spikes due to faulty equipment can also cause bits to be lost or changed during transmission.

All of us have placed long-distance phone calls where the connection is crystal clear, as if we're talking to someone across the street. If we used modems over a clear connection like that, we would probably never encounter data errors.

But we've also placed phone calls where the connection is terrible, filled with noise, static, echoes, and other sounds. If we used modems over this type of connection, we would likely encounter many errors. Humans can separate static and noise from actual conversation, but modems are easily confused by noise. As we discussed in the section on modulation in Chapter 4, modems may have to detect subtle frequency or phase shifts a 1000 times in 1 second. A "little static" that lasts a half-second can easily obliterate 4800 bits if we're transmitting at 9600 bits per second.

Error Control Approaches

Regardless of the source and cause of errors, we need some scheme to protect our data. These methods of maintaining data integrity are often called error control approaches. There are four common approaches in use today.

One approach is simply *not to check for errors*. This approach may sound frivolous, but it is used by some of the "dumb terminals" we introduced in Chapter 3. The device assumes that the terminal operator, and not the terminal itself, will be able to catch any errors. In this case, a conscious decision has been made that it's more important to build a cheap terminal than an error-free terminal.

For a human example of this approach, picture a court reporter writing down everything said in a courtroom. A witness uses the word "books" during testimony, but the courtroom is fairly noisy, and the reporter thinks he said "bucks." The reporter writes "bucks" into the court record and doesn't even know he's wrong. Hopefully, whoever reads the court record will notice the error and be able to understand the sentence. That's an example of not checking for errors.

A second approach is *error detection with flagging*. This approach requires that errors be detected, or noticed, when the data is received; it requires no correction of these errors, only an indication that an error exists. Some terminals will display a question mark, or sound a beep, when they receive a character they believe is in error. These terminals have no idea how to correct errors, but they are alerting the user that something has gone wrong.

In our previous example, the reporter knows that he didn't hear the word properly, but thinks he heard "bucks." He therefore writes it down, circles it, and puts a question mark above it, to alert whoever reads the record later that this word may not be correct. That's an example of error detection with flagging.

A third approach is *error detection with a request for retransmission*. After an error is detected by the receiver, some protocols ask the sender to retransmit the message. A terminal using one of these protocols would check all incoming messages, and if they contained errors, would ask the sender to transmit another copy of the message. The terminal would not display the message on the screen until it was received error-free.

In our courtroom example, the reporter knows that he didn't hear the word correctly, so he raises his hand and says, "Please repeat that sentence. I didn't quite get it the first time." That's an example of error detection with a request for retransmission.

A fourth approach is *forward error correction (FEC)*. In this case, the error is corrected by the receiving device. This method requires sufficient intelligence in the receiving device to determine not only where the error is, but also to correct it. In most cases, forward error correction is limited. For example, a scheme can be provided to correct 100% of single bit errors, where only one bit in a byte is incorrect, though the same scheme will not correct multiple bit errors in a byte.

Data Integrity and Security

In our previous example, the reporter realizes that he didn't hear the word correctly, because "bucks" doesn't make sense in the context of the sentence. The reporter decides that the witness must have said "books" and writes that down instead. That's an example of forward error correction.

Implementing Error Control:
The Technical Details

There are many ways to detect errors. The most common methods are echo checking, parity checking, checksums, and cyclical redundancy checks.

Echo checking. In *echo checking*, the receiving device repeats everything it receives to the transmitting device. If the characters "ABC" are transmitted to a device using echo checking, the receiver then transmits "ABC" back to the sending device. The sender can then determine if the data was received correctly, and can retransmit it if necessary.

Since echo checking requires every data bit to be repeated back to the originator, it at least doubles the time required for data transmission. Though this method guarantees that data will be received correctly, it is obviously inefficient and is used only in critical applications. For example, if the command "Lower landing gear" is being sent from an airplane's central computer to the landing gear controller, it is certainly worth repeating the command back and forth a few times to be sure that it has been properly understood.

Parity checking. *Parity checking* is the most commonly used error-checking method for asynchronous transmission. As we discussed in Chapter 3, in asynchronous transmission, a user might send one character now, ten characters 5 minutes from now, no characters for 1 hour, and then 1000 characters 3 minutes later. Any error detection scheme used with asynchronous transmission should be able to check each character as it arrives; it would be foolish to wait for a block of characters to perform a check, since we are not sure we will receive any more characters.

There are many types of parity checking, including even parity, odd parity, space parity, mark parity, and no parity (or ignored parity). Parity checking requires the transmitter to send an extra bit in each character to meet a certain parity requirement. *Even parity* requires an even number of ones in each byte. *Odd parity* requires an odd number of ones in each byte. *Space parity* uses a 0 for every parity bit, and *mark parity* uses a 1 for every parity bit.

Figure 6-1 shows examples of the letters "A," "B," "C," and "D" being transmitted, using ASCII code and even, odd, space, and mark parity.

For a parity-checking example, we will use a seven-bit ASCII character as discussed in Chapter 3. The letter "A" is represented by the 7 bits 1000001 in ASCII code. Since we are using even parity, there must be an even number of ones sent in every byte. There are already 2 ones in the sequence 1000001, so the parity bit will be 0, and 01000001 will be sent. The receiver counts the number of ones in the byte and assumes

FIGURE 6-1 ASCII CHARACTER TRANSMISSION WITH DIFFERENT PARITIES

ASCII Character	Even Parity	Odd Parity	Space Parity	Mark Parity
A	01000001	11000001	01000001	11000001
B	01000010	11000010	01000010	11000010
C	11000011	01000011	01000011	11000011
D	01000100	11000100	01000100	11000100

the data was received correctly, since there are two 1's in the sequence 01000001. Notice that the parity bit is placed in the leftmost position in ASCII code.

If an error occurs during transmission in the previous example (letter "A," ASCII, even parity = 01000001), and the sequence received is 01001001, the receiver counts the number of ones and determines that there are three ones in the sequence. The receiver recognizes that this is an error, since with even parity all characters received should have an even number of ones. In this case, even parity is able to detect that there is an error in the byte.

Odd parity functions in the same way as even parity, except that there is always an odd number of ones. The letter "A" using odd parity is transmitted as 11000001 using ASCII.

Even and odd parity have several limitations. First, it is critical that both the sending and receiving devices use the same parity checking method, be it even or odd. It makes no difference which method is used as long as the same method is used by both sender and receiver.

Second, this type of parity checking will detect only an odd number of bit errors in a byte. If an even number of bit errors occur, parity checking (even or odd) will not detect the error. The only way to be convinced of this is by repetition. Figure 6-2 shows several examples of transmission errors occurring in the letter "A" to demonstrate this point. If we expect that errors will occur in a random fashion, we have a 50% chance of detecting errors using either even or odd parity.

FIGURE 6-2 PARITY CHECKING AND BIT ERRORS

Character "A" Sent with Even Parity	Number of Ones Sent	Received As:	Number of Bit Errors	Number of Ones Received	Is Error Detected by Even Parity?
01000001	2	01000001	0	2	No
01000001	2	01100001	1	3	Yes
01000001	2	01110001	2	4	No
01000001	2	01110101	3	5	Yes
01000001	2	01110111	4	6	No
01000001	2	01111111	5	7	Yes
01000001	2	11111111	6	8	No
01000001	2	10111111	7	7	Yes
01000001	2	10111110	8	6	No

Space and mark parity are primitive parity-checking methods. In space parity, the sender always uses a 0 for the parity bit and the receiver always looks for a 0. If there is a drastic data error, wiping out enough of the byte to change the parity bit to a 1, space parity will detect the error. Otherwise, as long as the parity bit is 0, the receiving device is oblivious to any error. In fact, if we have only one bit error in the transmission of a byte, there is only a one in eight chance that it is the parity bit, giving us a 12.5% chance of detecting the error. In that case, we have actually detected an error in our parity bit when our data is fine! Mark parity functions in the same manner as space parity does; however, a 1 is substituted for the 0. Therefore, space and mark parity work only when a lot of bits are wiped out, and are not really useful for single bit errors.

No parity, or ignored parity, implies that a 0 will be sent as a parity bit, and the receiver will not even check the parity bit. This allows a receiver not capable of parity checking to communicate with another device that is using parity checking.

Cyclical parity. *Cyclical parity* is a less common variation of parity checking, but it increases the odds of detecting errors. Rather than using only one parity bit to detect errors in a byte, cyclical parity uses at least two parity bits. Each parity bit checks some of the bits in the byte. For example, if we wanted to send the six-bit sequence 101101, we could use cyclical parity checking as shown in Fig. 6-3. Bits 1, 3, and 5 are checked with the parity bit in position 7, and bits 2, 4, and 6 are checked with the parity bit in position 8. If we use odd cyclical parity checking, there must be an odd number of ones in bits 1, 3, 5, and 7 and in bits 2, 4, 6, and 8. In this example, bits 7 and 8 must both be 1 to provide an odd number of ones in both bit groups. The only way for errors to slip by this checking scheme is if errors occur in certain combinations of alternating bits.

Hamming code. *Hamming code*, a forward error correction code devised by Richard Hamming, allows the receiving device not only to detect a single bit error, but also to correct it with 100% accuracy. However, because this error correction ability requires several parity bits, it is not as widely used as other parity methods. Hamming code for a seven-bit ASCII character requires four parity bits, for a total of 11 bits. The parity bits are placed in bit positions 1, 2, 4, and 8 (all powers of 2). The data bits are placed in positions 3, 5, 6, 7, 9, 10 and 11 (none of these are powers of 2). Hamming

FIGURE 6-3 CYCLICAL PARITY CHECKING

Type of Bit	Bit Value	Bit Number
Data	1	1
	0	2
	1	3
	1	4
	0	5
	1	6
Parity	1	7
	1	8

code allows for either even- or odd-parity checking; we will use even-parity Hamming code for our example.

Figure 6-4 shows the ASCII letter "A," with its seven bits. Notice on the first line of the example that the seven data bits have been placed in the Hamming code data bit positions. Now we'll move to line 2 to fill in the parity bits. There must be an even number of ones in the following bit combinations:

Bits 1, 3, 5, 7, 9, 11 (checked with parity bit 1)
Bits 2, 3, 6, 7, 10, 11 (checked with parity bit 2)
Bits 4, 5, 6, 7 (checked with parity bit 4)
Bits 8, 9, 10, 11 (checked with parity bit 8)

FIGURE 6-4 HAMMING CODE

ASCII for letter "A" = 1 0 0 0 0 0 1

		1		0	0	0		0	0	1	Before
Bit No.	1	2	3	4	5	6	7	8	9	10	11	parity

0	0	1	0	0	0	0	1	0	0	1	After
Bit No.	1	2	3	4	5	6	7	8	9	10	11	parity

There are already 2 ones in bits 3, 5, 7, 9, and 11, so a device using Hamming code places a 0 in bit 1 to maintain an even number of ones in bits 1, 3, 5, 7, 9, and 11. There are already 2 ones in bits 3, 6, 7, 10, 11, so the device places a 0 in bit 2 to maintain an even number of ones in bits 2, 3, 6, 7, 10, and 11. There are no ones in bits 5, 6, 7, so the device places a 0 in bit 4 to maintain an even number of ones in bits 4, 5, 6, and 7. There is only a single 1 in bits 9, 10, 11, so the device places a 1 in bit 8 to give us 2 ones in bits 8, 9, 10, and 11.

The resulting sequence, 00100001001, will be transmitted, and the receiving device can check the four parity bits by the same method we used to create them; there should be an even number of ones in every group. If all of the parity checks are correct at the receiving end, there have been no errors (or more than one).

If a single bit is in error, one or more of the parity checks will fail. Add up the numbers of the parity bits that failed, and the position of the incorrect bit will be found. For example, if bit 6 was switched during transmission from a 0 to a 1, 00100101001 would be received. Parity check 1 would pass (even number of ones), parity check 2 would fail (odd number of ones), parity check 4 would fail (odd number of ones), and parity check 8 would pass (even number of ones). When we add up the parity checks that failed (2 + 4 = 6), the result is a clear indication that bit 6 is incorrect. Bit 6 can then be switched from a 1 to a 0, resulting in 00100001001, and the parity bits can be removed, resulting in 1000001, which is the data we sent originally.

Remember, this ingenious method is designed to correct single bit errors. If more than one bit error occurs, the results will not be predictable.

Data Integrity and Security

Checksums.   A *checksum* is a generic term referring to a type of error detection used when receiving blocks of characters rather than single characters. Large blocks are often sent in synchronous transmission, as we explained in Chapter 3. In a simple example, the transmitting device begins with a checksum equal to zero before transmitting a block of data. As each character in a block is transmitted, the transmitter takes the binary number representing that character (the ones and zeroes) and adds it to the checksum. When the entire block of characters has been sent, the checksum (or a portion of the checksum) is also sent. Meanwhile, the receiver adds up the ones and zeroes that it receives, creating its own checksum. When the checksum arrives, the receiver can then compare it to the checksum it calculated. If these do not match, the receiver knows that an error has occurred. Typically, checksums are used in protocols where the receiver can ask the sender to retransmit the data if an error has occurred.

Cyclical Redundancy Check.   The *cyclical redundancy check,* or *CRC*, is a variation on the concept of the simple checksum described above. Instead of simply adding up the ones and zeroes, the CRC uses a more complicated mathematical formula, combining division and addition. This formula helps exaggerate errors, preventing them from canceling each other out. In simple binary addition, as in the simple checksum discussed previously, a one turning to a zero in one byte can be hidden by a zero changing to a one in a later byte. Although the CRC is more complicated and expensive to implement, it is more reliable and provides a high degree of data integrity; almost no block of characters with an error can slip by a CRC without the error being detected.

SECURITY

Though accurate transmission of data is often essential, in some cases, data security can be even more important.

The Importance of Security

As computers take on a larger and larger share of business transactions, the need for data security becomes evident. Hardly a check or invoice is written today by medium-sized to large corporations without the assistance of computers. Even checks written by hand will probably be processed by a computer in the check clearing house.

Twenty years ago it was standard practice for clerks in the accounting department to keep financial records locked away. Similarly, today's computer users are accustomed to utilizing special *passwords* to help "lock up" important information. One common example of a password is the *PIN*, or *personal identification number*, employed in conjunction with our bank card to access an automated teller machine, or ATM. We tolerate the inconvenience of remembering and using this PIN because we recognize the need to safeguard our bank accounts.

Security Concerns

Data communications devices and links are often vulnerable to unauthorized access or intrusion. Many networks, both public and private, include microwave or satellite transmission at one point or another. Anyone with the necessary equipment can eavesdrop on this data, often without the user's knowledge. In addition, phone lines can be tapped, further eroding a data network's security.

There are two common concerns when considering security issues. First, do we expect accidental or intentional intrusions? Precautions taken to prevent someone from stumbling into our network will do little to foil a determined intruder.

Second, do we want simply to guard against others eavesdropping on our data, or do we expect someone to attempt data alteration? Advance knowledge of corporate strategies can be worth millions of dollars to competitors, making eavesdropping a very profitable endeavor for unethical individuals. Similarly, we could all add a few extra zeroes to the end of our bank account balances if we could alter the data on our bank's computer network. There are clearly many motives for breaching a network's security.

Security Goals

There are several goals to consider when safeguarding data. The *National Bureau of Standards*, or *NBS*, has identified five basic goals for proper data security. A secure data message should be sealed, sequenced, secret, signed, and stamped.

A *sealed message* cannot be modified by an unauthorized party. This is the data communications equivalent of the tamper-proof packaging used on many over-the-counter medications today. The receiver will be able to detect if a message has been tampered with.

A *sequenced message* is protected against undetected loss or repetition. This book is an example of a sequenced message; since the pages are numbered, the reader can determine if any pages are missing.

A *secret message* cannot be understood by an unauthorized party. Secret messages are often sent in coded or scrambled form.

A *signed message* includes proof of the sender's identity. A signature on a check is one example; it is recognizable by all, but reproducible only by the sender.

A *stamped message* guarantees receipt by the correct party. Sending a certified letter and requesting a return receipt with the receiver's signature is an example of a stamped message.

Security Measures

Most of today's networks do not meet all of these security goals. The level of protection used depends on the value of security in a given application.

Security measures are often distributed throughout data communications networks. These measures can be implemented in host computers, terminals, modems, special security devices, and even transmission facilities.

Secure transmission facilities.   One security approach that is often over-looked is selective use of transmission media. As we discussed in Chapter 4, the characteristics of the various transmission media differ widely. Twisted pair and coax can be tapped easily and cheaply, whereas unnoticed tapping of fiber optic lines requires extensive training and more expensive equipment. Satellite and microwave transmission are also completely vulnerable to tapping by anyone willing to invest in the appropriate receiving equipment. Sometimes the cost involved in making inexpensive services secure is greater than the economic benefits provided. Careful selection of transmission media is the simplest way to improve security.

Passwords.   *Passwords* are the most common form of security. The biggest drawback of passwords is the carelessness of many users. Some write down passwords where they can be discovered, and others choose a familiar word, like the name of their dog, which can easily be guessed.

Passwords are usually required by the host computer, but can also be required by special security *call-back devices*. These devices help increase the security provided by a password. Remote users attempting to access a host computer using a modem must first enter their password and name into a call-back device attached between the modems and the host. The device then checks the password for accuracy, and if it is correct, hangs up and calls the location programmed into the call-back device. In this case, an intruder must not only steal a user's password, but must also break into their home or office to be there when the call-back device telephones. Some front end processors have this call-back feature built in, and then a separate call-back device is not necessary. This feature provides increased security, but unfortunately has an important drawback: the call-back device must know in advance where the user will be calling from. The traveling salesman would have a hard time accessing the office computer if it is attached to a call-back device.

Another way to make passwords more secure is to incorporate special hardware into the terminal. For example, an ATM cannot be accessed with a PIN alone; a bank card must be inserted as well.

Historical and statistical logging.   Another security method is *historical logging*, a complete recording of all data passed through a particular device. All data passing between a terminal and a host computer can be captured in the historical log. Historical logging is usually performed by host computers or front end processors, though it can be accomplished at other points in the network. The data can be stored on a variety of devices, the most common of which are magnetic tapes or disks.

One example of historical logging is a student taping a professor's lecture. The tape is a complete record of the entire lecture and could be replayed the next week if the student wanted to review a particular topic. Similarly, if a company's personnel computer files have been mysteriously altered, it could replay the historical log in the front end processor the next day and determine which user changed everyone's salaries. The historical log would contain a complete record of the user's actions. By reviewing the log, the user's method of access can be determined, and hopefully the system can be made more secure against future intrusions.

Though this method provides total recall of system events, it also uses a great deal of storage space (disks and tapes). A more efficient but similar method is known as *statistical logging*, whereby statistics are kept on each data port. These statistics might include which users were logged on to which ports, the amount of time logged on, the files accessed, and other information about transactions that occurred. Like historical logging, statistical logging is often performed by host computers or front end processors, though it can be accomplished by other devices.

An example of statistical logging is a student trying to determine which topics a professor considers important. The student records in his notebook that the professor spent 10 minutes on topic A, 20 minutes on topic B, and then 10 minutes on topic C. The student can later look back at this record to determine what the professor emphasized. Similarly, the company with the mysteriously altered personnel files could look back at the statistical log to determine which user accessed the salary files. The statistical log would not indicate exactly what was done to the files; the offending user would be identified, but the exact events that occurred would not be recorded.

When comparing statistical and historical logging, remember that by the time a company consults its logs, the security breach has probably already occurred and the damage has been done. A statistical accounting showing which users may have caused the damage is probably just as useful as a play-by-play description of exactly what happened.

Closed user groups.   Many networks restrict user access by establishing *closed user groups*, or *CUGs*. A set of users who need to communicate only with each other and do not want other users to access their computers can form a closed user group. For instance, a company may want to allow its branch offices to connect to the corporate computer for sales price information, but at the same time ensure that competitors and customers cannot also access this information. The company can resort to a closed user group to ensure that only its branch offices have this access. Typically, closed user groups are employed with packet switching networks, which we discuss in detail in Chapter 8.

Encryption and decryption.   One of the most thorough and effective ways to improve data security is to use *encryption*. Encryption requires coding, or scrambling the data, before it is transmitted over the communications link. *Decryption* is the decoding, or descrambling, of the received data.

This encryption and decryption can be performed by host computers, front end processors, or special *encryption devices*. Although these devices actually perform both encryption and decryption, they are commonly referred to as encryption devices.

A terminal can transmit *clear text*, also known as *plain text*, to an encryption device, as shown in Fig. 6-5. The encryption device takes the clear or plain text and scrambles, or encrypts it, turning it into *cipher text*, before sending it on. At the other end of the communications link, the cipher text is decrypted by the encryption device and sent on to the host computer as clear or plain text (as originally transmitted).

The advantage of encryption is that those eavesdropping on the data transmission cannot understand the encrypted data. This allows use of public data networks, and even satellite or microwave links, without fear of security breaches. Of course, almost any code can be broken eventually, given enough time and a powerful enough computer; the method of encryption chosen determines if it will be practical for an eavesdropper to break a code.

Data Integrity and Security

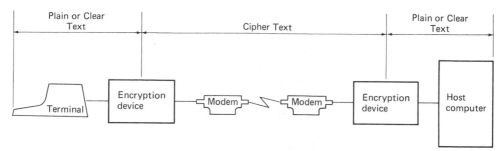

Figure 6-5 Encryption devices.

There are several terms describing the process of encryption. An *algorithm* is a set of instructions, in this case for scrambling the data. A *key* is a specific set of codes to be used by the algorithm to perform the encryption.

A child's plastic "code ring" offers a simple example of encryption. Typically, the ring contains the alphabet in proper order on the top row and the alphabet in scrambled order on the bottom. To send a coded message, the user simply finds each letter in the top row and sends the corresponding letter in the bottom row. The receiver must then have an identical ring and decode the message by looking at each letter in the bottom row and finding its counterpart in the top row.

An example of this simple type of encryption is shown in Fig. 6-6. In this example, the encryption algorithm would be "Find the letter in the top row and instead use the corresponding letter in the bottom row." The decryption algorithm is "Find the letter in the bottom row and instead use the corresponding letter in the top row." The key is the two-row alphabet chart. If we changed the order of the letters in the bottom row, we would still use the same algorithm, but we would be using a different key. In this example, the phrase "THIS IS SIMPLE ENCRYPTION" would be encrypted as "JDCU CU UCTNRS SGZYLNJCBG."

Secret keys.   The basis of all encryption systems is that even if the algorithm is known, without the appropriate key, an eavesdropper cannot interpret a message. In the example above, even with the algorithm, a code ring that is missing the bottom row is useless. We call this type of key a *secret key*; as long as we can keep the key a secret, our data is safe from eavesdroppers. Our example requires that the encryption devices store the entire alphabet and their corresponding code letters. Whereas our example uses only 26 letters, character codes like ASCII and EBCDIC have 128 or 256 characters, respectively. Storing all of these characters and their corresponding coded versions would take a lot of memory space in an encryption device. Therefore, most encryption algorithms and keys are based on mathematical formulas.

One example of an encryption algorithm is "Add the key to the character." The corresponding decryption algorithm is "Subtract the key from the character." For example, as shown in Fig. 6-7, if we choose 0010111 (23 is the decimal equivalent) as our key and

FIGURE 6-6 SIMPLE ENCRYPTION

Clear text:	A B C D E F G H I J K L M N O P Q R S T U V W X Y Z
Cipher text:	Q A Z X S W E D C V F R T G B N H Y U J M K I O L P

Data Integrity and Security

115

want to send the letter "A" in ASCII, which is represented by a 1000001 (65 decimal), we will send 1011000 (88 decimal). At the receiving end, the key will be subtracted from 1011000, resulting in the original 1000001, or the letter "A." Readers unfamiliar or uncomfortable with binary math can use the binary to decimal conversion charts in the Appendix, perform the arithmetic in decimal numbers, and then convert the numbers back to binary numbers to determine what pattern of ones and zeroes will be sent.

All future examples in this chapter will assume that keys used for encryption and decryption are binary numbers, like 10000001; the encryption algorithms are mathematical formulas that somehow combine the key with the data to result in cipher text. In some encryption devices the user can change the key used for encryption or decryption by setting certain switches on the device itself.

The advantage of this type of secret key system is that the key can be changed on a regular basis, to ensure our data is safe. If the transmitter changes the key, the receiver must be notified, or else the received data will not be decrypted correctly. The new key is often sent over a *secure channel*, if one is available. A secure channel is a communications link that is known to be safe from intrusion. More frequently a new key is sent by courier, or an arbitrary system can be used. For example, we can agree that our key will be the number of words in the first paragraph of column 1 of a particular newspaper's front page that day. As long as sender and receiver are using the same key and no one else knows what the key is or how the key is determined, the data is relatively safe, and the secret key is effective.

The reason the data is only "relatively" safe is that any code can be broken, given enough time, computing power, and a little luck. Entire wars have been won or lost by breaking codes. Our example, using an addition/subtraction algorithm, would not take long to break. Most algorithms are far more complicated, including multiplication, division, and exponents. As long as the keys are changed frequently enough, these complicated algorithms are more difficult to break. Today's computers are much faster than their counterparts of even five years ago; there is reason to believe their descendants will be even faster and therefore able to break codes more quickly. New algorithms are constantly being developed to outsmart the faster computers, and these algorithms must continue to evolve to ensure data security.

The Data Encryption Standard and Data Encryption Algorithm. A need for a standard, general-purpose encryption algorithm for use with secret keys was answered in the mid-1970s by the *Data Encryption Standard*, or *DES*. The DES was originally developed by

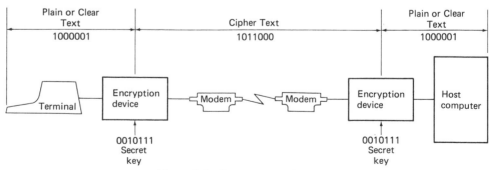

Figure 6-7 Secret encryption keys.

Data Integrity and Security

IBM, and later adopted by the National Bureau of Standards. The *American National Standards Institute*, or *ANSI*, adopted the same standard under a different name, the *Data Encryption Algorithm*, or *DEA*. The DES has also been endorsed by the *National Security Agency*, or *NSA*, for protecting information that is sensitive but not classified. Classified information is more likely to be encrypted with a secret algorithm, not a standard one like DES, to make unauthorized deciphering more difficult. The DES is relatively inexpensive to implement, and chips that use DES for encryption and decryption are widely available.

The adoption of DES set a clear direction for the communications industry. Government agencies and many commercial customers began to demand DES encryption of certain data. DES could be incorporated in an encryption device or in host computers, terminals, modems, or other equipment. The distribution of secret keys was still up to the individuals transmitting and receiving the data, but at least a standard for encryption devices was established.

Symmetric and asymmetric keys. We have already established that secret keys require both users to know which key is being used. The secret keys used in the examples cited so far were based on *symmetric keys*; both the sender and receiver used the same key to encrypt and decrypt the message. In some cases, *asymmetric* keys are used, where the sender and receiver use different keys.

Public keys. *Public keys* are a common use of asymmetric keys. Though secret keys are easy enough to implement between two users, what if we need to contact many different users, and all of the messages need to be encrypted? It is inefficient to call each person, and make up a new secret key, for each transmission. These calls also jeopardize key security.

The public key encryption method uses asymmetric keys to eliminate this problem. Imagine a company with 100 employees. In the company phone book, in addition to an employee's name and phone number, there is another entry for the employee's unique public key. This public key is used to encrypt messages sent only to that employee. These messages can only be decrypted using that employee's secret key (known only to the employee).

It is assumed that everyone in the company uses encryption devices with the same algorithm. To transmit data to another employee's host computer, we need to enter that employee's public key into the encryption device, as shown in Fig. 6-8. However, the cipher text that emerges can only be decrypted with the receiver's secret key. Everyone knows the

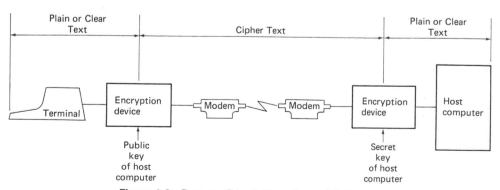

Figure 6-8 Data confidentiality using public keys.

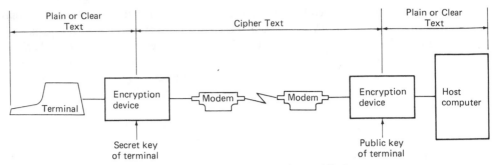

Figure 6-9 Digital signatures using public keys.

public key, but only the particular receiver knows the secret key.

A public key system requires that the algorithm use asymmetric keys; a different key is used to encrypt and decrypt the data. An eavesdropper who tries to decode cipher text with the receiver's public key will not obtain clear text. The public key system is secure because the public keys used to encrypt the data will not also decrypt the data.

All of the encryption methods we have discussed thus far are intended to protect data confidentiality. What about verifying the identity of the sender? A *digital signature* can be obtained by using the reverse of the system just described. If we encrypt data using our secret key, anyone can decrypt it with our public key, as shown in Fig. 6-9. With this method we lose all data confidentiality, since the key used for decryption is now public, but we now are assured that no other user can masquerade as us. For example, if someone tries to forge a memo purported to come from us, they would need to know our secret key to encrypt it properly so that others decrypting the message with our public key would obtain plain text.

DATA CONFIDENTIALITY
AND IDENTITY VERIFICATION

The two systems just described can be combined to obtain both confidentiality and identity verification. We prepare our memo and then encrypt a certain portion, say the last paragraph, using our secret key. Then we encrypt the entire memo again with the receiver's public key. The receiver will then use his secret key to decrypt the message. The resulting message will all be in plain text, except for the last paragraph, which we *double encrypted*.

The receiver then decrypts this paragraph using our public key. If the resulting paragraph is then in plain text, it is proof that the message was sent by us; only someone knowing our secret key could have encrypted that paragraph in a way that our public key would decrypt it. This double encryption method requires both parties to agree in advance on which part of the message will be double encrypted.

Hardware, software, and firmware encryption. In our examples, we used a method known as *hardware encryption*, where a separate encryption device encrypted and decrypted the data. To change the encryption algorithm, the user must usually purchase a new device.

Data Integrity and Security

The key can often be changed using special switches on the device itself. This method is fairly secure, because it is hard to determine an algorithm by looking at an encryption device.

Host computers and intelligent terminals can perform encryption and decryption themselves if they are appropriately programmed. This is known as *software encryption*, and no separate encryption devices are needed. The algorithm can be changed by changing the software. The keys are usually also contained in the software. However, this method is vulnerable, because anyone obtaining a copy of the software knows not only the algorithm, but also the key, and can decipher all messages.

A compromise between these two methods is using *firmware encryption*. In this case, the software containing the algorithm or the keys can be stored on preprogrammed chips which can be inserted into an encryption device. If there are suspected security breaches, a new set of chips, containing new software, can be installed in the encryption device, thereby changing either the algorithm or the key. This combines the security of hardware encryption with the flexibility of software encryption.

SUMMARY

Data integrity and security are both important concerns in today's data communications networks. There are many approaches to error control. Errors can simply be detected and flagged. Another approach is to request retransmission when errors are detected. Sophisticated receiving devices can actually correct some errors (forward error correction). Methods for implementing error control include echo checking, parity checking, cyclical parity, the Hamming code, and various checksums, including the cyclical redundancy check (CRC).

Equally important is data security. Ideally all messages are sealed, sequenced, secret, signed, and stamped. Security measures include the use of appropriate transmission facilities, passwords, historical and statistical logs, closed user groups, and encryption.

Encryption is performed using instructions known as an algorithm, and with a specific code, known as a key. Secret keys can be used for data confidentiality. The DES, or DEA, is a standard secret key algorithm. Public keys can be combined with secret keys to provide not only data confidentiality, but also a digital signature. Finally, encryption can be performed using hardware, software, or firmware methods.

TERMS FOR REVIEW

Algorithm	*Checksum*	*Cyclical parity*
American National	*Cipher text*	*Cyclical redundancy check*
Standards Institute	*Clear text*	*Data Encryption Algorithm*
ANSI	*Closed user group*	*Data Encryption Standard*
Asymmetric keys	*CRC*	*DEA*
Call-back device	*CUG*	*Decryption*

DES
Digital signature
Double encrypted
Echo checking
Encryption
Encryption device
Error detection with a
    request for retransmission
Error detection with
    flagging
Even parity
FEC
Firmware encryption
Forward error correction
Hamming code

Hardware encryption
Historical logging
Key
Mark parity
National Bureau of
    Standards
National Security Agency
NBS
NSA
Odd parity
Parity checking
Password
Personal identification
    number
PIN

Plain text
Public key
Sealed message
Secret key
Secret message
Secure channel
Sequenced message
Signed message
Software encryption
Space parity
Stamped message
Statistical logging
Symmetric keys

EXERCISES

6-1. Why is data transmission more sensitive than voice transmission to errors?

6-2. How is error detection with flagging different from error detection with a request for retransmission?

6-3. What is the advantage of forward error correction over other error control approaches?

6-4. What is echo checking?

6-5. How does even-parity checking detect errors? Odd-parity checking? Is one method better than the other?

6-6. If errors occur transmitting bits 3 and 4, will even-parity checking detect the error? How about even cyclical parity?

6-7. What type of bit error does the Hamming code correct?

6-8. How is a simple checksum different from the cyclical redundancy check?

6-9. Explain the major goals of proper message security.

6-10. Which transmission media are the most secure? Which are the least secure?

6-11. What is the difference between historical and statistical logging?

6-12. Explain the difference between clear text and cipher text.

6-13. Compare secret and public keys. How is each used for encryption and decryption?

6-14. What is the difference between symmetric and asymmetric keys?

7

ARCHITECTURES
AND PROTOCOLS

We have already discussed host computers, front end processors, terminals, modems, multiplexers, and many other devices used for data communications. Communications architectures and protocols enable these devices to communicate in an orderly manner, defining precise rules and methods for communications, and ensuring harmonious communications among them.

ARCHITECTURES

A *communications architecture* is a manufacturer's strategy for connecting its host computers, terminals, and communications equipment. It defines the elements necessary for data communications between devices. One of the advantages of a well defined communications architecture is that it cleanly separates the function of communications from the host computer's other functions. Specifically, a communications architecture may describe special functions that the host computer's hardware and software must perform to allow applications programs to communicate with the outside world.

For example, there may be many different types of terminals attached to a single host computer. A programmer who is writing accounting software for the host computer does not need to know how to communicate with these different terminals. The programmer formats the data in a special manner defined by the host computer's communications architecture; the accounting program then passes the data to the communications software, which will in turn translate it to a format for each of the different terminals. The architecture defines the precise role of each program; the accounting program calculates profits and losses, and the communications program sends data to the terminals. Similarly, the author of a word processing program doesn't need to understand how particular terminals function; the programmer simply follows the rules spelled out by the communications architecture and then passes the data onto the communications program for further processing.

An analogy for a communications architecture can be found in a televised football game. The referee calls a penalty and uses hand signals to indicate the infraction and the offending team. The announcer sees these hand signals and translates them into words for the television viewers. In this communications architecture, it is the function of the referee to call the penalty and explain it by using hand signals, and the announcer is responsible for translating the hand signals into words and adding further explanation. Similarly, in communications architectures, each piece of hardware and software has its own task, and for communications to occur, they must all function in harmony.

Separating the communications functions of a host computer from its other functions adds flexibility. For example, if we later want to modify our architecture to include other types of terminals and devices, we do not need to modify all of the host computer's software. Since all applications programs communicate through the communications software, only the communications software needs to be modified to accept the new devices. Referring back to our analogy, to televise the same football game in Spain, we would not need to teach the referee to speak Spanish; since only the announcer speaks to the viewers, only the announcer needs to know Spanish.

Thus far in this book we have considered host computer-to-terminal communications. Users often want to connect host computers to other host computers, to allow them to share information, transfer files, and so on. A communications architecture describes this type of communications, in addition to host computer-to-terminal communications.

Currently, each host computer manufacturer uses its own architecture. Unfortunately, though all architectures perform similar functions, they are rarely compatible. For example, connecting IBM host computers to each other may be easy; connecting DEC host computers to each other may also be easy. Connecting DEC host computers to IBM host computers, however, may require special conversion devices that can communicate successfully in both architectures. Before we discuss individual manufacturers' particular architectures, we will consider an international standard that may allow all future host computers, regardless of manufacturer, to communicate with each other.

THE OPEN SYSTEMS INTERCONNECTION MODEL

The International Standards Organization (ISO) has developed a universal architecture for computer communications. This standard, known as the *Open Systems Interconnection Model*, or *OSI model*, breaks down the task of communications into seven independent layers, each with its own tasks. OSI's purpose is to permit communications among devices made by many manufacturers. The exact methods for performing these tasks, including protocols we discuss later in this chapter, are still evolving. Almost all of the major host computer manufacturers have supported the concept of OSI in principle, even though their current product offerings may not yet comply with OSI. The *Corporation for Open Systems,* or *COS,* is a nonprofit corporation formed in 1985 consisting of representatives of major host computer manufacturers, including Control Data, DEC, Hewlett-Packard, Honeywell, IBM, NCR, Tandem, Unisys, Wang, Xerox, and others. The corporation's purpose is to facilitate the evolution of inter-vendor compatibility from a model to a reality.

The seven layers of OSI are shown in Fig. 7-1. Each layer represents a particular function. Sometimes, each function is performed by a separate piece of hardware or software. Other times, a single program may perform the functions of several layers. All of the layers are necessary for communications to occur. The different layer classifications are somewhat arbitrary, and a different standards committee might have chosen to break the communications function into more or fewer layers. For example, we might describe the process of driving to work as "(1) Open the car door. (2) Sit down. (3) Close the door. (4) Insert the key. (5) Turn the key." And so on. Another person might describe the same process by saying "(1) Get in the car. (2) Start the car. (3) Put the car in gear." And so on. We are all describing the same task, and both descriptions are correct and accurate; however, each description chose to break up the process of driving to work into different tasks. Similarly, the ISO-OSI model chooses to divide the function of computer communications into seven layers, though more or fewer layers could easily have been chosen. Rather then examine each layer's functions in detail, we will merely highlight its most important functions.

The lowest layer, known as the *Physical Layer,* or *Layer 1,* is responsible for transmission of bits. The Physical Layer is always implemented by using hardware; this layer encompasses the mechanical, electrical, and functional interface. This layer is the interface to the outside world, where ones and zeroes leave and enter the device, usually using electronic signals as specified by interface standards. Examples of Physical Layer standards are RS-232-C and RS-449/RS-422-A/RS-423-A.

The *Data Link Layer,* or *Layer 2,* is responsible for ensuring error-free, reliable transmission of data. The Data Link Layer scrutinizes the bits received to determine if errors occurred during transmission. This layer is able to request retransmission or correction of any errors using protocols such as BSC, SDLC, and HDLC, presented later in this chapter.

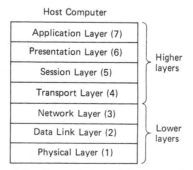

Figure 7-1 Layers of the Open Systems Interconnection model.

Architectures and Protocols

The *Network Layer,* or *Layer 3,* is responsible for setting up the appropriate routing of messages throughout a network. This is the only layer that is concerned with the types of switching networks used to route the data. The routing of data between networks, and through packet switching networks, is also handled by the Network Layer. We discuss packet switching networks further in Chapter 8.

These layers of OSI (Physical, Data Link, and Network) are usually referred to as the *lower layers.* Layers 4 through 7 (Transport, Session, Presentation, and Application) are usually referred to as the *higher layers,* or *upper layers.*

The *Transport Layer,* or *Layer 4,* is responsible for isolating the function of the lower layers from the higher layers. This layer will accept messages from higher layers, and break them down into messages that can be accepted by the lower layers. For example, the file being transferred may contain thousands of characters; the lower layers may be transmitting data 100 characters at a time, so this layer breaks the file into many blocks, each 100 characters long. If communications technology changes, and longer messages can be accepted in the future, only the Transport Layer will need modification. The Transport Layer is also responsible for monitoring the quality of the communications channel, and for selecting the most cost efficient communication service based on the reliability required for a particular transmission.

The *Session Layer,* or *Layer 5,* requests that a logical connection be established based on the end user's request. In this case, an end user might be the terminal operator using the computer. For example, if the user wants to transfer a file, the Session Layer is informed of the location of the file on the user's system, and the location of the destination file on the remote host computer. Any necessary "log-on" and password procedures are also usually handled by this layer. The Session Layer is also responsible for terminating the connection.

The *Presentation Layer,* or *Layer 6,* provides format and code conversion services. For example, if the host computer is connected to many different types of printers, each printer may require different character sequences to invoke special features, such as boldface and italics. The Presentation Layer handles all the necessary formatting. In addition, if files are being transferred from the host computer of one manufacturer to the host computer of another, there may be different file formats, or even different character codes. The Presentation Layer would handle any necessary conversion (e.g., ASCII-to-EBCDIC conversion).

The *Application Layer,* or *Layer 7,* provides access to the network for the end user. The user's capabilities on the network are determined by the Application Layer software, which can be tailored to the needs of the user. Some Application Layer software might permit remote terminals only to access a host computer; other Application Layer software might also permit file transfers. Network management statistics, diagnostics, and other on-line monitoring capabilities can also be implemented in this layer.

We have already mentioned that the Physical Layer must be implemented in hardware. Since this layer is the only part of the model where bits are actually transmitted, it is also the only part of the model requiring hardware implementation. The other layers all manipulate the data in some way, perhaps adding to it, or modifying it, but all of these techniques can generally be performed using software. However, since functions can be performed more efficiently and inexpensively by hardware than by software, some

Architectures and Protocols

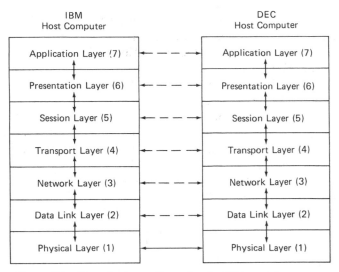

Figure 7-2 Transferring a file under the OSI model.

functions of the Data Link and Network Layers are sometimes implemented in hardware. The higher layers are almost always implemented in software.

OSI IN ACTION

Few of today's host computers fully implement OSI functions that allow for complete inter-vendor compatibility. Assuming that some day all host computer manufacturers will adopt OSI, how would a common transaction, like a file transfer, then take place? We'll trace a file transferred from an imaginary IBM host computer of the future to a DEC host computer of the future, using the OSI model as a reference.

We will begin by examining the path of the data through the layers of the IBM host computer. As illustrated in Fig. 7-2, a user of a word processing program on the IBM host computer issues the file transfer command to the Application Layer. The Application Layer then passes the file to the Presentation Layer, which may reformat the data. The data is then passed to the Session Layer, which requests that a connection be provided to the destination host and passes the data to the Transport Layer. The Transport Layer breaks the file into manageable chunks of data for transmission and passes them to the Network Layer. The Network Layer selects the data's route and then passes the data to the Data Link Layer. The Data Link Layer adds extra information to the data so that it can be checked for errors at the receiving end, and passes the data to the Physical Layer. The Physical Layer takes the resulting data stream and transmits it across the physical link to the other host computer.

The data transmitted by the Physical Layer includes not only the file from the Application Layer, but all the extra information added by each of the other layers. Each layer performs its function by modifying the data. For example, the Network Layer adds extra bits to the data that specify the route the data is to take. The data finally transmitted by the Physical Layer could be twice as long as the original data, but these extra ones and zeroes each perform valuable functions. The receiving host computer's different layers will each examine the ones and zeroes related to their functions, and will remove their data before passing the remaining data to the next higher layer. By the time the message reaches the Application Layer on the destination host computer, it is the same length as the message originally sent by the Application Layer on the originating host computer.

The DEC host computer's Physical Layer receives the bits and passes them on to its Data Link Layer. The Data Link Layer verifies that no errors occurred, and then passes the data onto the Network Layer. The Network Layer ensures that the selected route is proving reliable, and then passes the data on to the Transport Layer. The Transport Layer reassembles the small chunks of data into the file being transferred, and then passes it onto the Session Layer. The Session Layer determines if the transfer is complete, and if so, may break down the session, in effect ending communications. The data is then passed on to the Presentation Layer, which may reformat it, performing any necessary conversion, and then pass it on to the Application Layer. The DEC host computer users can then access the transferred information through the Application Layer software.

In this example, the transfer of data went smoothly. What if an error had occurred? For example, if the DEC host computer's Data Link Layer detects any errors, it might request that the data be retransmitted. This retransmission request would be sent back over the DEC Physical Layer to the IBM Physical Layer, which would pass it on to the IBM Data Link Layer. The IBM Data Link Layer would respond to the retransmission request, since this layer is responsible for error-free transmission. The IBM Data Link Layer retransmits the data to the IBM Physical Layer, which transmits the data over the physical link. The data is received by the DEC Physical Layer, and passed on to the DEC Data Link Layer. If there are still errors, the entire retransmission process is repeated. If the data is now error-free, the file transfer continues as described previously, with the data being passed on to the higher layers.

The OSI model provides for *peer-level* communication between the layers. The Physical Layers of the two host computers are the only parts of the two devices that communicate directly. The other layers communicate indirectly, through the lower layers, and eventually through the Physical Layer. For example, the Data Link Layer on the IBM host computer adds bits to the message for error detection that are interpreted by the DEC Data Link Layer. Similarly, each layer on the IBM host computer contributes bits which are interpreted by the corresponding layer on the DEC host computer. Although only the Physical Layers communicate directly, all of the layers communicate indirectly with their peers on the other host computer by modifying the data, sending messages for interpretation by their counterparts. This peer-level communication is shown with dashed lines in Fig. 7-2.

Our discussion so far has assumed that two host computers are directly connected to each other. Sometimes, in a network with many host computers, there may be intermediary devices between the two host computers trying to communicate. Each device on a network can be referred to as a *node*. For example, a message being routed from a host computer in San Francisco to a host computer in New York might pass through a switch-

Architectures and Protocols

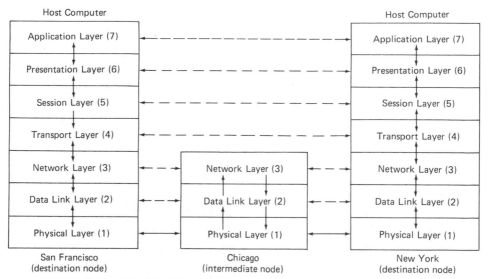

Figure 7-3 Multiple node communications under OSI.

ing node in Chicago. In Fig. 7-3, there are nodes in New York, San Francisco, and Chicago. The nodes at the far ends of the connection, in this case in San Francisco and New York, are sometimes referred to as the *destination nodes*. The intermediate devices, known as *intermediate nodes,* support only the first three layers of the OSI model. The node in Chicago must receive the message from San Francisco with its Physical Layer, verify with its Data Link Layer that there are no errors, and then determine, with its Network Layer, the appropriate routing to the destination host computer in New York. Error correction information is then added back to the message by the Chicago node's Data Link Layer before it is retransmitted to New York by the node's Physical Layer. Intermediate nodes must support the lower three layers, which are necessary for data transmission and routing. The intermediate node may have higher layers, but since it is not the destination device, the message in this case never reaches those layers in the intermediate node. The Network Layer at the host computer in New York recognizes the message has reached its destination, and does not send the message to another node, but instead to its own higher layers.

TODAY'S COMMUNICATIONS ARCHITECTURES

Today's communications architectures typically have a sole purpose in mind: to allow a single vendor's devices to communicate with each other. Host computers, front end processors, terminals, and other devices are all linked in accordance with the rules spelled out in a communications architecture. Attachment of devices from other vendors requires the use of special converters and adapters. For example, a Hewlett-Packard terminal might connect to a Honeywell host computer using a special protocol converter.

Typically, a device attached with a converter will be limited in its communications capabilities. In our example, the HP terminal might be able to perform basic text communications, but might be unable to perform graphics functions on the Honeywell host computer.

Since it may be many years before OSI is implemented on all devices, today we are still bound by the limitations of today's communications architectures. There are many different communications architectures offered by different vendors today, but one architecture is by far the most widely used.

Systems Network Architecture

IBM's *Systems Network Architecture,* or *SNA,* introduced in 1974, has become the most widely used communications architecture in the world. SNA's success is usually attributed to its ability to connect a wide variety of devices, each with different capabilities, in a homogeneous network whose workings are hidden from the end user. SNA allows customers to start with a small network and increase its size in a modular fashion. SNA networks can also be connected to other SNA networks. Finally, SNA includes sophisticated network management functions to simplify fault isolation and problem determination, as well as provide reports on network usage. We explain these functions in Chapter 9.

Like OSI, SNA functions can be divided into different layers. These layers roughly parallel the OSI model, but some SNA layers perform more or fewer functions than the corresponding OSI layers. The SNA layers are shown in Fig. 7-4, along with a rough approximation of their OSI equivalents.

SNA Layers	OSI Layers
Transaction Services	Application Layer
Presentation Services	Presentation Layer
Data Flow Control	Session Layer
Transmission Control	Transport Layer
Path Control	Network Layer
Data Link Control	Data Link Layer
Physical Control	Physical Layer

Figure 7-4 SNA layers vs. OSI layers.

Because of SNA's flexibility and complexity, a thorough discussion would require several volumes. We will therefore concentrate on some of the basic terminology and language of SNA, as well as its major functions. Since SNA is the architecture of a particular manufacturer (IBM), some of the terminology is slightly different from the terminology used previously in this book. For example, what we have often called host computers are known in SNA as *Host Processors.* Similarly, SNA *Workstations* are equivalent to the devices we have called terminals.

The structure of SNA. The components or devices interconnected by an SNA network are known as *Nodes*. The Nodes are connected by data communications *Links*. For instance, a Host Processor and Workstation could be considered Nodes in SNA, and the two Nodes are connected by a communications Link. The *network* includes the components and the communications Links.

SNA clearly separates the network from the users. In other words, the users do not have to understand how the network functions to use the network. For example, assume an accountant is using a Workstation in an SNA network to access an accounting program on a Host Processor in the same network. There are two *End Users* in this communications path, the accountant and the accounting program. The accountant sends data to the SNA network and receives data from the SNA network. Similarly, the accounting program, which is a specific *Application Program* on the Host Processor, also sends data to the SNA network, and receives data from the SNA network. The two End Users, the Application Program and the accountant, are isolated from the routing and transmission of data, which is handled entirely by the SNA network. Neither the accountant nor the accounting program need to understand how their data is routed or transmitted.

Often there will be a *Communications Controller* between the Host Processor and the Workstation, as illustrated in Fig. 7-5. The Communications Controller's responsibilities include routing data through a network and controlling the communications Links. For example, the Communications Controller could be linked to several other Host Processors, allowing the same Workstation user to access several different computers.

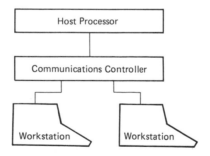

Figure 7-5 Using a Communications Controller in an SNA network.

Cluster Controllers are often added to allow several Workstations to share a single point of access to the network, as shown in Fig. 7-6. A Cluster Controller is similar in function to the generic remote intelligent controller we presented in Chapter 5. The Cluster Controller is often located many miles from the Communications Controller; the length of the communications Link is not important, and Links may even include telephone circuits and modems.

There are different types of Nodes in SNA, depending on their function. For example, as illustrated in Fig. 7-7, the Host Processor is often referred to as the *Host Node*. A Communications Controller is referred to as the *Communications Controller Node*. A Workstation, or a Cluster Controller with several Workstations, is referred to as

Architectures and Protocols   129

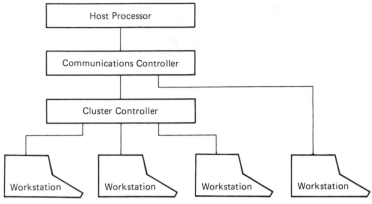

Figure 7-6 Using a Cluster Controller in an SNA network.

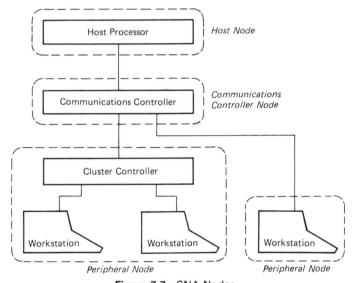

Figure 7-7 SNA Nodes.

a *Peripheral Node.* A Peripheral Node is always the source and destination of data. Another type of Peripheral Node is a *Distributed Processor,* which is similar to a Host Processor, through more limited in function.

Network Addressable Units.   The SNA network components we have already discussed can be further broken down into the various functions they perform. Each Node may contain several *Network Addressable Units,* or *NAUs.* Network Addressable Units have unique addresses, so that data can be routed to a particular NAU. Network Addressable Units are a combination of hardware and/or software in a Node managing a particular function. There are three types of Network Addressable Units, known as a *Logical Unit,* a *Physical Unit,* and a *System Services Control Point.*

A *Logical Unit,* or *LU,* is the End User's access point to an SNA network. For example, the End User of a Workstation in a Peripheral Node types data on the keyboard, which is then passed to the Logical Unit for routing to its destination, which is a Host Node in the SNA Network. When the data reaches the Host Node, it is passed to the Logical Unit in that Host Node. At the Host Processor, the End User is an Application Program, so the Application Program receives the data from a Logical Unit on the Host Node. Data enters and leaves the SNA network at the Logical Unit.

End Users are not part of the SNA network; they each communicate with the SNA network through the network's Logical Units. When two End Users communicate in *SNA* through their respective Logical Units, it is known as an LU-LU *Session,* as shown in Fig. 7-8. An SNA session is a communications path through an SNA network.

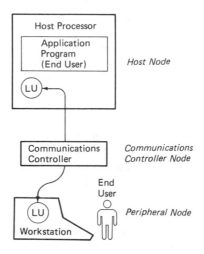

Figure 7-8 SNA LU-LU Session between Logical Units in the Workstation and Host Processor.

Workstations that are capable of communicating directly with an SNA network contain a Logical Unit. Some Workstations do not possess sufficient intelligence to communicate directly with the SNA network, and are instead attached to a Cluster Controller; in this case the Cluster Controller contains the Logical Unit, as illustrated in Fig. 7-9. Notice that the Communications Controller does not contain a Logical Unit, because there are no End Users at the Communications Controller Node, and data is only routed through the Communications Controller.

Every Node contains a *Physical Unit,* or *PU,* which manages and monitors that Node's resources. For example, the telephone lines and modems connecting two Nodes are not part of the SNA network. The Physical Unit represents these devices to the network, in much the same way that the Logical Unit represented the End User to the network. A simple SNA network with its Physical Units and Logical Units is shown in Fig. 7-10. Notice that the Workstations connected to the Cluster Controller do not contain a Physical Unit, because the Cluster Controller is managing that Peripheral Node's physical resources.

Architectures and Protocols

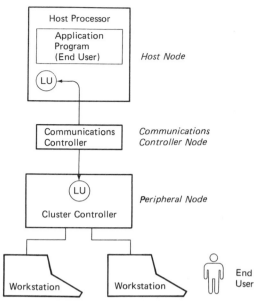

Figure 7-9 SNA LU-LU Session between Logical Units in the Cluster Controller and Host Processor.

Finally, the *System Services Control Point,* or *SSCP,* is a part of the Host Node that acts as a central control point for monitoring and controlling a network's resources. The System Services Control Point communicates with all of the Physical Units in the Network using SSCP-PU Sessions, and all of the Logical Units in the Network using SSCP-LU Sessions. The SSCP can communicate with the PUs and LUs, ensuring that they are operating properly; any malfunctions can be logged by the SSCP. Finally, the SSCP can help establish sessions between two LUs, thereby allowing End Users to communicate.

Domains and Subareas. The SSCP can be thought of as the king of the SNA network, commanding all the PUs and LUs in its *Domain.* Each domain has only one SSCP. To establish an LU-LU Session where each LU is in a different Domain, the SSCPs of each Domain must first communicate through an SSCP-SSCP Session. Two SSCPs and their respective Domains are illustrated in Fig. 7-11.

Domains can be subdivided into *Subareas,* each containing a *Subarea Node* and the resources that Node controls. Host Nodes and Communications Controllers are both classified as Subarea Nodes. Therefore, as shown in Fig. 7-12, each Host Processor is a Subarea, and each Communications Controller with its attached Workstations and Cluster Controllers also comprise a Subarea. Also shown in Fig. 7-12 are the Links between Subarea Nodes. These Links are known as *Transmission Groups.* If there are several Links in a Transmission Group, and one should fail, communications will automatically be routed over one of the other Links in the Transmission Group.

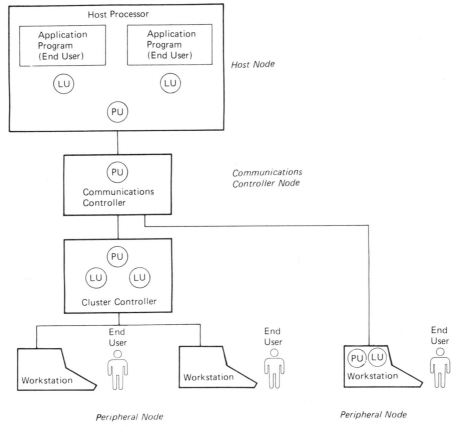

Figure 7-10 SNA network with its Physical Units and Logical Units.

Other Communications Architectures

Almost all computer manufacturers have an architecture for computer communications. It is hard to classify any one architecture as superior to another. Each is designed to allow a particular manufacturer's devices to communicate with each other. Until OSI unifies future communications architectures, there will continue to be compatibility problems. Some of the more popular communications architectures are listed in Fig. 7-13.

PROTOCOLS

While architectures provide a broad framework for communications, describing how different components can be connected together, *protocols* precisely define the methods

Architectures and Protocols

used to communicate. Almost all architectures require the use of certain protocols to ensure reliable data transmission. Protocols are a set of rules for transmitting and receiving data between devices. Sometimes called *line disciplines,* protocols spell out the specific character or bit patterns required for communications between two devices.

An example of a human communications protocol can be found in a classroom. Typically, a professor begins a lecture, and controls the communications path. If a student wants to communicate, the student must wait until the professor asks "Any questions?", raise his hand, and wait for permission to communicate. The professor can then call on the student, granting control of the communications line to the student. The student then asks his question, and grants control of the communications path back to the professor for the response. The protocol in this case is that the student speaks only when called upon; it is customary that the student doesn't interrupt the professor, and vice versa. The type of protocol commonly used in data communications is known as a *link-level protocol*, because it precisely defines methods for communicating over a link.

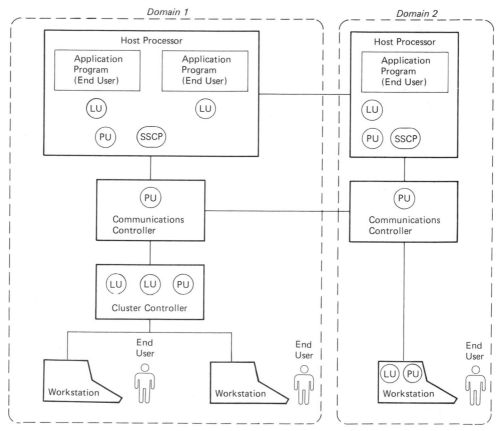

Figure 7-11 Two-Domain SNA network.

Architectures and Protocols

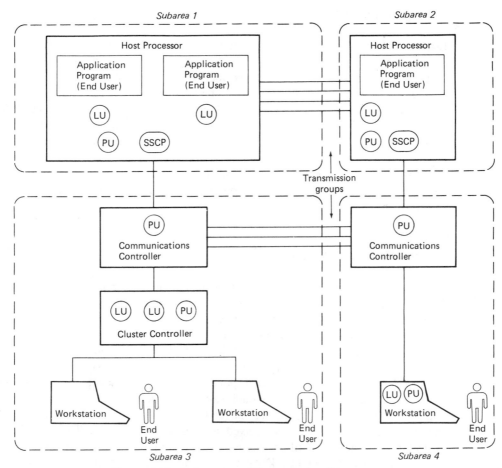

Figure 7-12 Subareas and Transmission Groups.

FIGURE 7-13 POPULAR COMMUNICATIONS ARCHITECTURES

Vendor	Architecture
DEC	Digital Network Architecture (DNA)
Hewlett-Packard	AdvanceNet
Honeywell	Distributed Systems Architecture (DSA)
IBM	Systems Network Architecture (SNA)
Unisys (Burroughs)	Burroughs Network Architecture (BNA)
Unisys (Sperry)	Distributed Communications Architecture (DCA)
WANG	Wang Systems Networking (WSN)

Polling and Selecting

Establishing rules for sharing the communications path, known as *communications line control,* is one of the major functions of a link–level protocol. Often this is accomplished by using polling and selecting methods, mentioned previously in Chapter 5.

Polling occurs when the host computer or front end processor asks the terminal, "Do you have any data to send?" At this point, a smart terminal might send data, or simply answer "No." *Selecting* occurs when the front end processor or host computer asks the terminal, "Can you accept data now?" A smart terminal might then answer "Go ahead" or "Not now, I'm busy." Only smart or intelligent terminals can respond to these messages; dumb terminals cannot be controlled by polling and selecting. Protocols define the exact characters or bit patterns that must be sent to perform this polling and selecting.

Automatic Repeat Request

Finally, almost all protocols provide for some *error detection and correction* capability. Most protocols use an *automatic repeat request* system known as *ARQ.* In these systems, when the receiving device recognizes an error, it automatically requests that the data be retransmitted. Both the transmitting and receiving devices usually detect errors by using a checksum or cyclical redundancy check method, as described in Chapter 6.

There are two common types of ARQ in use today. One type, known as *stop-and-wait ARQ,* requires that the receiver respond to each block of data before the next one can be sent. A human example of stop-and-wait ARQ would be an inexperienced secretary taking dictation; after each sentence spoken by the boss, the secretary may say "Okay," indicating that the sentence was received and transcribed properly. The boss does not go on to the next sentence until hearing the "Okay." In addition, a secretary who doesn't understand a sentence might ask "What?". This is a request for the boss to repeat the transmission. Similarly, with stop-and-wait ARQ, a device will not transmit the next sentence until it has received confirmation that the last message was received correctly; it will also repeat messages that were not understood.

In the other method, known as *continuous ARQ,* a device continues sending messages without waiting for confirmation that the last message was received. For example, a boss dictating a letter to a very experienced secretary would probably not pause between sentences to wait for the secretary to say "Okay." We'll assume that this boss is in the habit of rattling off several sentences at a time, sometimes getting far ahead of the secretary's ability to transcribe. Even though the secretary may continue to say "Okay" after each sentence is transcribed, the boss may already be in the middle of the next sentence. As long as the secretary doesn't say "What?", the boss keeps talking.

There are two types of continuous ARQ protocols. If the secretary asks "What?", there are two possible reactions by the boss. The first, known as *go-back-N continuous ARQ,* would have the boss return to the last sentence the secretary understood, and begin retransmitting the misunderstood sentence, as well as any that followed. Another possible response, *selective repeat continuous ARQ,* would require the boss to repeat only the

Architectures and Protocols

misunderstood sentence; the subsequent sentences would not have to be retransmitted. In either case, the advantage of continuous ARQ protocols over stop-and-wait ARQ protocols is that the sending device does not have to wait for permission from the receiving device before sending the next block of data. With either type of continuous ARQ, as long as no errors occur, data transmission is never delayed. Continuous ARQ therefore is more efficient than stop-and-wait ARQ, where the transmitter must wait for an acknowledgment before proceeding to send the next data block.

COMMON COMPUTER PROTOCOLS

All common computer protocols allow devices to share a communications path, and detect and correct errors. There are two common classes of communications protocols, byte-oriented protocols and bit-oriented protocols.

In both types of protocols, the devices must exchange *control information* along with the data transmitted. This control information includes the queries and responses used for polling and selecting, as well as the error-checking information necessary for all types of automatic repeat request. In *byte-oriented protocols,* also known as *character-oriented protocols,* all control information and data are encoded using entire bytes. *Bit-oriented protocols,* on the other hand, may use single bits to represent both control information and data. Most older protocols were byte or character-oriented, and almost all major character sets, including ASCII and EBCDIC, include control characters.

We will choose two commonly used protocols, BSC and SDLC, for examples. There are many other protocols in use today, and surely new ones will be proposed in the future. However, these two protocols illustrate classic features. One is byte-oriented, and the other is bit-oriented; one uses stop-and-wait ARQ, and the other uses continuous ARQ; one allows only half duplex transmission, and the other permits half duplex or full duplex.

Binary Synchronous Communications

The most widely used byte or character-oriented protocol is IBM's *Binary Synchronous Communications,* or *BSC* (often referred to as *Bisync*). BSC is a half duplex, stop-and-wait ARQ protocol. It permits point-to-point communications, for example, a terminal connected to a host computer. BSC also permits multipoint communications.

In multipoint use, there is a single *Control station,* and many *Tributary stations.* The Control station can communicate with any of the Tributary stations, and any of the Tributary stations can communicate with the Control station, but the Tributary stations cannot communicate with each other. For example, in Chapter 5, we described a host computer connected to several terminals attached to a line splitter. In this case the host computer is acting as the Control station, and the terminals as Tributary stations.

BSC was originally designed to accommodate three specific character codes: ASCII, EBCDIC, and Transcode. We have already presented ASCII and EBCDIC in Chapter 3; Transcode is a seldom-used six-bit code. The major functions of BSC and other link-level protocols are sharing the communications circuit among two or more devices, and ensuring error-free transmission. Because BSC uses half duplex transmission, along with stop-and-wait ARQ, it is not well suited to use over satellites or any other transmission media subject to long delays.

For example, if we used BSC to communicate over satellites, a block of data, known as a *frame,* is sent from a host computer over the satellite to a terminal. The message might take a quarter of a second to get to the terminal, at which point the terminal determines if the frame contains any errors. Assuming that there are no errors, the terminal sends an *acknowledgment* that the frame has been properly received, and this acknowledgment message goes back up over the satellite to reach the host computer, taking another quarter of a second. During this round trip of a half-second, the host computer is not permitted to send any more data, and must wait for the return acknowledgment. We have not even included any line turnaround time required due to the half duplex nature of the conversation. These delays make BSC unsuitable for satellite transmission.

The BSC frame.   During our discussion of character codes in Chapter 3 we mentioned that special control codes included in character codes were used by certain protocols. BSC uses many of these control codes to permit devices to exchange *control information,* like an acknowledgment message, and to help divide a BSC frame into several parts. We will present here only the basic elements of a BSC frame, and only a limited number of BSC features. The purpose of this book is not to make the reader fluent in the BSC protocol, but to introduce the types of messages used in a character-oriented protocol.

There are two basic types of BSC frames, one containing user data, and the other containing control information. User data frames contain data actually typed by the terminal user, or sent from the host computer's applications program. Additional information, known as a *header,* may be included in the user data frame by the BSC protocol, to allow for addressing the message to one of several terminals. Some error-checking information may also be included in the user data frame.

The other type of frames, known as control information frames, are passed between the terminal and the host computer to perform polling and selecting, as well as to determine if errors have occurred. A BSC terminal user does not personally type any control information. The terminal itself is programmed to respond to BSC control information, but not to pass this information to the user. A BSC terminal and host computer actually carry on their own private conversation about the data's accuracy and each other's status, without the knowledge or intervention of the terminal user.

For example, the terminal user types data on the keyboard and then hits the ENTER or XMIT (transmit) key. The BSC terminal sends the data, along with a header, to the host computer. The host computer checks the message for errors, and if it is satisfied that none have occurred, will send back the acknowledgment message; this acknowledgment message is control information, which will be received by the terminal. The terminal now is certain that its message was received by the host computer, and the message can be erased from its memory; if the host computer had found errors, the terminal would at this point retransmit the message. This exchange of control information occurs between the host computer and terminal, but the terminal will not pass the acknowledgment message to the terminal user. The only way an end user will know that an error has occurred is if he hits the ENTER key again very quickly and doesn't receive a response; this indicates that the terminal may be busy retransmitting the last message.

CHARACTERS IN A BSC FRAME

What characters actually make up a BSC frame? We'll begin with a control information frame, which contains the following characters:

PAD SYN SYN {control information} PAD

The *PAD* character is simply a special pattern of ones and zeroes used at the beginning and end of a frame. The only purpose of the PAD character is to allow time for the transmission line to stabilize. We'll assume eight-bit characters are being used for our example, so each PAD character will be eight bits in length.

Following the PAD characters are two *SYN* characters, which allows the receiver to "sync up" to the incoming signal and prepare to receive real data. The SYN character can be found in almost all character codes. Since this is a control frame, it contains control information, followed by a PAD character to conclude the frame. Remember that none of these special characters is ever seen by the user, but is part of the frames sent between the BSC terminal and host computer.

What characters make up control information? That depends on whether we are using BSC for point-to-point or multipoint configurations. Each device is sometimes referred to as a communications *station* in BSC. In point-to-point use, there are only two stations, and the most commonly used control information is "Can I send now?" This question is known as an *enquiry*, and the *ENQ* character is used in the control information portion of the frame. An enquiry frame would be

PAD　　SYN　　SYN　　ENQ　　PAD

The device receiving the enquiry can reply with an *ACK0*, a *NAK*, or a *WACK*. An ACK0 is a type of acknowledgment indicating that the device is ready to receive; a NAK is a negative acknowledgment indicating that the device is not ready to receive; a WACK indicates that the device is temporarily busy, but will be ready soon. These three possible responses are

PAD	SYN	SYN	ACK0	PAD
PAD	SYN	SYN	NAK	PAD
PAD	SYN	SYN	WACK	PAD

Remember that if we are using an eight-bit character code, the ENQ, ACK0, NAK, and WACK characters may each have an eight-bit representation. If any of these special characters are not available in a character code, a combination of two other characters can be used instead. Assuming that ACK0 was the response, the transmitter can now send data using a data frame, which we will explain soon. After the data transmission is complete, the transmitter sends an *EOT,* indicating an end of transmission

PAD   SYN   SYN   EOT   PAD

At this point, either of the two devices could ask permission to send, using the ENQ character.

Multipoint use complicates the control information exchanged, because there is now a single Control station, and several Tributary stations. Typically, a host computer is the Control station, and the terminals are Tributary stations. The Control station will perform all of the polling and selecting in multipoint use. The polling and selecting is performed by using the ENQ character, plus the address of the Tributary station. Selected stations can respond with acknowledgments, indicating their readiness to receive data. Polled stations will send data if they have any to send, or otherwise indicate they are done transmitting with a simple EOT message

PAD   SYN   SYN   EOT   PAD

So far we have considered only control information. How is data transmitted? After a terminal user hits the ENTER key, the BSC terminal assembles the data into a data frame. A typical data frame in BSC looks like

PAD SYN SYN SOH {header} STX {data} ETX BCC BCC PAD

The PAD and SYN characters perform the same functions as before. The *SOH* character indicates the start of the header, which contains addressing information. The *STX* character indicates the start of the text, or user data, and is followed by the actual user data. The *ETX* character signifies the end of the data, and is followed by two *BCC*, or block check characters, and a final PAD character. The BCC characters vary with each transmission, containing checksums for error correction, like the cyclical redundancy check (CRC) discussed in Chapter 6. There are other possible data frames which allow control characters to be sent as data, in a special *transparent data mode*. This is an exception, however. Most data is transmitted as described in the previous frame.

BSC, like any protocol, is a systematic method for insuring reliable communications over a shared communications link. There is an appropriate query and response for every possible situation, though we have covered only some basic examples. A comparison of these two most common types of BSC frames is presented in Fig. 7-14.

Figure 7-14 Binary Synchronous Communications frames.

PAD	SYN	SYN	control information	PAD

PAD	SYN	SYN	SOH	header	STX	Data	ETX	BCC	BCC	PAD

Synchronous Data Link Control

One of the most widely used bit-oriented protocols is IBM's *Synchronous Data Link Control, or SDLC*. SDLC is similar to the ISO *High-level Data Link Control, or HDLC*, which contains some additional features. Another very similar protocol is the ANSI *Advanced Data Communications Control Procedures, or ADCCP*. Another bit-oriented protocol is the CCITT *Link Access Procedure—Balanced, or LAP-B*. Many vendors have bit-oriented protocols similar to SDLC, but SDLC is probably the most widely used because it is the protocol used by IBM's popular SNA.

SDLC is most often used in full duplex, though it can be used in half duplex mode. Since it uses go-back-n continuous ARQ, it is suitable for use over satellite links or other transmission media with long delays. With continuous ARQ, the host computer does not have to wait for an acknowledgment of the first message before sending more data.

In a full duplex SDLC link, the transmitter can send data continuously, while simultaneously receiving acknowledgment messages from the receiver. On a half duplex SDLC link, up to seven frames can be sent, at which point the line is turned around, and a single acknowledgment message can be sent for all seven frames. This is more efficient than BSC, where half duplex must always be used, the line must be turned around after each frame, and each frame is acknowledged separately.

In SDLC, as in BSC, the control information passed between the host computer and terminal never reaches the end user. The user is shielded from all errors by the protocol's ability to correct them, and control information is passed efficiently between stations, using only a few bits. The greatest advantage of SDLC, however, is that it contains continuous ARQ and full duplex capability; this allows its use with a wide range of transmission media, regardless of delays. The customer can choose the transmission media based on cost, desired reliability, and bandwidth, and not be concerned about the effect of delays on the protocol's performance.

The terminology in SDLC is slightly different from that used in BSC. Rather than using Control and Tributary Stations, SDLC uses *Primary* and *Secondary stations*. All communications is between the single Primary station and the one or many Secondary stations.

The SDLC frame.   SDLC, like BSC, also sends data in frames, but data and control information are sent a bit at a time, not a character at time. There are three basic frame formats in SDLC, known as *Information, Supervisory,* and *Unnumbered*. As in our discussion of BSC, we will consider only the most basic elements of SDLC.

Information Format Frames, or *I-Frames*, are used to send and receive data. *Supervisory Format Frames*, or *S-Frames*, are used to transfer control information, including acknowledging the accurate receipt of data. *Unnumbered Format Frames*, or *U-Frames*, are used for special functions, including establishing connections, reporting procedural problems, and special cases of data transfer. The I-Frames and S-Frames are most commonly used together to send data and ensure reliable transmission.

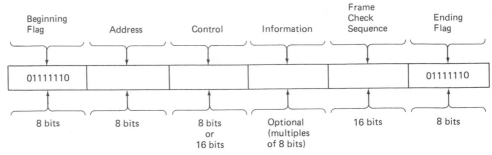

Figure 7-15 Synchronous Data Link Control Frame.

BITS IN AN SDLC FRAME

All three frame formats follow the pattern shown in Fig. 7-15. Each type of frame begins with a *Flag*, which is a pattern of eight ones and zeroes (01111110). Then there is the eight-bit *Address Field*, containing the address of the Secondary station. Since all communications is between a Primary and Secondary station, this address is the destination of a message when the Primary station transmits, and the source of the message when the Secondary station transmits. This addressing method allows for proper routing of data to and from Secondary stations in multi-point configurations.

After the address field comes the *Control Field*, which contains either eight or 16 control bits, depending on the mode of operation. The function of these control bits will differ depending on whether this is an I-Frame, an S-Frame, or a U-Frame. After the Control Field is the *Information Field*, which occurs only in certain I-Frames and U-Frames. The Information Field is used to transmit data, and is variable in length, depending on the amount of data being transmitted. The length of the Information Field is always a multiple of eight bits.

Next in the frame is the *Frame Check Sequence Field*. The Frame Check Sequence, or *FCS*, contains 16 bits for error checking; the bits are calculated using the Cyclical Redundancy Check (CRC) method presented in Chapter 6. The frame concludes with the ending Flag, also a pattern of eight ones and zeroes (01111110).

Notice that the Flags of SDLC perform a similar function to the PAD and SYN characters in BSC. The FCS is also very similar to the BCC characters used in BSC. Both BSC and SDLC contain addresses. However, the control information in SDLC is passed in a very different manner than in BSC.

Each bit in the Control Field has a special meaning. For example, Supervisory Format Frames are used to acknowledge receipt of data. The SDLC *Receiver Ready*, or *RR*, is similar to the BSC ACK, indicating that data has been successfully received. An SDLC *Reject*, or *REJ*, is similar to a BSC NAK, indicating a retransmission is necessary. An SDLC *Receiver Not Ready*, or *RNR*, is similar to a BSC WACK, indicating a temporary busy condition. These different conditions are represented by only a few bits in the SDLC Control Field, rather than using entire eight-bit characters, as in BSC.

The remaining bits in the Control Field can be used for other functions. For example, in all types of SDLC frames, the Control Field contains a *P/F bit*. The Primary station can require the Secondary station to respond by setting the P/F bit, in this case the Poll bit. The Secondary station can then transmit data, and when finished, can also set this bit; when the Secondary station sets the P/F bit, it is now the *Final* bit, indicating that transmission is complete. This single bit is used for two functions, compared to the BSC use of eight bits for a single function. This high efficiency is another of the advantages of SDLC.

Protocol Converters and Code Converters

If two SDLC devices need to communicate, the SDLC protocol will ensure reliable and accurate data transmission. What if a dumb asynchronous terminal needs to communicate with a host computer using SDLC? A separate device, known as a *protocol converter*, can act as a translator between the two devices, taking asynchronous data from the terminal, packaging it into SDLC frames, and transmitting it synchronously to the host computer. Data from the host computer will be removed from its frame and transmitted asynchronously to the terminal. The same function could be performed for a BSC host computer, as well as almost any other protocol.

In some cases the terminal may use a different character code from the host computer. A *code converter* can be used to translate the characters from one character code to another. For example, data sent from an ASCII terminal can be translated for reception by an EBCDIC host computer. Sometimes a *protocol converter* will perform both protocol and code conversion. Also, either or both of these conversion functions may at times be performed by front end processors, as discussed in Chapter 5.

SUMMARY

A communications architecture is a manufacturer's strategy for connecting its equipment. Most good communications architectures cleanly separate the function of communications from the host computer's other functions. Currently, each manufacturer has its own communications architecture, but ISO has developed a model for standardizing future communications between devices of all manufacturers. The ISO Open Systems Interconnection (OSI) model breaks down the task of communications into seven independent layers, each with its own roles. The Corporation for Open Systems (COS), a group of major computer vendors, is facilitating the implementation of inter-vendor compatibility.

The seven layers of the ISO model, from lowest to highest, are the Physical Layer, the Data Link Layer, the Network Layer, the Transport Layer, the Session Layer, the

Presentation Layer, and the Application Layer. The tasks of each layer are clearly defined in the OSI model. Even though the only actual transmission of data occurs at the Physical Layer, all of the other layers communicate with their peers on other devices by modifying or adding to the data being transmitted.

IBM's Systems Network Architecture (SNA) is the most widely used communications architecture. SNA functions can also be divided into layers, namely Physical Control, Data Link Control, Path Control, Transmission Control, Data Flow Control, Presentation Services, and Transaction Services. SNA networks are made up of many components, including Host Processors, Workstations, Communications Controllers, Cluster Controllers, and Distributed Processors. SNA networks can be further broken down into different Nodes, including Host Nodes, Communications Controller Nodes, and Peripheral Nodes. Each Node may contain several Network Addressable Units (NAUs), of which there are three basic types: a Logical Unit (LU), a Physical Unit (PU), and a System Services Control Point (SSCP). End Users, such as Workstation users or Application Programs on Host Processors, can communicate with the SNA Network through LUs. A PU exists in each Node to manage the Node's physical resources. An SSCP provides central control and monitoring of a network. Each SSCP is responsible for a certain Domain, which can be further divided into Subareas. Subareas are connected by Transmissions Groups. SNA is only one manufacturer's architecture; many others are also in use today.

Protocols precisely define the methods used for communications between devices. Most protocols, also known as line disciplines, provide for polling and selecting. Polling is a request for data transmission, and selecting is a request for data acceptance. Most protocols also use some form of automatic repeat request (ARQ) for error correction. There are different types of ARQ, including stop-and-wait ARQ, where each frame is acknowledged before the next is sent, and continuous ARQ, where the next frame can be sent before the previous frame is acknowledged. Continuous ARQ includes go-back-N continuous ARQ, which requires retransmission of all frames after an error, and selective repeat continuous ARQ, which requires only retransmission of the frame in error. There are two common classes of protocols, byte- or character-oriented and bit-oriented.

IBM's Binary Synchronous Communications, or BSC, is an example of a character- or byte-oriented protocol. BSC is a half duplex, stop-and-wait ARQ protocol, and is therefore not well suited for satellite transmission. BSC frames can contain user data or control information; control information is sent using entire characters. BSC has a single Control station and one or more Tributary stations.

IBM's Synchronous Data Link Control, or SDLC, is an example of a bit-oriented protocol. SDLC can be used in half duplex or full duplex mode, and uses go-back-N continuous ARQ; it can therefore be used for satellite transmission. SDLC frames can be Information Format Frames, Supervisory Format Frames, or Unnumbered Format Frames. In all frames, control information is sent by using individual bits. SDLC has one Primary station and one or more Secondary stations.

BSC and SDLC are just two examples of common protocols; many other protocols are also in use today. Devices using different protocols can be connected by using protocol converters; devices using different character codes can be connected by using code converters.

Architectures and Protocols

TERMS FOR REVIEW

Acknowledgment
ACK0
ADCCP
Address Field
Advanced Data
  Communications Control
  Procedures
Application Layer
Application Program
Architecture
ARQ
Automatic repeat request
BCC
Binary Synchronous
  Communications
Bisync
Bit-oriented protocol
BSC
Byte-oriented protocol
Character-oriented protocol
Cluster Controller
Code converter
Communications
  architecture
Communications Controller
Communications Controller
  Node
Communications line control
Continuous ARQ
Control Field
Control information
Control station
Corporation for Open
  Systems
COS
Data Link Layer
Destination node
Distributed Processor
Domain
End User
ENQ

Enquiry
EOT
Error detection and
  correction
ETX
FCS
Final
Flag
Frame
Frame Check Sequence
  Field
Go-back-N continuous ARQ
HDLC
Header
Higher layers
High-level Data Link
  Control
Host Node
Host Processor
I-Frame
Information Field
Information Format Frame
Intermediate node
LAP-B
Line discipline
Link Access Procedure—
  Balanced
Link-level protocol
Link
Logical Unit
Lower layers
LU
NAK
NAU
Network
Network Addressable Unit
Network Layer
Node
Open Systems
  Interconnection model
OSI model

PAD
Peer level
Peripheral Node
P/F bit
Physical Layer
Physical Unit
Polling
Presentation Layer
Primary station
Protocol
Protocol converter
PU
Receiver Not Ready
Receiver Ready
REJ
Reject
RNR
RR
SDLC
Secondary station
Selecting
Selective repeat continuous
  ARQ
Session
Session Layer
S-Frame
SNA
SOH
SSCP
Station
Stop-and-wait ARQ
STX
Subarea
Subarea Node
Supervisory Format Frame
SYN
Synchronous Data Link
  Control
System Services Control
  Point

Systems Network
  Architecture
Transmission Group
Transparent data mode

Transport Layer
Tributary station
U-Frame
Unnumbered Format Frame

Upper layers
WACK
Workstation

EXERCISES

7-1. What is a communications architecture?

7-2. Name the layers of the ISO-OSI model. Which are the lower layers and which are the higher layers?

7-3. Explain the functions of each of the layers of the ISO-OSI model.

7-4. What is SNA?

7-5. What connects two Nodes in an SNA network?

7-6. Define the following SNA terms: Host Processor, Workstation, and End User.

7-7. What is the purpose of an SNA Communications Controller? A Cluster Controller?

7-8. What is the difference between a Host Node, a Communications Controller Node, and a Peripheral Node?

7-9. Compare each of the different types of NAUs.

7-10. Compare Subareas and Domains in SNA.

7-11. What is a protocol?

7-12. Explain the difference between polling and selecting.

7-13. What is ARQ? Compare the different types of ARQ.

7-14. What is the difference between a byte-oriented protocol and a bit-oriented protocol?

7-15. What are the different types of basic frames in BSC? In SDLC?

7-16. Is BSC or SDLC better suited for satellite transmission? Why?

Architectures and Protocols

8

DATA TRANSPORT NETWORKS

Data transport networks connect a wide variety of devices located in the same building or across the world. In most cases, data transport networks are not limited by a single vendor's architecture, or to a single vendor's equipment, because they provide only the means for transmitting and receiving the data. Data transport networks provide only the OSI model's lower-layer functions. As long as the two devices can perform the higher-layer functions in a compatible manner, they can use data transport networks to perform the lower-layer functions of transmitting and receiving the data.

For example, two French-speaking Americans can send letters written in French to each other through the U.S. Postal Service. The mail carriers do not need to understand French, because they only transport the mail. Packet switching networks and local area networks are two examples of data transport networks.

PACKET SWITCHING NETWORKS

One popular data transport network often used for long-distance data transmission is a *packet switching network*, or *PSN*. Packet switching networks provide a *switched service*; for example, a terminal user can connect to one host computer now, and a host computer at a different location later. Data is separated into *packets*, or blocks, and sent through the packet switching network to the destination. At the destination, the packets are combined to form the original stream of data.

Packet switching networks provide a *virtual circuit* between two devices, rather than a continuous connection. In other words, when a packet of data is given to the packet switching network, the network will route the data to its destination. However, if no data is being transmitted, there will be no transmission resources wasted on the connection. Compare this to the telephone network, where we can call someone and stay on the line, not saying anything, but still tying up a circuit. We call a packet switching network's connection a virtual circuit, because to the users, it virtually appears they have a continuous connection, and their data always gets to the destination.

Many of today's packet switching networks span great distances. Each location in the network is known as a *switching node*, or simply a *node*. The switching nodes are connected by *interexchange circuits*, or *IXCs*. A simple packet switching network is presented in Fig. 8-1. These networks can be customer-owned, or someone else's packet switching network service can be leased.

Communicating through packet switching networks requires that the devices at each end send data in specially formatted packets. Devices that can communicate by

Figure 8-1 Simple packet switching network.

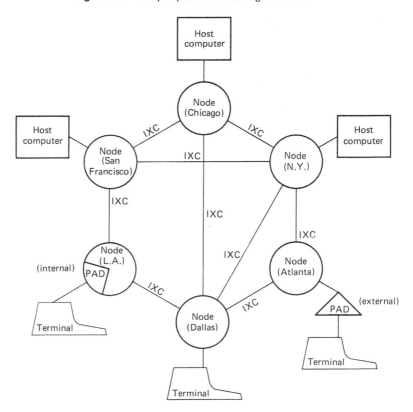

Data Transport Networks

using these packets can be directly attached to a packet switching network. A device known as a *PAD*, or *packet assembler disassembler*, is used to connect devices to a packet switching network if these devices cannot perform the special packet formatting on their own. A PAD takes data from a terminal or host computer, assembles it in a special packet format, and passes it on to the PSN node. Data coming from the packet switching network is disassembled from its packet by the PAD, and can then be routed to the host computer or terminal.

The PAD might be on the premises of the end user or at the packet switching node itself. A PAD that is part of the packet switching node is often called an *internal PAD*, while a PAD on the premises of the user is often called an *external PAD* or *terminal handler*. Placement of both types of PADs is also shown in Fig. 8-1.

PSNs combine the advantages of many other transmission methods, and add some of their own. Packet switching provides the reliability of a dial-up network, because each packet of data can take a different route. For example, a packet of data could be routed directly from San Francisco to New York, or it might be routed through Chicago. If the transcontinental IXC is not functioning, there are still alternate routes for the packets. Packet switching also has the flexibility of the dial-up network, because users can connect to a different host computer with each call.

These networks also provide error detection and correction. Packets are checked for errors during transmission, and if necessary, packets are retransmitted. The packet switching network guarantees that the data received at the destination node will be the same as the data transmitted at the source node. The error detection and correction performed by the packet switching network nodes ensures reliable transmission even if the source and destination devices do no error checking themselves.

Public Packet Switching Networks

Packet switching networks that are owned and operated by service providers for use by their customers are known as *public packet switching networks*. These networks often have entire operations staffs monitoring the network's health. This provides a high level of service equivalent to the reliability of the public telephone network. Many of these public packet switching networks have nodes and PADs in numerous cities, affording easy access. For example, a traveling salesman could access pricing information in a host computer in the company's home office from anywhere in the country, simply by making a local call to the nearest node of the public packet switching network.

One of the first large-scale packet switching networks, known as *ARPANET*, was established to connect U.S. government computing facilities. Two of the largest commercial public packet switching networks in the United States are the *Telenet* and *Tymnet* networks, operated by GTE and McDonnell-Douglas, respectively. Each network uses proprietary methods to communicate between packet switching nodes, but they both support similar interface standards.

Packet switching networks are a very cost-effective method of transmitting data. Since no permanent connection is ever established between two devices, users of these networks are typically charged on a per packet basis. This charge is usually less expensive than comparable dial-up telephone line charges, because the packet switching network effectively shares its bandwidth among many users. For example, the IXCs can be high-bandwidth media, like satellites, microwave, or T-1 circuits. These economies of scale can be passed on to the end user of packet switching networks in the form of lower per packet costs.

One disadvantage of all packet switching networks, both public and private, is that certain delays may occur, because data may be routed through many nodes before reaching its destination. If an IXC uses satellite transmission, delays are increased even further. A terminal user in San Francisco, communicating with a host computer in New York, might notice a 1- or 2-second delay when using the packet switching network. However, the added benefits of low cost, high reliability, flexibility, easy access, and guaranteed error-free transmission usually outweigh the delay problem in most applications.

The X.25 Standard

The most commonly used standard for connecting to packet switching networks is the CCITT *X.25* standard. Packet switching networks do not have to comply with this standard, but most do. The X.25 standard, which describes all the functions necessary for communicating with a packet switching network, is divided into three levels. These three levels are similar in function to the lower three layers of the OSI model.

The lowest level, known as the *Physical Level*, describes the actual interface; it conforms to the CCITT V.24/V.28 standard, which is similar to the ANSI RS-232-C discussed in Chapter 4. The second level, or the *Frame Level*, is the CCITT LAP-B bit-oriented data link protocol that handles error detection and correction; it is very similar to the SDLC protocol explained in Chapter 7. The third level, or the *Packet Level*, provides for network level addressing and call connections.

The X.25 standard defines two types of devices, DTEs, or data terminal equipment, and DCEs, or data circuit-terminating equipment. The packet switching network itself presents an X.25 DCE interface; a host computer or terminal that attaches to the packet network presents an X.25 DTE interface. For example, a host computer presenting an X.25 DTE interface would provide a V.24/V.28 type of physical interface, use the LAP-B protocol for transmitting and receiving bits, and add special packet-level information regarding call setup and addressing.

In addition to the X.25 standard, CCITT developed three standards for describing the operation of an internal PAD. The *X.3* standard defines the PAD's functions and parameters; the *X.28* standard describes the PAD-to-terminal protocol; the *X.29* standard describes the PAD-to-host computer protocol.

The relationship between the X.25, X.3, X.28, and X.29 standards is illustrated in Fig. 8-2. Since we are for the time being considering only the packet switching network interface standards and protocols, we will consider the entire network as a single entity, ignoring the various nodes and IXCs inside.

In Fig. 8-2, terminal A and host computer A both communicate to the packet switching network using X.25. Terminal B, however, is not X.25 compatible, and must

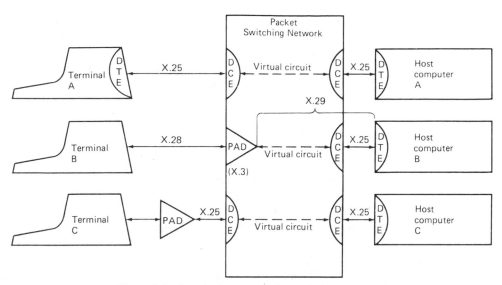

Figure 8-2 Interfacing to a packet switching network.

be attached to the packet switching network through a PAD. Terminal B communicates with the internal PAD using the X.28 protocol; the PAD's function and parameters are described by X.3; the PAD communicates with host computer B using the X.29 protocol. Notice that host computer B is X.25 compatible, and therefore communicates with the network using X.25. Terminal C is attached to an external PAD on the user's premises; since the X.25 conversion is done on the user's premises, the packet switching network thinks that terminal C is X.25 compatible. To the packet switching network, the connection from terminal C to host computer C is no different than the connection from terminal A to host computer A. These are just a few combinations, and others are certainly possible.

Packet Switching Network Services

Many optional services can be provided by packet switching networks. For instance, a *closed user group* allows users to specify that they want to communicate only with certain users. This is one security measure to ensure that only authorized users can access a particular host computer. For example, a company linking its branch office computers with headquarters could connect all of its computers through the packet switching network in a closed user group; this permits communication among company computers, but prevents others from accessing these computers. Other possible security services include allowing DTEs to accept *incoming calls only*, or place *outgoing calls only*, depending on the application.

There are two data transmission-related services that can be provided by packet switching networks. *Flow control negotiation* allows the DTEs to specify the size of the packet and other parameters. Another service, known as *throughput class negotiation*, allows the DTE to negotiate for a certain bandwidth on a virtual circuit.

Finally, many packet switching networks provide for *reverse charging*, or *collect calls*. This is the PSN equivalent of a toll-free number, allowing users to contact a particular DTE, with the receiver paying for the service.

Routing Data in a Packet Switching Network

Perhaps the most interesting facet of packet switching network operation is the routing of data. Earlier we mentioned that a packet from San Francisco destined for New York might take a direct route or might be routed through a node in Chicago. If we are sending a large block of data through a packet switching network, it will be divided into many packets, or *packetized*. Packets are usually a fixed length, like 128 bytes. In fact, each packet may take a different route from the source to the destination!

For example, as shown in Fig. 8-3, packet 1 may leave San Francisco and be routed through Chicago to New York, because the direct transcontinental route to New

Figure 8-3 Routing data in a packet switching network.

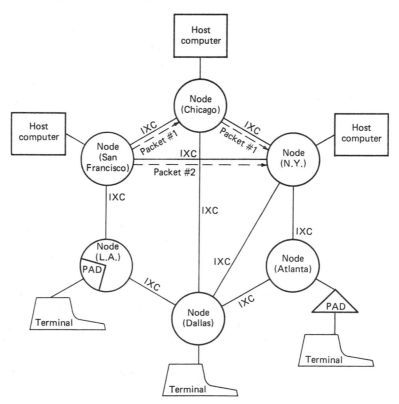

Data Transport Networks

York may be busy at that moment with other traffic. Packet 2, transmitted a tenth of a second later, may take the direct route to New York, because at the moment of transmission, that circuit is available. Because of the delays involved in routing, it is possible that packet 2 will arrive in New York before packet 1.

This is analogous to the traveler changing planes in Chicago; not only is the route traveled longer than the direct route, there may be some time wasted in Chicago. Traveler 1 may leave San Francisco at 9 AM, change planes in Chicago, and arrive in New York at 7 PM. Traveler 2 may leave San Francisco at 10 AM, take a nonstop flight, and arrive in New York at 6:30 PM. Traveler 2 left later than traveler 1, but arrived in New York earlier. If these travelers were packets, the second 128 bytes of the message would have been received before the first 128 bytes. This would be the equivalent of reading the second sentence of this chapter before the first. Therefore, the node in New York is holding, or *buffering*, packet 2 until it receives packet 1, and then send the packets to the host computer in New York in the proper order. All packets must therefore be *numbered*, and destination packet switching nodes must provide *buffering* and *resequencing* of packets.

Packet switching networks are typically used over wide areas, and are a type of *wide area network*, or *WAN*. There is another type of data transport network used for local data transmission.

LOCAL AREA NETWORKS

A *local area network*, or *LAN*, is a privately owned data communications system that provides reliable high-speed, switched connections between devices in a single building, campus, or complex. Networks that extend outside a single building, campus, or complex are no longer considered local area networks. Like packet switching networks, local area networks provide switched connections, allowing users to connect to different computers at different times. The transmission speed of local area networks is often many millions of bits per second, providing high-bandwidth connections suitable for almost any application, including lengthy file transfers. The limited geographic area of a local area network usually allows the customer to own all of the wiring; therefore, the speed of the LAN is limited largely by the bandwidth of the chosen transmission media.

Most of today's local area networks are highly reliable, with extremely low error rates. Since few local area networks span more than a mile or two, the probability of transmission errors is much smaller than in a wide area network. Local area networks are typically used to connect desktop computers, known as *personal computers*, with each other or with other host computers; terminals and larger host computers can also be connected. A typical application with personal computers is the file transfer mentioned previously.

Users of a local area network can exchange files as well as share resources. One example of resource sharing is when several personal computers share a single high-speed laser printer; each user prints infrequently, but may need the special features and speed of the laser printer. The printer is generally attached to a personal computer, which is also attached to the network. We say that this personal computer acts as a *print server* for the network, because it provides access to the printing services for other users. Sometimes an entire department will access a single file storage device, like a high-volume disk attached to one user's personal computer; this personal computer acts as a *file server*. Providing access to remote resources located off the network is the job of a *communications server*. Typically, a communications server is a personal computer attached to both a modem and the network, thereby allowing network users to use the modem to access remotely located computers and services. There are other specialized server functions that can also be provided on a local area network. The servers may be personal computers used for other functions as well as being servers.

Local area networks can be implemented using two different types of control. *Centralized control* requires a single device that controls the entire network. Failure of this controller will disable the entire network. Changing the number or configuration of devices on the network will require more than simple rewiring. The central controller will need to be notified of any adding, removing, or moving of devices in the network.

Distributed control, used by most of today's local area networks, requires no central device; instead, all of the devices attached to the network actually run the network. The instructions for transmitting and receiving messages must be built into all the devices attached to the network, usually with a combination of hardware and software. For example, ten personal computers in a local area network using distributed control all share the responsibility of running the network; each personal computer usually contains a special network interface card, and uses a special network software program.

One advantage of distributed control is that adding another user to the network only requires installing the interface card and software in the new user's personal computer and attaching the personal computer to the network. There is no central processor or controller that needs to be notified of the addition, because each device speaks for itself on the network, and shares in the task of operating the network. These networks can therefore be expanded incrementally; the network hardware cost for 101 users is only 1% more than for a network of 100 users. Companies can start with small networks and enlarge them as needs change. There is an upper limit to the number of users on all networks, but this varies, depending on the bandwidth of the media, as well as the applications used.

The major disadvantage of distributed control is that if one device attached to the network malfunctions, it can throw the entire network into disarray. Many local area networks make some provision for a centralized monitoring function to shut down network stations that are causing problems.

Local Area Network Topologies

Local area networks can take many different forms or shapes, known as *topologies*. Some of these topologies are illustrated in Fig. 8-4.

In a *mesh network*, each device is connected by a cable to every other device in the network. This may be convenient for small networks, but becomes awkward and expensive as the network grows to more than a few devices.

In a *star network*, all the devices are connected by cable to a single central point.

Data Transport Networks

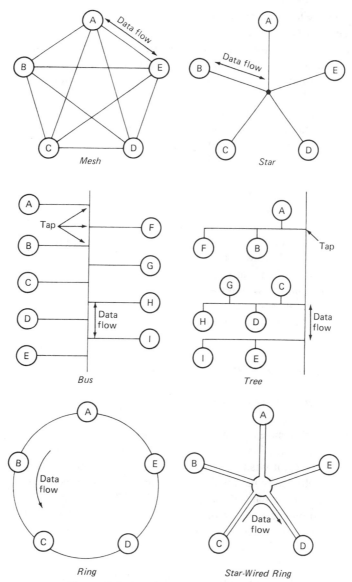

Figure 8-4 Local area network topologies.

Some type of a controller is located at this central point; this centralized control requirement is an often-cited disadvantage of star networks. In a star network, all data is routed through the central point.

A *bus network* has many devices connected to a single cable, known as the bus. Typically there are limitations to the length of the bus in these networks. The point at which devices connect to a bus is known as the *tap*. A *tree network* is similar to a bus network, except that there may be many different branches off the main bus. This allows many closely located devices to attach to the network with only a single tap on the main bus. There is no central control point in a bus or tree network, so new devices can be added by simply tapping onto the network at any point; disconnecting a tap removes a device from the network. In bus and tree networks, data typically flows in two directions; this is accomplished using two separate cables, or dividing a single cable into two channels.

A *ring network* connects all devices in a continuous loop, though it doesn't have to be a perfect circle. Data in a ring network usually flows only in one direction; therefore, data may circle around 90% of the ring to reach a neighboring device. There is no central controller in a ring network, either, so devices can be added simply by inserting them anywhere in the ring, or removed from the network by disconnecting them from the ring and closing the ring at that point.

A *star-wired ring network* is a special type of ring network, often used when wiring already exists between a central point and the users. The data still flows one way in a continuous loop, though between each device it returns to the central area. Many buildings already have wire running to each office; this is a convenient way to implement a ring network when star-shaped wiring already exists. Users can be removed from, added to, and moved within the star-wired ring by moving wires at the center of the ring. A network monitoring device can be optionally placed at the center to automatically disconnect a failed device from the star-wired ring.

Baseband vs. Broadband Transmission

There are two basic types of local area network transmission. *Baseband* local area networks transmit digital signals directly on the cable, while *broadband* local area networks use carrier frequencies to modulate the signal. Whereas baseband LANs allow only a single data conversation or channel at any given time, broadband LANs can be divided into many different channels, allowing for multiple data conversations simultaneously.

Typically baseband local area networks are less expensive to implement, but they are limited in their capacity and length. Broadband local area networks, though more expensive to purchase and maintain, usually provide higher bandwidth transmission and have less restrictive length limitations. Neither type is clearly superior; the user's applications and cost requirements will determine the appropriate choice.

The transmission media chosen will depend on whether the LAN is baseband or broadband, as well as on the bandwidth needed. Most local area networks use twisted pair wire or coaxial cable, though some use fiber optic cable for high-speed applications. The relative bandwidth of various transmission media was presented in Chapter 4.

Local Area Network Access Methods

When more than one device needs to share a communications line, *access methods* are required to specify which devices can transmit data at any given moment. We have already discussed one such method, known as *polling and selecting*. This technique is not often used in local area networks, because a central controller is required to poll and select the devices.

Some broadband networks use *frequency division* and separate the communications line into many different frequency channels. Many baseband networks employ *time division* techniques, allocating time slots to each device for transmission. These local area network access methods are similar to their point-to-point multiplexing counterparts, frequency division multiplexing and time division multiplexing, explained in Chapter 5.

Contention.   Among the most common types of access methods in use today are the *contention* methods. The various contention methods allow devices to transmit if the line is free; if the line is busy, devices must wait before transmitting. Contention methods are effective because local area networks use high-bandwidth transmission, and a typical message will be relatively short. For example, a 40-page file may contain 120 kilobytes, or 960 kilobits, of data; a 10 Mbps local area network could transmit the entire file in less than a tenth of a second. Since most messages are shorter than a 40-page file, and typical devices only use the network occasionally, the network is available most of the time.

Infrequently, two devices will transmit at the same time, and a *collision* occurs. Collisions cause data to be lost, and the way the network recovers from a collision depends on the access method. If too many devices are placed on a contention network, many collisions will occur and the network's performance will deteriorate; a few devices transmitting many large files will have the same effect.

One contention method is *random access*, where devices transmit whenever they please. With this method, devices assume that the line is free, because statistically, the network is free most of the time. For this method to succeed, there must be some acknowledgment by the receiver that the message arrived; otherwise, the sender cannot be sure that a collision didn't occur.

If we think of a three-way telephone conference call, random access is the equivalent of persons who speak whatever is on their minds, without regard to whether anyone else is talking or not. If they don't get an answer, they try speaking again.

A more refined contention method is known as *carrier sense multiple access*, or *CSMA*. In CSMA, the device with data to transmit listens to the network to determine if it is being used. If the network is free, the device transmits all the data, and waits for an acknowledgment from the receiving device. Once the transmitter begins sending data, other devices, also using CSMA, will not transmit, because they will be listening and know the network is busy. Occasionally, if two devices begin transmitting at exactly the same time, collisions may still occur.

When collisions occur, the transmitted data is garbled and the acknowledgment message will not be returned by the receiver. Eventually, after a set time limit, the transmitter gives up waiting for the acknowledgment and retransmits the message. CSMA is an improvement over random access, because at least the transmitter makes an attempt to check if someone else is using the network before sending data. However, the transmitter must still wait a period of time before deciding that the acknowledgment is not forthcoming due to a collision.

Returning to our three-way telephone conference call example, CSMA is the equivalent of a person who checks to see if anyone is talking, and if not, begins speaking and stops listening. After speaking, this person begins listening again.

CSMA is a type of contention method that uses *collision avoidance* techniques. A further improvement on CSMA adds *collision detection*. In this method, known as *carrier sense multiple access/collision detection*, or *CSMA/CD*, the device not only listens before transmitting, but also while transmitting. The device will first check to be sure that the network is free, and then begin transmitting. If all goes well, the transmitting device will hear its own transmission loud and clear. However, if another device began transmitting at the same instant, both transmitters will hear not only their own signals, but both signals, or some mixture of the two. Both of the transmitters will hear the collision and immediately stop transmitting. After waiting a certain period of time, the transmitters will again attempt to send the message. After a collision is detected, this process of halting transmission, waiting, and then retransmitting, is known as *backoff*.

The same method will be used for the retransmission after a collision: the transmitter will listen both before transmitting, to avoid another collision, and during transmission to detect if another collision occurs. Remember that collisions are relatively infrequent, since they occur only when two devices begin transmitting at exactly the same time.

In our conference call example, CSMA/CD is the equivalent of a person who first listens to be sure that no one else is talking, and then begins speaking. This person keeps listening while talking and will realize that someone else started speaking at the same time. Both people are using CSMA/CD, and both will stop talking, back off, and wait a little while before speaking again. Typically the more aggressive person will jump in almost immediately and start talking again, while another person might wait longer.

An essential aspect of CSMA/CD is determining how long a device must wait after detecting a collision before attempting retransmission. Clearly, this waiting time must be different for the two transmitters that collided; otherwise, they would continue to repeat their collision forever. For instance, in our conference call example, if the two people's statements collided, and each person waited exactly 10 seconds after the collision to speak again, the collision would occur again.

PRIORITY AND RANDOM BACKOFF

It is possible to build devices with different retransmission times, thereby creating a *priority backoff* scheme. After a collision, the device with the shortest retransmission time would always get to retransmit first, and the device with the longest retransmission time would retransmit last. This would be the equivalent of aggressive and shy people. More typically, a *random backoff* process is used, where each device picks a random amount of time to back off for each collision. This ensures fairness, and as long as the devices are good at picking truly random numbers for each collision, practically eliminates the possibility of repeated collisions.

The difference between priority backoff and random backoff is presented in the two diagrams in Fig. 8-5. An ''A'' represents a transmission completed successfully by device A, a ''B'' indicates a transmission completed successfully by

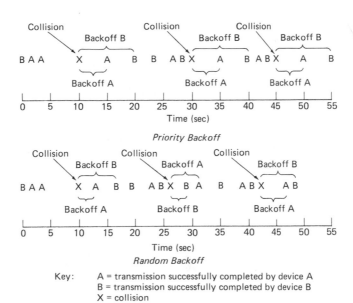

Figure 8-5 Priority and random backoff.

device B, and an "X" represents a collision between the two devices. As long as each device transmits at a different time, there are no collisions. When a collision does occur, notice that with priority backoff, device A has a higher priority and always gets to retransmit first. In random backoff, sometimes device A gets to retransmit first after a collision, and sometimes device B gets to retransmit first. This random backoff CSMA/CD method is one of the most popular methods in use today for LANs, particularly for bus networks.

These different contention methods regulate when devices can transmit and how they recover from collisions. How, though, do devices know when to receive data? Whether a network is using random access, CSMA, or CSMA/CD, when a device is not trying to transmit data it must listen to all data on the network. Each message will contain a unique address, specifying the intended destination. All devices except the receiver will simply ignore the message.

Token passing. The only LAN access method besides contention in wide-spread use today is known as *token passing*. A *token* is simply a pattern of ones and zeros with a special meaning, much like the control information used in the link-level protocols presented in Chapter 7. Two common types of tokens are *free tokens* and *busy tokens*; each is a different pattern of bits. All devices in a token passing network constantly listen to the network. A device can only transmit when it sees a free token.

We will assume a ring topology for an example because this is the easiest to visualize. The various steps of transmission using a *token ring network* are shown in Fig. 8-6. Initially, there is a free token circulating around the ring in Fig. 8-6. This indicates

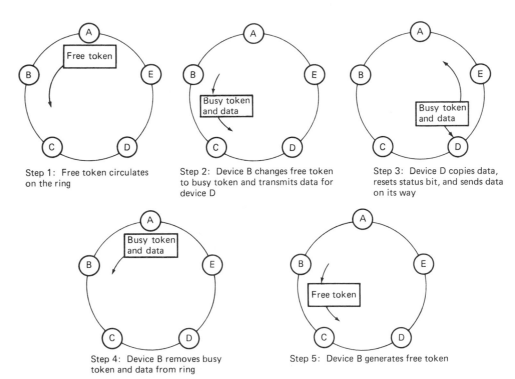

Step 1: Free token circulates on the ring

Step 2: Device B changes free token to busy token and transmits data for device D

Step 3: Device D copies data, resets status bit, and sends data on its way

Step 4: Device B removes busy token and data from ring

Step 5: Device B generates free token

Figure 8-6 Operation of a token ring.

that the network is free and available for use. A device wanting to transmit data must wait for the free token to reach it.

In step 2 of Fig. 8-6, device B sees the free token that is circulating and decides to transmit. Device B then changes the free token to a busy token, adds the data to be transmitted, along with the address of the recipient (device D), its own return address, and some bits for error checking and monitoring. This new package of data now circulates on the ring, and any other devices wanting to transmit data will have to wait, because there is no free token on the ring. When the data reaches its destination, the receiver (device D) recognizes its address.

As shown in step 3 of Fig. 8-6, device D then copies the data, changing some status bits to indicate the data was received, and lets the data continue around the ring. When the data reaches the original transmitter, as shown in step 4 of Fig. 8-6, the transmitter will remove the data from the ring. The transmitter can then release the network by generating a free token, as shown in step 5. The free token then circulates around the ring as before, and other devices can transmit their data in the same manner. We are now back to step 1, and the network is free again.

The token passing networks have several features to maintain order in the network. Notice that the data makes a complete circle around the ring, giving the transmitter confirmation that the data was not lost. Also, transmitters cannot monopolize the network; they must generate a free token after a certain time period. One of the devices on the network, known as the *active monitor device*, in addition to being a user of the network, is responsible for monitoring the network. An active monitor provides the first free token when the network is started. In addition, if a free token is lost due to a transmission error, the active monitor will generate a new free token. Other devices on the network act as *standby monitors*, waiting to step in and fill the role of the active monitor if it should fail. Token passing networks are one of the more popular methods in use today.

Local Area Network Standards

Local area networks provide physical transmission of data, as well as error detection and correction. Therefore, we often think of local area networks as providing the Physical Layer and Data Link Layer functions of the OSI model.

Many of the local area networks standards were developed by an IEEE committee called *IEEE 802*. This committee divided the Data Link Layer function of local area networks into two main parts. The first, known as *Medium Access Control*, or *MAC*, describes the access methods used in a network, like CSMA/CD or token passing. The second, known as *Logical Link Control*, or *LLC*, describes other functions that are common to all access methods, like error checking and reliability. Together, the Medium Access Control and Logical Link Control standards describe the way local area networks implement the Data Link Layer of the OSI model.

Each of the IEEE 802 subcommittees formulates standards on different areas. The *IEEE 802.1* standard provides an overview of local area networks as well as methods of connecting networks and systems management. The *IEEE 802.2* standard describes the Logical Link Control methods common to all IEEE 802-compatible networks. The *IEEE 802.3* standard describes the CSMA/CD Bus Medium Access Control method already discussed. The *IEEE 802.4* standard describes the *token bus* method for Medium Access Control; the token bus is a variation on the token ring, which is described by the *IEEE 802.5* standard. The *IEEE 802.6* standard describes Medium Access Control methods for a *metropolitan area network*, or *MAN*. A metropolitan area network is larger in geographical scope than a classic local area network and is not considered a local area network at all by many experts.

There are other IEEE advisory groups making recommendations about specific local area network topics that may affect all the other subcommittees, though they may not result in standards themselves. These include the *IEEE 802.7* committee for broadband transmission, the *IEEE 802.8* committee for fiber optics, and the *IEEE 802.9* committee for integrating voice and data on local area networks.

There is one ANSI standard for local area networks that has received much attention. ANSI's *Fiber Distributed Data Interface*, or *FDDI*, uses fiber optics to operate at speeds of up to 100 Mbps per channel using a token ring topology similar to IEEE 802.5. FDDI uses two channels, forming an inner and outer ring. This high bandwidth network is suitable for high-speed mainframe computer communications, as well as many other applications.

The *Manufacturing Automation Protocol*, or *MAP*, is a user-defined networking standard originally developed by General Motors. The MAP standard describes a token bus network, like IEEE 802.4. MAP is designed to integrate operations on the factory floor by tying together control computers, robot welders, and other intelligent devices that previously operated independently. Many products are already built by automated equipment; the MAP network ties all of this equipment together, allowing an engineer making a design change to communicate the change automatically to the equipment on the production line in seconds. Many users are demanding MAP compatibility for all future factory equipment.

Another user-defined standard, known as the *Technical and Office Products* specification, or *TOP*, was developed by Boeing Computer Services. TOP is similar to MAP, though it uses the CSMA/CD bus, much like IEEE 802.3. TOP is designed with the office and computing environment in mind, rather than the factory floor.

Widely Used Local Area Networks

There are many different types of local area networks in use today. Two of these, however, have captured the largest share of the market. Equipment compatible with these networks, *Ethernet* and the *IBM Token Ring Network*, is available from many different vendors.

Ethernet was originally used by Xerox, DEC, and Intel, among others. Ethernet is a bus network, using a CSMA/CD access method very similar to IEEE 802.3. Ethernet baseband transmission rates of 10 Mbps using coaxial cable are common. The use of different transmission media can increase this bandwidth.

The *IBM Token Ring Network* is an IBM local area network offering which uses a star-wired ring configuration. Token passing is accomplished by a method similar to the IEEE 802.5 standard. The IBM Token Ring Network uses baseband transmission to transmit data at 4 Mbps using unshielded twisted pair cable. Different transmission media, such as shielded twisted pair or fiber optic cable, could potentially increase the bandwidth of a token ring network.

There arc many other local area networks in use today. Another network, the *IBM PC Network*, is a 2 Mbps network available in baseband and broadband CSMA/CD versions. A.T.&T. also has two local area networks; A.T.&T.'s *Starlan Network* is a star network designed mainly for connecting personal computers in the office environment. A.T.&T.'s *Information Systems Network*, or *ISN*, provides connections to a wide variety of devices, including host computers, terminals, and personal computers, by using a combination of local area network and packet switching network transmission methods.

Literally dozens of vendors produce devices compatible with the networks mentioned, particularly Ethernet and the IBM Token Ring. There are also many different special-purpose, proprietary networks that do not meet any particular standard. Most large users, however, prefer to choose a standard network.

INTERNETWORKING

The two data transport networks we have presented, packet switching networks and local area networks, can each operate separately. However, there are many applications for *internetworking*, or connecting two networks.

Two separate networks, each using different communications methods, can be connected using a *gateway*. A gateway may be a dedicated device, similar in function to a protocol converter. Sometimes a personal computer is equipped with the hardware and software needed to perform this function. For example, users on an Ethernet local area network could communicate with users on an IBM Token Ring Network through a gateway. Similarly, Ethernet users could access a host computer on a packet switching network through a gateway connecting these two networks. Both of these examples are illustrated in Fig. 8-7.

Two separate networks, each using the same communications method, can be connected by using a *bridge*. A bridge is similar to a gateway, though the two networks must already be compatible. For example, Ethernet is limited to a set distance from one end of the bus to the other. Over longer distances, two separate Ethernet networks are attached with a bridge, giving users on each network access to the other network. Similarly, two packet switching networks that both use the X.25 standard could also be connected with a bridge, allowing users on each network to access users on the other network. Two token rings could also be connected with a bridge. These examples are also shown in Fig. 8-7.

One of the most popular methods of internetworking is to use local area networks

Figure 8-7 Internetworking with gateways and bridges.

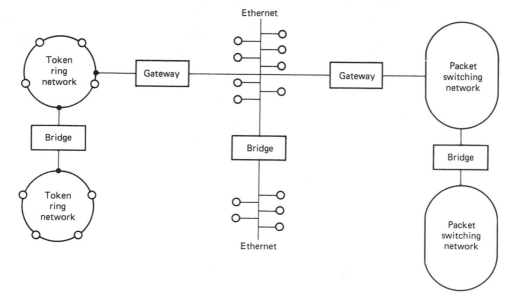

Data Transport Networks

within each location, and connect the LANs to remote locations by using packet switching networks. This configuration provides high-bandwidth transmission within each location through local area networks, and takes advantage of the economies of packet switching networks for remote transmission.

SUMMARY

Data transport networks provide the lower-layer OSI model functions. Packet switching networks and local area networks are two examples of data transport networks.

Packet switching networks are often used for long-distance data transmission, and provide a virtual circuit between devices. Packets are routed from one PSN node to another node over interexchange circuits. Devices unable to communicate using packets can be attached to a PAD, which performs the necessary translation. The PAD can be part of the network, or completely external and on the user's premises. PSNs provide the reliability of the dial-up network at a reduced cost, since permanent connections are never established. Packet switching networks can be customer-owned, or operated by service providers for use by the public. These public PSNs typically charge users on a per packet basis.

Most packet switching networks comply with the X.25 standard. This three-level standard specifies the Physical Level, Frame Level, and Packet Level procedures and protocols for connecting to a packet switching network. There are other related standards explaining the PAD function, known as X.3, X.28, and X.29. PSNs can provide additional services, such as closed user groups, incoming or outgoing calls only, flow control or throughput class negotiation, and reverse charging. The routing of data in a packet switching network may cause delays, and packets may arrive out of sequence. Therefore, the destination node must be able to buffer and resequence the packets before transmitting them to the end user. Packet switching networks are one type of wide area network.

A local area network is a privately owned data communications system that provides reliable high-speed, switched connections between devices in a single building, campus, or complex. LAN users typically transfer files or share resources known as servers. LANs can be designed using centralized or distributed control. LANs can also be designed using many different topologies, including a mesh, star, bus, tree, ring, or star-wired ring. Both baseband and broadband transmission can be used in LANs.

The access methods used in LANs also vary widely. LANs can be designed to use polling and selecting, time division, or frequency division, though contention or token passing methods are more commonly used. Contention methods include random access, CSMA, and CSMA/CD. The most important aspect of these contention methods is the backoff procedure used; it is typically either priority backoff or random backoff. Token passing methods use free and busy tokens to control access to the network; active and standby monitor devices help maintain a reliable token passing network.

The IEEE 802 committee is responsible for many LAN standards, encompassing both Medium Access Control and Logical Link Control. The ANSI Fiber Distributed Data Interface standard describes a high-speed fiber optic LAN. The General Motors

Manufacturing Automation Protocol, or MAP, is a user-defined standard for a token bus LAN in the factory environment. Another user-defined standard, Boeing Computer Services' Technical and Office Products specification , or TOP, describes a CSMA/CD bus LAN for the office and computing environment. The Ethernet and the IBM Token Ring Networks are two of the most widely used LANs today.

There are many applications for internetworking, or connecting two networks. A gateway connects two different types of networks, while a bridge connects similar networks. One typical internetworking application involves a multiple-site customer, with LANs at each location and all of the LANs connected by a PSN.

TERMS FOR REVIEW

Access method
Active monitor
ARPANET
Backoff
Baseband transmission
Bridge
Broadband transmission
Buffering
Bus network
Busy token
Carrier sense multiple
   access
Carrier sense multiple
   access/collision detection
Centralized control
Closed user group
Collect calls
Collision
Collision avoidance
Collision detection
Communications server
Contention
CSMA
CSMA/CD
Data transport network
Distributed control
Ethernet
External PAD
FDDI
Fiber Distributed Data
   Interface

File server
Flow control negotiation
Frame Level
Free token
Frequency division
Gateway
IBM PC Network
IBM Token Ring Network
IEEE 802
IEEE 802.1
IEEE 802.2
IEEE 802.3
IEEE 802.4
IEEE 802.5
IEEE 802.6
IEEE 802.7
IEEE 802.8
IEEE 802.9
Incoming calls only
Information Systems
   Network
Interexchange circuit
Internal PAD
Internetworking
ISN
IXC
LAN
LLC
Local area network

Logical Link Control
MAC
MAN
Manufacturing Automation
   Protocol
MAP
Medium Access Control
Mesh network
Metropolitan area network
Node
Numbered
Outgoing calls only
Packet
Packet assembler
   disassembler
Packet Level
Packet switching network
Packetized
PAD
Personal computer
Physical Level
Polling
Print server
Priority backoff
PSN
Public packet switching
   network
Random access
Random backoff
Resequencing

Reverse charging
Ring network
Selecting
Standby monitor
Star network
Starlan Network
Star-wired ring network
Switched service
Switching node
Tap

Technical and Office
   Products
Telenet
Terminal handler
Throughput class negotiation
Time division
Token
Token bus
Token passing
Token ring network

TOP
Topology
Tree network
Tymnet
Virtual circuit
WAN
Wide area network
X.3
X.25
X.28
X.29

EXERCISES

8-1. What is a virtual circuit in a packet switching network?

8-2. What are the functions of PSN nodes, IXCs, and PADs?

8-3. What are the advantages and disadvantages of a PSN?

8-4. What are the levels of the X.25 standard? What other standards are similar to the lower levels of the X.25 standard?

8-5. What are the different internal PAD standards?

8-6. What is a closed user group in a PSN?

8-7. Explain why packet resequencing may be necessary at the destination node in a PSN.

8-8. What is a LAN?

8-9. What is the function of a server? Describe several different servers.

8-10. What is the difference between centralized control and distributed control in LANs? What are the advantages and disadvantages of each method?

8-11. Describe the different LAN topologies. Which topology usually requires centralized control?

8-12. How do baseband LANs differ from broadband LANs?

8-13. What is an access method?

8-14. What is contention? What is a collision?

8-15. Describe random access, CSMA, CSMA/CD, and backoff.

8-16. Describe how token passing can control access to a LAN. What happens if the free token is somehow lost during transmission?

8-17. What are the two most widely used LANs today? Which IEEE standards best describe these networks?

8-18. What is internetworking? Describe the difference between a bridge and a gateway.

Data Transport Networks

9

NETWORK MANAGEMENT

Any network, whether it is a LAN, a PSN, or an SNA network, is really a collection of individual components working in harmony. *Network management* helps maintain this harmony, ensuring consistent reliability and availability of the network, as well as timely transmission and routing of data.

NETWORK MANAGEMENT FUNCTIONS

Network management can be accomplished by dedicated devices, by host computers on the network, by people, or by some combination of all of these. No matter how network management is performed, it usually includes several key functions: *network monitoring, network control, network troubleshooting*, and *network statistical reporting*. These functions assume the role of network "watchdog," "boss," "diagnostician," and "statistician," respectively. All of these functions are closely interrelated, and often many or all of them are performed by the same device.

The most important function of network management is *network monitoring*. This function constantly checks on the network, and reports on any problems, acting as the network "watchdog." A reported malfunction may be as serious as a completely inoperative communications link to a host computer, and might require immediate action.

Another possible report might indicate an unusually high error rate between two modems, indicating either modem problems or a possible degradation in the telephone circuit. Such a report would allow the problem to be corrected before the communications link becomes completely inoperative.

Another function of network management is *network control*. This function, acting as the network "boss," allows for the activation and deactivation of network components and features. Deactivating a faulty modem to prevent network users from accessing it is an example of network control. Network control also allows components to be re-configured; for example, an intelligent terminal might have its address changed using network control.

There is another network management function, known as *network troubleshooting*, that works closely with the network monitoring and control functions. For example, after network monitoring determines the link to a host computer is not operating properly, the network control feature could be used to deactivate that link. The network troubleshooting function, acting as the network "diagnostician," could then be used to isolate the exact cause of the problem. Diagnostic tests could be run on all of the devices in the communications link, perhaps including the cables, modems, and telephone circuits.

Resolving network operations problems almost always requires a combination of the network monitoring, control, and troubleshooting functions. Even if the network is operating flawlessly, there may still be delays, or resources may be inadequate for the user's data traffic. The *network statistical reporting* function can then be one of the most useful in network management.

The network statistical reporting function, acting as the network "statistician," can pinpoint exactly which parts of a network are being utilized and how often particular components are being used. Over-utilization and under-utilization problems can be identified and corrected. For example, statistics might reveal that there are not enough communications links between two host computers, because the existing links are constantly busy and data is being delayed. Similarly, infrequently used resources can be identified and perhaps taken out of service or used elsewhere.

Working in conjunction with the network monitoring function, information about the performance of specific circuits in a network can be collected. Network statistical reporting can then reveal if the network's overall performance requirements are being met.

SERVICE LEVELS

Some criteria for the successful performance of a network are clear-cut; a link that isn't working at all obviously needs to be reported. But in the case of occasional data errors, how many errors are acceptable? What are the criteria for these subjective network management functions?

The performance of a network is typically judged by comparing it to acceptable *service levels* in several key areas. In some areas, there are industry-accepted standards for reasonable service levels; other areas require the user to specify a service level based on the particular application.

Availability

The most important area in which to measure a network's success is its *availability*. We consider the time when it is working properly its *uptime*, and the time when the network is not working properly its *downtime*. Availability is the ratio of uptime to total uptime and downtime, as shown in Fig. 9-1. A network that works properly for 99 hours and is then down for 1 hour has an availability of 99%.

FIGURE 9-1 AVAILABILITY

$$\text{Availability} (\%) = \frac{\text{uptime}}{\text{uptime} + \text{downtime}} \times 100\% = \frac{\text{MTBF}}{\text{MTBF} + \text{MTTR}} \times 100\%$$

MTBF = Mean time between failures
MTTR = Mean time to repair

Since networks are not likely to fail at a set time each day, we usually deal with the average failure rate of a network. The *mean time between failures*, or *MTBF*, is the average time between network failures. Interpreted in a more positive way, MTBF is the uptime, or the average time a network works properly.

In general, the longer the MTBF, the better, though it depends how crucial the component is. For example, the MTBF of a light bulb may only be 1000 hours; that's usually acceptable, because light bulbs are easy to replace. However, the MTBF of twisted pair local loops is expected to be many years; that's important, because it's not practical to dig up streets to repair telephone wire every few months.

To the network user, the downtime is as important as the uptime. The *mean time to repair*, or *MTTR*, is the average time required to diagnose and correct a problem. The corrective action may be either a repair or a replacement of the defective component. In general, the shorter the MTTR, or downtime, the better. A host computer with an MTBF of nine years may seem outstanding, but if its MTTR is 1 year, the availability is only 90%. Some components, like modems, are easily and quickly replaced, provided that spares are kept on hand. Because of this low MTTR, a lower MTBF may be tolerated; it may be acceptable that a modem has an MTBF of only 1 year, since the MTTR may be only 1 day. The availability of this modem could be 364/365, or 99.7%. A summary of the relationship between MTBF, MTTR, and availability is provided in Fig. 9-1.

The MTBF and MTTR of a network are based on the MTBFs and MTTRs of all the components in the network. A sophisticated host computer with a long MTBF may sit idle due to a cheap protocol converter with a low MTBF. There is no industry-accepted level of availability for a data communications network; it simply depends on the applications of the end users in a given environment.

The higher a network's availability, the more often the components in the network are functioning properly. There are some components that cannot be judged by availability alone. For example, during a thunderstorm some static may occur on a telephone line. This is usually not classified as a failure, because the telephone line is working, though its performance is momentarily degraded, causing a brief period of errors.

Reliability

A data communications network's *reliability* is usually measured by its ability to pass data without errors. Acceptable error rates are usually specified for each communications link in the network. Locally, this link might be a coaxial cable; remotely, the link usually includes telephone circuits and modems.

A special test, known as a *bit error rate test*, or *BERT* test, can be performed to determine a communications link's reliability. Typically, a known pattern of ones and zeroes is continually transmitted on the link, and proper reception is verified at the other end. If 1000 bits are transmitted and two bit errors are detected, the bit error rate for that circuit is .002. An acceptable bit error rate for modems using voice-grade circuits might be about one bit in a million, or 0.000001. Most modems perform better than this under ideal conditions, and worse than this under poor conditions.

Another measure of reliability, known as a *block error rate test*, or *BLERT* test, measures the ability of a link to pass entire blocks of data, rather than just bits. When using protocols, the BLERT test may be more appropriate than the BERT test, since protocols automatically correct errors anyway, using retransmission. The only issue with protocols is how often the blocks need to be retransmitted.

A BLERT test is more indicative of actual link reliability when using protocols, because even if only a single bit error occurs, the entire block of data will need to be retransmitted by the protocol. In addition, a BLERT test will distinguish between bit errors spread randomly during transmission, and errors that are clustered together in the same block. When using protocols, randomly dispersed errors are more troublesome, because many blocks may have to be retransmitted. A comparison of BERT and BLERT is presented in Fig. 9-2.

FIGURE 9-2 RELIABILITY

$$\text{BERT} = \frac{\text{number of bit errors detected}}{\text{total number of bits received}} = \text{bit error rate test}$$

$$\text{BLERT} = \frac{\text{number of block errors detected}}{\text{total number of blocks received}} = \text{block error rate test}$$

Response Time

In some networks, a consistent *response time* is critical. The definition of response time depends on the devices being used. For example, consider a smart terminal connected to a host computer through a network. The time between the instant when the terminal user hits the Enter key and when the reply message is received from the host computer is known as the response time. In this case, response time is really a summation of the time it takes the message to travel from the terminal to the host computer, the processing time at the host computer, and the travel time of the reply. This formula is summarized in Fig. 9-3.

If there are many terminals being polled, three response times are usually considered. There is a *minimum response time*, if the terminal is polled immediately after the user hits the Enter key. The *maximum response time* assumes that the terminal was polled just before the Enter key is hit, and therefore must wait until all the other terminals are polled before it will get another chance to transmit. The *average response time* is halfway between the minimum and the maximum response times, assuming that all terminals are using the network equally.

A small local area network might have a response time of only a few hundred milliseconds. On the other hand, a packet switching network with many nodes might have response times of a second or more.

Response time may or may not be important to a user, though for most common applications, a 2-second response time is considered adequate. A clerk typing payroll data into a terminal may not mind waiting an extra few seconds for the next screen of information to be transferred from the host computer. However, a nuclear power plant operator needs to communicate with the control computer instantly in an emergency, and even a few seconds can be critical.

FIGURE 9-3 RESPONSE TIME

Response time = travel time from terminal to host computer +
                                processing time at host computer +
                                travel time from host computer to terminal

Throughput

Perhaps even more important than response time as a measure of network transmission speed is *throughput*. Throughput is the net bandwidth of a network; it is a measure of the number of information bits per second that can be accepted and transmitted by a network. This rate is typically less than the transmission speed of the individual links. For example, in a network, a particular communications link with 9600 bps modems may have an average throughput of only 6000 information bits per second, because some of the available bandwidth is used for the extra bits, or *overhead*, associated with protocols. This overhead may include error checking and addressing information, and is necessary for data transmission with protocols, though not part of the actual user's data.

Throughput is often referred to as *net bandwidth*, rather than simply *bandwidth*, because it considers only the number of information bits transmitted per second. Bandwidth considers all of the bits transmitted, including the overhead bits.

One standard measure of throughput is calculated using the ANSI formula for *TRIB*, or *transfer rate of information bits*. This formula, shown in Fig. 9-4, provides a throughput rate in bits per second. It calculates the average rate at which users can expect the network to transport actual information bits to their destination. Throughput is an excellent measure of the efficiency of a particular network or communications link.

Network Management

FIGURE 9-4 THROUGHPUT

$$TRIB = \frac{\text{number of information bits transferred}}{\text{time required for the information bits to be transferred}}$$

TRIB = transfer rate of information bits
         (bits per second)

NETWORK MANAGEMENT APPROACHES

Setting standards for adequate service levels in the availability, reliability, response time, and throughput areas is an important first step in network management. After these thresholds are in place, the next logical step is to judge the network against these levels.

Although many different methods are used in network management, there are three basic approaches, using varying degrees of automation.

Non–automated Network Management

The first approach uses minimal automation and requires users to call a network control center to report problems. There is little or no automated network monitoring and control equipment. However, when network problems are reported, specialized test equipment can be used to isolate the problem. This approach relies on users to monitor the network and report problems, and requires technicians trained in the test equipment to isolate and diagnose the problems. This specialized network test equipment is usually portable, and can be taken to possible trouble spots in the network. We discuss some different types of network test equipment later in this chapter.

Unfortunately, in a large network it is often difficult to determine where to place test equipment to start isolating the problem. A typical user might report "I keep getting disconnected from the computer." There may be twenty links and ten nodes between the user and the computer. Where does the technician start? It's the equivalent of a driver complaining that there was a pothole somewhere on a 50-mile commute, and expecting the highway department to find and repair it.

This minimal automation approach has the advantage of requiring little or no investment in network management tools. However, ongoing cost in maintaining the network is high, since problems can be difficult to diagnose and locate. Network problem reporting is completely in the hands of the users, and technicians must isolate and diagnose all problems themselves.

Semi–automated Network Management

The second approach uses automatic network monitoring equipment for parts of the network. For example, a host computer might have network management capabilities

Network Management

that trigger alarms when an unusual number of bit errors occur. In this case automation is used to report a problem, but a technician still must use specialized test equipment with the host computer to isolate and diagnose the problem. The problem could be occurring at the computer, at the end user's terminal, or at any of the links or nodes in between.

This compromise approach takes advantage of built-in network management capabilities already in some devices, without the expense of updating the entire network. Some problems will still be difficult to locate, and the burden of fault isolation and troubleshooting still falls largely on the network technician. A network's reliability is improved somewhat with this approach because problems are detected quickly. However, isolating and troubleshooting many problems will still require much expertise on the part of technicians.

Integrated Network Management

The most advanced network management approach ties all equipment in a network together using special network management protocols. Network management functions are integrated into every component of the network, and software used in one host computer continuously monitors the network; this host computer acts as a control center. Test messages are sent to each device periodically, and any transmission errors are reported to the control center. The control center software may operate on a mainframe, minicomputer, or even personal computer, depending on the size of the network.

In this integrated approach to network management, a single technician, using the control center host computer, can perform all of the major network management functions. The technician can monitor the network, is instantly alerted to all network problems, and can usually perform network control functions. Typically, diagnostics can be run directly from the control center, and devices can be deactivated or re-configured if necessary to work around a simple link problem. Many problems will still require that a technician be dispatched to investigate with specialized test equipment, but in almost all cases, the technician at the control center will know about problems before the users do, or at least at the same time.

Many of today's integrated network management tools use graphics extensively to display network status, actually highlighting problem areas on a map of the network to aid in troubleshooting. Some of these control centers actually use artificial intelligence computer software, known as *expert systems*, to help diagnose and isolate problems. Ideally, a technician's job is simplified by these tools because a defective component is already isolated, or at least the choice is narrowed down to one or two components. The technician can then use the specialized test equipment to determine which of the devices is actually causing the problem.

The integrated network management approach can also provide access at the control center to extensive network statistics on all devices in the network. Such network-wide statistics are almost impossible to compile without an integrated network management approach.

It should be noted that with an integrated network management approach, however, all devices in the network must be compatible with the control center's network management protocols, so they can report their problems and statistics. Clearly, a single vendor could establish network management protocols and implement them in all of its devices. However, for integrated network management to be successful, not all the equipment needs to be from the same vendor; only compatibility is necessary.

For example, IBM's host computer-based network management software, known as *Netview*, can interface to another IBM software product, known as *Netview/PC*. This personal computer-based software allows any device that conforms to IBM's standard set of protocols to report network management information to Netview. Many vendors have already adopted the Netview/PC protocols, in order to fully participate in IBM's integrated network management approach. Netview is just part of IBM's family of *Communications Network Management (CNM)* tools.

A.T.&T. has also defined its own network management structure, known as the *Unified Network Management Architecture*, or *UNMA*. UNMA allows for network management at the customer site or at an A.T.&T. control center. UNMA defines specific network management protocols for vendors of computer and communications equipment. Other vendors besides A.T.&T. and IBM have defined their own integrated network management schemes.

DIAGNOSTIC METHODS

The different network management approaches vary slightly in their methods of diagnosing problems. One of the most common techniques is *loopback testing*, or *echo testing*. Typically, loopback testing is used to test modems or dumb terminals, though other devices can also be tested this way.

For example, a dumb, asynchronous, RS-232-C-compatible terminal can be loopback tested with a specially wired connector. This connector, known as a *loopback plug*, has the Transmitted Data and Received Data pins wired together; in addition, several control signals are connected together to simulate normal operation. If a technician suspects that a terminal is not operating properly, the cable attached to the terminal can be disconnected and the loopback plug attached instead.

Figure 9-5 RS-232-C asynchronous terminal loopback plug.

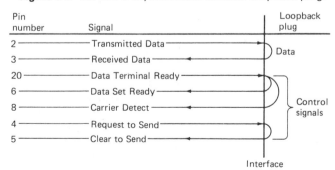

Network Management

The terminal user types characters, which are translated into bits, and then sent over the RS-232-C Transmitted Data pin as positive and negative voltages. Since the Transmitted Data pin is wired to the Received Data pin, the terminal receives the characters it just transmitted. If the terminal is functioning properly, the typed characters will be received and then appear on the screen. A typical RS-232-C loopback plug configuration is illustrated in Fig. 9-5; details on the RS-232-C interface itself are provided in Chapter 4.

A loopback test is the equivalent of a person putting one end of a garden hose up to his mouth and the other end up to his ear; when talking into one end of the hose, he hears his voice at the other end of the hose.

ANALOG AND DIGITAL
MODEM LOOPBACK TESTING

Many modems are designed with internal loopback testing capability because users usually are unable to identify where the problem with a data link lies; the problem could be in the local modem, in the remote modem, or in the phone line itself. The loopback testing capability is usually activated by depressing a switch on the modem or by issuing a special command, and can be performed by a user or a technician.

To help isolate modem problems, there are two types of modem loopback testing, the *local analog loopback test* and the *remote digital loopback test*. Neither test verifies all of a modem's functions, but the two combined will reveal almost any modem problem. Modems usually have switches, or commands, to activate each test. To understand these two tests, we will take a brief look inside a modem.

As shown in Fig. 9-6, in normal operation, square waves from a DTE (perhaps a terminal) enter the modem's *decoder* circuitry. At this point, the square waves are translated into an internal representation of ones and zeroes used by the modem. The *modulator* circuitry then translates these ones and zeroes into an analog signal, usually a sine wave. This analog signal is then sent out on the telephone line.

At the receiving modem, the sine waves enter the *demodulator* circuitry, where they are translated into ones and zeroes. This digital data then enters the *driver* circuitry, which produces a square wave at the appropriate voltage levels.

If a modem uses an RS-232-C interface, its decoders must be able to receive and interpret RS-232-C square waves, and its drivers must be able to transmit these waves. Similarly, another type of interface could be used simply by changing the decoder and driver circuitry.

In the local analog loopback test, a terminal is attached to a single modem with a cable, as illustrated in Fig. 9-7. When the local analog loopback switch is depressed, the analog signal is looped back before ever leaving the modem. In a successful test, a user types a key on the terminal, the terminal generates a square wave, the data enters the modem and reaches the decoders, is converted to digital

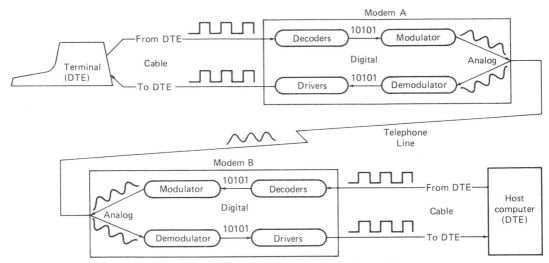

Figure 9-6 Normal operation of a modem.

form and sent to the modulator, where it is converted to analog form. The analog sine wave is then looped back into the demodulator—hence the name *analog loopback*.

In the demodulator, the analog signal is converted back to digital form and passed on to the driver, where it can be translated back to a square wave with the appropriate voltage levels and sent back to the terminal.

The character then appears on the terminal screen, and the test is complete. This test verifies the operation of almost all of one modem's components. Some parts of the modem, including some of the wiring from the modulator/demodulator circuitry to the phone jack are not tested, however; nor is the phone line itself tested. "Local" refers to the fact that the analog loopback test can be performed locally without another modem, and without any phone line. A successful analog loopback test confirms a modem's, decoders, drivers, modulators, and demodulators are probably functioning properly; it also confirms that the terminal and cable are working.

A remote digital loopback test can test the phone line itself as well as parts of the modem not covered in the local analog loopback method. In this case, two

Figure 9-7 Local analog loopback test.

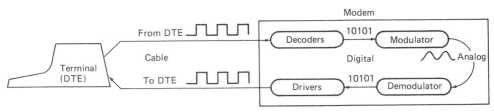

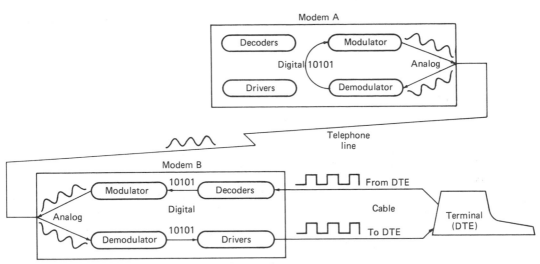

Figure 9-8 Remote digital loopback test.

modems, a terminal, a cable, and a phone line are required, as shown in Fig. 9-8. The remote digital loopback switch is pressed on modem A; modem B is in normal operation mode. The terminal user strikes a key and the data is sent by modem B in analog form to modem A, where it enters the demodulator and is translated to digital form. The digital signal is looped back—hence the name *digital loopback*.

The digital signal enters the modulator and is translated back into analog form and sent back over the phone line to modem B and the terminal. A successful test confirms the operation of the terminal, the phone line, all of modem B, and the modulator/demodulator circuitry of modem A. The term *remote* in this case simply means that another modem is required at the other end of a telephone line.

By using the local analog loopback and the remote digital loopback testing capabilities of most modems, many obvious problems can be isolated without specialized test equipment. Intermittent problems, and problems caused by large volumes of data, will not usually be detected by these tests. Also, it is sometimes difficult to determine whether problems lie in the data link, or in the attached equipment, like host computers. These cases still require specialized data communications test equipment.

DATA COMMUNICATIONS
TEST EQUIPMENT

Regardless of which network management approach is chosen, specialized test equipment is sometimes necessary to isolate and confirm the cause of a problem. Networks using the integrated network management approach may seldom need to use specialized test equipment, while networks managed without automation will almost always need this equipment to resolve network problems.

The Breakout Box

The simplest form of data communications test equipment is called a *breakout box*. A breakout box typically can be attached at a data communications interface, perhaps between a terminal and a modem. A breakout box contains light bulbs, called *LEDs*, or *light-emitting diodes*, to monitor interface signals. For example, an RS-232-C breakout box might contain 25 LEDs, one for each signal on the DB-25 connector. A positive voltage might cause the LED for that signal to light; a negative voltage might cause it to turn off. In this way, the status of control signals can be monitored. Data being transmitted by the terminal will cause the Transmitted Data LED to flash on and off, but at a rate much too fast to be read by humans.

The main purpose of the LEDs on a breakout box is to allow monitoring of the control signals, which typically are either on or off, and do not change as frequently as the data signals. Breakout boxes can therefore be used to determine if a particular device is presenting a DTE or DCE interface, based on the control signals turned on. This knowledge helps users connect this device to other devices.

Breakout boxes get their name from their switches and jumper wires, which allow technicians to "break out" individual signals. For example, in normal position, all switches are closed and signals are passed straight through the breakout box. However, the switches for the Transmitted Data and Received Data signals can be opened and wires used to cross these signals. In this way, custom cables can be tested to determine the most suitable configuration for connecting two devices. The "breaking out" of signals in this manner is known as interface modification.

Some breakout boxes contain a small battery for use in testing cables. A simple continuity test can be performed on each wire in a cable; a lit LED indicates that a wire is conducting electricity, a LED that doesn't light indicates that a wire is broken.

To summarize, a breakout box is often used for monitoring control signals, DTE/DCE determination, interface modification, and cable testing.

The Datascope
or Protocol Analyzer

A more sophisticated device is a *datascope* or *protocol analyzer*. Like a breakout box, a datascope can be placed in the data communications circuit for monitoring purposes. The datascope generally has all of the features of a breakout box, including switches and jumper wires, and can perform all breakout box functions. However, a datascope also has its own display screen to allow technicians to observe the data being transmitted and received.

Datascopes are often called protocol analyzers because they let users see not only the data typed at a terminal, but the special control information added by a protocol.

Only the actual data typed by the terminal user, or sent by the host computer, will appear on the terminal screen; however, all transmitted data, including the control information, is visible on the datascope's display screen, and this can aid in troubleshooting network problems.

In addition to monitoring the data transmitted, many datascopes have features that allow data to be trapped in memory when certain conditions or errors occur. When troubleshooting intermittent conditions, datascopes can be left in place and configured to sound alarms when protocol errors are detected. Some datascopes, when attached to a phone line, will even call a remote office when errors are observed.

Most datascopes can perform the BERT and BLERT tests we mentioned earlier. Typically, after a communications problem is isolated and repaired, a datascope is used to run a BERT or BLERT test to verify that the problem is corrected.

Some datascopes can even be programmed to simulate or mimic the operation of host computers. For example, a datascope can be programmed to poll a smart terminal to test its operation.

Since datascopes typically contain their own microcomputers, their features are limited only by the software used in them.

Analog Test Equipment

Finally, since almost all data communications networks include analog telephone circuits at some point, *analog test equipment* is often used. For example, analog test equipment can determine if a particular analog leased line is providing the expected bandwidth. A wide variety of analog test equipment exists today, capable of measuring distortion, noise, loss, gain, and many other analog circuit characteristics.

SUMMARY

Network management helps maintain network harmony, ensuring consistent availability and reliability, as well as timely transmission and routing of data. Network monitoring, network control, network troubleshooting, and network statistical reporting are the key functions of network management. These functions assume the role of network "watchdog," "boss," "diagnostician," and "statistician," respectively.

Appropriate service levels need to be established for a network in the areas of availability, reliability, response time, and throughput. Availability is the ratio of a network's uptime to its total uptime and downtime. Uptime is also called the mean time between failures, or MTBF; downtime is also called the mean time to repair, or MTTR. Reliability is often measured by using a bit error rate test (BERT) or a block error rate test (BLERT). Response time is the time between the instant when a user strikes the Enter key and when the reply message is received from the host computer. This includes the round-trip travel time as well as any processing time at the host computer. If there are many terminals being polled, there will be a minimum, average, and maximum response time. Throughput is a measure of the net bandwidth of a network. The ANSI standard measure of throughput is known as the transfer rate of information bits, or TRIB. TRIB is the ratio of the number of information bits transferred to the time required for these bits to be transferred.

There are several different approaches to network management, including non—automated, semi—automated, and integrated network management. Non—automated network management relies on people to report, isolate, diagnose, and correct problems. Semi—automated network management relies on automation to report many problems, but still requires people to isolate, diagnose, and correct problems. Integrated network management employs automation to report, isolate, diagnose, and assist technicians in correcting network problems. Many vendors use an integrated network management approach; examples are Netview and Netview/PC, both part of IBM's family of Communications Network Management (CNM) tools, and A.T.&T.'s Unified Network Management Architecture (UNMA) protocols.

One of the most popular diagnostic methods in use today is loopback testing. Dumb asynchronous terminal loopback testing can be accomplished with a simple loopback plug, while modem loopback testing capability is typically built into the modem itself. There are two common types of modem loopback tests, the local analog loopback test and the remote digital loopback test. A combination of these tests can verify the operation of the different parts of a modem, including the decoders, drivers, modulators, and demodulators, as well as the terminal, cable, and phone line itself.

Sometimes specialized data communications test equipment is needed to solve problems. The breakout box is used for monitoring control signals, DTE/DCE determination, interface modification, and cable testing. The datascope or protocol analyzer is a more sophisticated device which can perform all of the breakout box functions, as well as monitor data on a display screen. Using a datascope, a technician can view protocol control information, set alarms, trap data, perform BERT/BLERT tests, and program complex simulations. For telephone line problems, analog test equipment is used to measure distortion, noise, loss, gain, and other analog circuit characteristics.

TERMS FOR REVIEW

Analog test equipment	Communications Network	LED
Availability	Management	Light-emitting diode
Average response time	Datascope	Local analog loopback test
BERT	Decoder circuit	Loopback plug
Bit error rate test	Demodulator circuit	Loopback testing
BLERT	Downtime	Maximum response time
Block error rate test	Driver circuit	Mean time between failures
Breakout box	Echo testing	Mean time to repair
CNM	Expert system	Minimum response time

Modulator circuit
MTBF
MTTR
Netview
Netview/PC
Network control
Network management
Network monitoring

Network statistical reporting
Network troubleshooting
Overhead
Protocol analyzer
Reliability
Remote digital loopback test
Response time
Service level

Throughput
Transfer rate of information
  bits
TRIB
Unified Network
  Management Architecture
UNMA
Uptime

EXERCISES

9-1. Explain each of the key functions of network management.

9-2. What is the difference between availability and reliability?

9-3. What is MTBF? MTTR? When is a short MTBF acceptable?

9-4. What is response time?

9-5. What is throughput? Why is it sometimes referred to as net bandwidth?

9-6. Compare the different network management approaches.

9-7. Which of the network management approaches is the most economical to implement initially? In the long run?

9-8. Does integrated network management require that all the equipment in the network be supplied by a single vendor? Why or why not?

9-9. What are the major uses of a breakout box?

9-10. What are the major uses of a datascope? Why is it sometimes called a protocol analyzer?

10

THE FUTURE
OF DATA
COMMUNICATIONS

This book began with a discussion of telecommunications, and went on to examine various aspects of data communications. Basic data communications concepts, transmission, interfaces, efficiency, security, integrity, architectures, protocols, transport networks, and network management were all considered at length.

As we near the end of the twentieth century, telecommunications and data communications are converging. In Chapter 2, voice communications technology was presented as a predecessor to data communications. In fact, many of today's voice communications systems involve some digital equipment. Both customer premises equipment and transmission facilities are increasingly using digital technology.

DIGITAL CUSTOMER PREMISES EQUIPMENT

The PBX, discussed in Chapter 2, is perhaps the most widespread customer-premises equipment in use today. Almost all major PBX vendors are currently offering digital PBXs; voice is *digitized*, or translated from analog form into ones and zeroes. We present a method for digitizing voice later in this chapter.

By providing a single digital controller for both voice and data, a digital PBX offers a customer equal flexibility for both voice and data communications. When voice

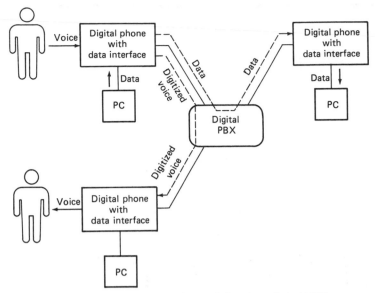

Figure 10-1 Integrated voice and data in a digital PBX.

is digitized, voice and data can be transmitted over the same transmission path. Typically, a *digital phone* converts the voice into digital form for transmission to the PBX. A digital phone should not be confused with the DTMF or rotary phones described earlier, which are analog voice communications devices that send dialing signals using tones or pulses. Digital phones uses ones and zeroes to transmit voice as well as signaling information. Computer data can also be transmitted through a digital phone as well.

For example, a digital phone equipped for both voice and data communications allows a personal computer user to place a voice call to one person, while simultaneously transferring files to the personal computer of another person. This integration of voice and data in a single device, the digital phone, is shown in Fig. 10-1.

Another device, known as an *integrated voice/data terminal*, or an *IVDT*, usually combines the capabilities of a digital phone with those of a terminal. Many of today's digital PBXs can be equipped with IVDTs.

While digital PBXs are increasingly being used to integrate voice and data, some data communications applications demand an extremely high bandwidth. In these cases, the LAN, discussed in Chapter 8, is the most popular data communications solution. LANs can be connected to PBXs, allowing LAN users access to host computers, terminals, and modems attached to the PBX; PBX users can also access devices on the LAN. Both LANs and PBXs are often connected to packet switching networks for economical long-distance data communications. These connections are shown in Fig. 10-2.

Another aspect of today's communications industry, known as *facsimile*, or *FAX*, was originally an analog communications method for transmitting an image of a printed page. Newer digital facsimile machines convert the image into ones and zeroes, allowing

The Future of Data Communications

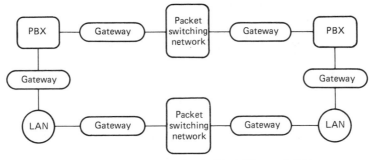

Figure 10-2 Interconnecting PBXs, LANs, and PSNs.

high-speed facsimile transmission over digital communications networks, including PBXs, LANs, PSNs, and other digital transmission facilities.

Transmission of moving images, known as *video transmission*, was originally only an analog technology, like FAX. Conventional cable television is an example of analog video transmission. Digital transmission of video is now possible, though it requires a very high digital bandwidth (many Mbps).

Digitizing Voice Using
Pulse Code Modulation

In Chapter 4, we explained various modulation methods that allowed us to transmit data over analog telephone lines. When digital customer-premises equipment and transmission facilities are used, it becomes necessary to transmit analog signals, like voice, over digital communications facilities; this requires the reverse approach, because the analog signals must now be converted to digital signals for transmission.

Normal telephone conversation can be digitized by using a technique known as *pulse code modulation*, or *PCM*. In PCM, an analog signal is converted to a digital signal for transmission; typically, the analog signal is sampled 8000 times a second, and an eight-bit representation of the signal is recorded for each *sample*, for a total of 64 kbps. Think of a sample as an audio equivalent of a snapshot of the signal at a given moment; if someone is speaking and we freeze their voice at a given instant, we can assign a number that represents the amplitude of the voice signal at that moment. If we do this 8000 times per second, we can then transmit these numbers in binary form, and at the other end, reconstruct the voice by converting the digital representation back into an analog signal. A simplified, four-bit version of PCM is shown in Fig. 10-3.

The receiver cannot detect any interruptions in the voice, because there are so many samples each second. This is the same principle as that on which movies are based. The camera really records many individual snapshots each second on the moving film. When the film is replayed on a projector, it appears that motion is continuous, because the eye cannot detect the slight jumpiness in the motion between each frame.

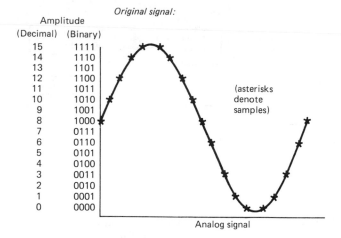

Original signal:

(asterisks denote samples)

Analog signal

Converted to digital form:

1000 1010 1100 1110 1111 1111 1110 1100 1010 1000 0110 0011 0001 0000 0000 0001 0011 0110 1000

Converted back to analog form:

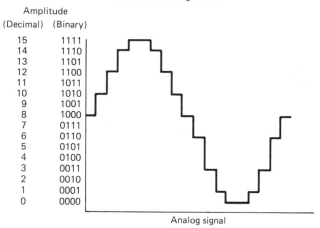

Analog signal

Figure 10-3 Pulse code modulation.

High-Bandwidth Digital Transmission Facilities

High-bandwidth digital transmission facilities are playing a major role in communications today. In Chapter 4, we briefly mentioned *T-1 carrier* service. The T-1 standard, developed by A.T.&T., provides a 1.544 Mbps digital path now available from almost all of the common carriers. The electrical characteristics, including the voltage levels for T-1 bit transmission, are specified by the *DS-1* standard. Typically, the 1.544 Mbps is divided into 24 separate channels, using time division multiplexing.

The Future of Data Communications

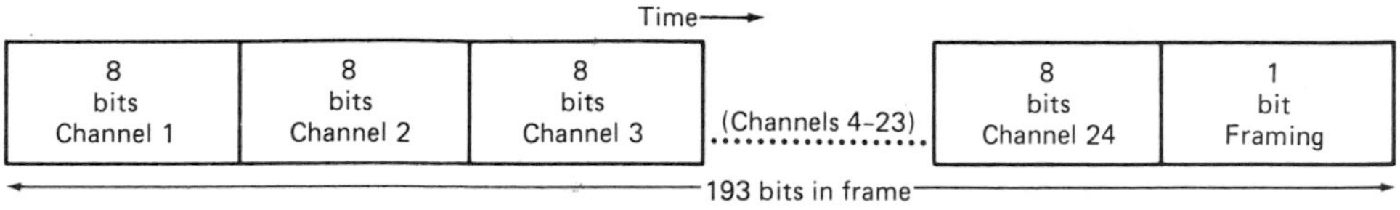

Figure 10-4 T-1 Frame.

T-1 frames.   Data is transmitted in *frames*, each 193 bits long; 8000 frames are transmitted each second in a T-1 carrier (1,544,000/193 = 8000). A typical T-1 frame is illustrated in Fig. 10-4. Notice that each of the 24 channels transmits eight bits per frame; in addition, one bit per frame is a *framing bit*, used for *synchronization*, and sometimes for error checking. The 8000 frames per second include 8 kbps of synchronization and 24 channels each of 64 kbps, adding up to a total of 1.544 Mbps. Each of these 24 channels can be used for either data or digital voice communications.

T-1 applications.   By combining T-1 carrier with PCM, 24 voice conversations can be simultaneously transmitted over a single T-1 circuit, which requires only two twisted pairs. With analog voice transmission, 24 pairs would be required. This 12-to-1 advantage does not come without a price, however. Since T-1 is a digital signal, repeaters need to be used after a certain distance to prevent the signal from fading, as discussed in Chapter 4. In addition, special digital transmission equipment is required at each end of a T-1 circuit. Analog transmission requires less expensive amplifiers and devices known as *loading coils*, instead of digital repeaters.

Even with the added costs of T-1 repeaters and other digital equipment, a T-1 circuit may cost only as much as a dozen analog leased lines, depending on the distance involved. In this case, T-1 offers 24 connections for the price of 12, over only 2 pairs of wires instead of 24 pairs; this results in a 2-to-1 price advantage and a 12-to-1 advantage in terms of wiring requirements. Also, a digital circuit, because of its many repeaters, is less likely to be affected by small amounts of noise. For this reason, a digitized long-distance voice circuit will usually be free of any static. In an analog circuit, static and other noise will usually be amplified and carried with the signal.

A common application of T-1 is presented in Fig. 10-5 (page 188), where two PBXs, each at a different site, are connected using a T-1 circuit through a central office. This allows a customer to provide 24 channels between the two PBXs for far less than the cost of 24 analog leased lines. Our figure shows 24 phones at each PBX, implying digitized voice communications on all of the T-1 channels. However, some of these channels could be used to transmit digitized voice, while others are being used simultaneously to transmit data.

T-1 SIGNALING

In Chapter 2, we discussed signals passed through the communications network. These analog signals included on-hook/off-hook, dialing signals, busy signals, and so on. Since T-1 is a digital transmission method, these signals must be passed by using a few bits of the 1.544 Mbps. The 8 kbps of synchronization information is

The Future of Data Communications   187

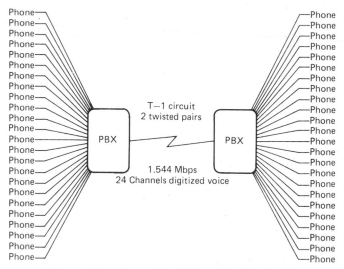

Figure 10-5 Connecting PBXs with a T-1 circuit.

required to separate one frame from the next; therefore, a bit may occasionally be "stolen" from one of the 24 channels for signaling purposes. One of the most common T-1 signaling methods, known as *robbed bit signaling*, allows signaling to occur simultaneously with digitized voice or data transmission.

If a particular channel has a bit robbed for signaling, this channel only has seven bits left instead of eight during this frame. With digitized voice, losing an occasional sample does not affect voice quality, since there are 8000 samples per second; this is equivalent to a speck of dust on one frame of a movie film each second.

However, if a T-1 channel is used to transmit data from a high-speed terminal to a computer, the bit robbed for signaling purposes will cause data errors. Therefore, when actual data, rather than digitized voice, is transmitted via T-1 carrier, only seven bits per channel should be used for actual data; the eighth bit can be used for signaling when necessary. With 8000 frames a second, and seven actual data bits per channel in each frame, this results in an actual data rate of 56 kbps per channel. With an analog line and modems, it very expensive to achieve even 19.2 kbps reliably, and 56 kbps is practically impossible to achieve with today's technology. Therefore, the 56 kbps capacity of a T-1 data channel is still a boon to data communications users.

Ironically, with robbed bit signaling, a digital transmission medium appears to provide 64 kbps per channel for digitized voice, but only 56 kbps per channel for data. In reality, the same bandwidth exists in both cases, but data transmission will fail at 64 kbps with robbed bit signaling, while voice transmission will not be noticeably impaired. The difference is that a missing bit is always noticed in data transmission.

The Future of Data Communications

There have been several generations of T-1, known as *T-1/D1*, *T-1/D2*, *T-1/D3*, *T-1/D4*, *T-1/D5*, and so on. The "D" part of the T-1 standard specifies exactly how the 1.544 Mbps can be subdivided into separate channels—the voice digitization and signaling methods used. T-1 continues to evolve as user requirements change.

T-1 multiplexers and submultiplexing. Though voice may be neatly digitized into 64 kbps channels, there are many data communications devices that operate at lower speeds, such as 9600 bps or 1200 bps terminals. Usually the T-1 transmission rate of 1.544 Mbps is broken into 24 separate channels using a device known as a *T-1 multiplexer*. Any of these channels can be further broken down by *submultiplexing*. Since we've agreed that for data transmission, 56 kbps is the limit of a T-1 channel, five 9600 bps terminals could be submultiplexed onto a single channel with bandwidth to spare. Submultiplexed in this manner, the entire T-1 circuit could carry 120 simultaneous 9600 bps terminal-to-host computer connections, all on two pairs of wires.

Voice and data compression. Even greater economies can be achieved by using a more efficient method than standard PCM to digitize voice. There are methods that can digitize voice using only 32 kbps or 16 kbps. As technology improves, these numbers will be driven even lower. However, there is already a great deal of 64 kbps PCM equipment installed, and compatibility is often more important than efficiency in telecommunications.

Data compression, explained in Chapter 5, can also be used in conjunction with T-1 circuits. This can greatly increase the effective bandwidth for certain applications.

Beyond T-1 speeds. While T-1 offers a 1.544 Mbps digital path, there are other, less widely used, higher-bandwidth standards. *T-1C* has a bandwidth of 3.152 Mbps and offers 48 channels. *T-3* offers 672 channels and a 44.736 Mbps bandwidth. However, few companies need 672 links between two locations; clearly, T-1 provides ample bandwidth for all but the largest organizations. The bandwidth of the T-1C and T-3 standards are not exact multiples of the T-1 bandwidth, because they require extra bits for framing and synchronization.

Digital Networks

Today, digital customer-premises equipment is often combined with digital transmission facilities to form a completely digital private telecommunications network. For example, a company with digital phones attached to digital PBXs at two locations can connect the two PBXs by using a T-1 circuit.

Many companies still use analog equipment in at least part of their network. For example, most digital PBXs today still use analog lines for central office trunks. In addition, almost all residential customers still use analog telephone service. The technology is available, however, to create an entirely digital public telecommunications network, serving businesses of all sizes, as well as residential customers.

INTEGRATED SERVICES DIGITAL NETWORK

The *Integrated Services Digital Network*, or *ISDN*, is an evolving set of standards for a digital network carrying both voice and data communications. Today most residential and small business communications are carried over analog local loops. Only large businesses with high volumes of telecommunications traffic currently use digital transmission facilities, in the form of T-1 carrier. ISDN extends the advantages of digital transmission to all users, large and small, by including many different sizes of digital transmission paths.

The CCITT is taking the lead in defining international ISDN standards. The ISDN standards are really a collection of many standards, specifying interfaces for connecting to the public network, as well as a set of services the network will provide to users. By standardizing interfaces through ISDN, the CCITT hopes someday to make end-to-end digital connections between all devices a reality. Communications networks operated in different countries could all be connected under ISDN standards, allowing for a worldwide, integrated digital network. In addition, ISDN will provide special services to the users, such as call forwarding, voice-mail, and calling party identification. How fast ISDN will be welcomed by different countries, and by the users within those countries, is still not known.

We will discuss only the more common ISDN standards here. As ISDN standards are implemented worldwide, it is expected that many modifications and additions will be necessary. Variations are expected in different countries; in fact, even in the United States, services are expected to differ regionally. However, the fundamental interfaces should be the same, allowing device portability and universal attachment. This is equivalent to today's modular jack, which is accepted as the universal method for attaching a telephone to the public network. Ideally, ISDN will allow terminals, computers, and telephones to attach to the network with similar ease.

ISDN Channels

To accommodate large and small users, ISDN provides different sizes of transmission paths, known as *channels*. These channels can be combined in different ways to satisfy user requirements.

The *B-channel*, also called the *bearer channel*, is a 64 kbps digital channel. The B-channel can carry user data or digitized voice.

The *D-channel* is a digital channel used to carry signaling information. The capacity of the D-channel can be 16 kbps or 64 kbps, depending on the type of circuit used. These bits are reserved for signaling information, such as on-hook/off-hook status, dialing information, busy signals, and so on, also used in T-1 signaling. However, most T-1 transmission uses *in-band signaling*, where the signaling bits are interspersed in the same channels as the data bits. ISDN uses *out-of-band signaling*, or *common-channel signaling*, meaning that a separate channel (the D-channel) is used for the signaling bits.

Since most signaling typically occurs at the beginning and end of a connection, the D-channel may be idle most of the time. Therefore, certain low-priority user data can also be passed on the D-channel when it is free. A typical example of low-priority data for the D-channel might be electronic mail sent in a packet format; there is usually no urgent need for rush delivery, so these messages can be sent when the D-channel is available, rather than using the high-speed B-channel.

The B-channel and D-channel are the basic building blocks of ISDN transmission, though there are several other channels already defined. The *A-channel* is similar to today's analog telephone circuit, and provides a means for analog signals to be carried in an ISDN. Since not everyone will discard their analog customer-premises equipment overnight, some method of carrying analog signals will still be necessary (hence the need for the A-channel). Another channel, known as the *C-channel*, provides a low speed (up to 16 kbps) data channel for older, pre-ISDN data devices, such as many of today's dumb terminals. A summary of the ISDN channel types is provided in Fig. 10-6.

The Basic-Rate Interface

ISDN will provide service to residential and business users with the *basic-rate interface*, or *BRI*. This interface consists of two B-channels and a single D-channel. Usually, one B-channel is used for digitized voice, the other B-channel is used for high-speed data, and the D-channel is used for signaling and low-speed data packets. The basic-rate interface is commonly referred to as *2B + D*.

In the basic-rate interface, the D-channel can carry 16 kbps of signaling information, and each B-channel can carry 64 kbps of data or digitized voice, for a total of 144 kbps. However, an additional 48 kbps is used for overhead, which includes synchronization and framing bits. Therefore, the basic-rate interface requires 192 kbps of digital transmission capacity, though the effective bandwidth is actually 144 kbps.

The basic-rate interface is intended to provide voice and data transmission to the office desktop or the home for the typical individual user. A 64 kbps data transfer rate is adequate for almost all terminal and PC applications, though as processor speeds increase, higher bandwidth may be desirable. The basic-rate interface provides the user with simultaneous voice and data communications capability, along with advanced sig-

FIGURE 10-6 ISDN CHANNEL TYPES

Channel	Type	Bandwidth	Typical Use
A	Analog	Voice grade	Voice
B	Digital	64 kbps	Digitized voice or high-speed data
C	Digital	Up to 16 kbps	Low-speed data
D	Digital	16 or 64 kbps (depending on circuit type)	Signaling or data packets

naling capability. The 64 kbps data rate is far superior to today's data transmission, which uses low-speed modems and analog lines; much of the signaling information in the basic-rate interface is not available to the user in today's public network. Certainly the basic-rate interface is a marked technological improvement over today's analog local loops. If all countries adopt the same basic-rate interface in their implementations of ISDN, worldwide device compatibility is within reach.

The Primary-Rate Interface

ISDN will also provide a higher bandwidth service for business users, known as the *primary-rate interface*, or *PRI*. This interface will normally be used to connect PBXs to central offices, PBXs to PBXs, PBXs to LANs, LANs to LANs, and in other high-bandwidth applications. The primary-rate interface consists of either 23 or 30 B-channels for user data and a single 64 kbps D-channel for signaling.

In North America and Japan, where T-1 transmission is already popular, the *23 B + D* method will be used. Since the capacity of each of the 23 B-channels is 64 kbps, and the D-channel capacity is also 64 kbps, existing T-1 transmission equipment that transmits 24 channels of 64 kbps each can also accommodate this primary-rate interface. Since a separate D-channel is used for signaling, no bits are taken from the B-channel for this purpose, and each B-channel has a full 64 kbps capacity, unlike the channels in T-1. A framing arrangement similar to that found in T-1 transmission is used in this version of the primary-rate interface. Therefore, there are 24 channels each of 64 kbps, and an additional 8 kbps used for framing, for a total of 1.544 Mbps.

In Europe, where high-speed digital transmission is done today using 2.048 Mbps, the *30 B + D* arrangement will be used. Though at first this may seem to cause a fundamental incompatibility between North American and European networks, this is not the case. Each country, or continent, can use its own methods for digital transmission, as long as gateways exist to connect the different networks. It certainly makes sense to maximize the use of existing digital transmission equipment between central offices and toll offices in each country, and the two different primary-rate interfaces permit this.

Other Channel Arrangements

The A-channel and C-Channel will be combined in a *hybrid interface* to allow users without ISDN phones and terminals to receive at least some of the ISDN features. These users will have voice and data, but will not have access to some of the ISDN services.

Individual channels may be offered separately, to comply with regulatory requirements in the United States and other countries. For example, a customer may be able to lease 35 B-channels and 6 D-channels. However, it is expected that initially most customer premises equipment will be designed to take advantage of either the basic-rate or primary-rate interfaces. A comparison of typical ISDN interfaces is shown in Fig. 10-7.

The Future of Data Communications

FIGURE 10-7 TYPICAL ISDN INTERFACES

Name	Channel Composition	Bandwidth Needed	Typical Use
Basic-rate interface	2B + D	192 kbps	Desktop or residence use; one digitized voice and one data channel
Primary-rate interface	23B + D or 30B + D	1.544 or 2.048 Mbps	PBX to PBX, PBX to CO, PBX to LAN, LAN to LAN
Hybrid interface	A + C	Analog voice and up to 16-kbps data	Used during the transition to ISDN

ISDN Equipment Functions and Reference Points

The equipment is an ISDN network and attached to an ISDN network is classified by the functions it performs. We will consider only the customer-premises equipment, not the details of the central office in the ISDN environment. On the customer's premises, there is both ISDN *Terminal Equipment*, or *TE*, and *Network Termination Equipment*, or *NT*.

There are different types of ISDN Terminal Equipment. In this case, the word *terminal* does not refer only to the dumb, smart, or intelligent terminals discussed so far in this book. Instead, terminal equipment in the ISDN nomenclature refers to any device attached to the end of an ISDN circuit; this could be a dumb terminal, but it could also be a telephone, a personal computer, or any device attached to the ISDN network that transmits or receives voice, data, or other information.

Terminal equipment that is compatible with the ISDN network is known as *Terminal Equipment Type 1*, or *TE1*. An ISDN-compatible digital telephone, an ISDN-compatible personal computer port, and an ISDN-compatible workstation are all examples of TE1. A device that is not compatible with ISDN, such as an RS-232-C dumb terminal, is known as *Terminal Equipment Type 2*, or *TE2*. This equipment can be attached to an ISDN network only by using a special *Terminal Adapter*, or *TA*, which acts as a converter between the TE2 and the ISDN network.

The TE1, or TE2/TA combination, is attached to the Network Termination equipment, as illustrated in Fig. 10-8. The point between the Network Termination equipment

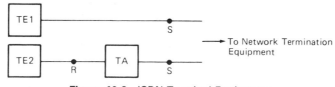

Figure 10-8 ISDN Terminal Equipment.

and the TE1 or TA is known as the *S reference point*. The point between the TE2 and the TA is known as the *R reference point*.

There are also several different types of Network Termination equipment. They provide functions similar to those found in the lower layers of the ISO-OSI model, and some users need only certain functions. *Network Termination 1* equipment, or *NT1*, provides only OSI layer 1 (Physical Layer) functions, including the electrical and physical termination of the network on the customer's premises. The NT1 function allows the rest of the customer-premises equipment to be isolated from the technology used in the local loop. For example, if the local exchange carrier currently uses twisted pair wire for local loops, an NT1 compatible with this transmission medium can be used. If fiber optic local loops later become available, only the NT1 needs to be changed, since it is the only equipment that attaches directly to the circuit.

There is no real equivalent of the NT1 in our homes today in the analog telephone network; however, imagine a box in our house where the local loop from the phone company is connected to our house telephone wiring. This box, terminating the public network circuit, is the equivalent of the NT1. It is similar in function to the CSU discussed in Chapter 4.

Network Termination 2 equipment, or *NT2*, can provide OSI layers 2 and 3 (Data Link and Network Layer) functions, including concentration and switching, if needed. LANs, PBXs, and other controllers are examples of NT2 equipment. While residential users would rarely need their own NT2 equipment, business users would, for the economical and practical reasons previously explained.

Finally, *Combined Network Termination 1 and 2*, or *NT12*, contains both NT1 and NT2 functions in a single device. Some economies can be gained by purchasing a single device that performs both functions, but if the local loop transmission technology changes, the entire NT12 may need to be replaced. Though less flexible than separate NT1 and NT2 devices, some users may choose NT12 for economical reasons.

The relationship between the Network Termination equipment is shown in Fig. 10-9. The point between the NT1 and the rest of the ISDN network is known as the *U reference point*. The point between the NT1 and the NT2 (if an NT2 is used) is known as the *T reference point*. If an NT1 is used without an NT2, the S and T reference points coincide where the NT1 is connected directly to the terminal equipment.

In the United States, both TE and NT are usually considered customer premises equipment. Outside the United States, however, the NT1 function is almost always

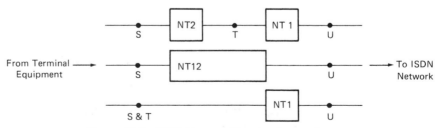

Figure 10-9 ISDN Network Termination equipment.

The Future of Data Communications

provided by the local exchange carrier. Even in the United States, the customer usually has the option of leasing some of the NT functions from the local exchange carrier.

The current ISDN standards specifies that the S and T reference points require two twisted pairs for transmission, while the U reference point requires only one. The exact nature of transmission at the S, T, and U reference points is clearly defined in the CCITT standards. The standard at the R reference point depends on the interface standard of the TE2.

Understanding the details of the CCITT S, T, and U reference point standards is not as important as understanding the functions performed by the TE1, TE2, TA, NT1, NT2, and NT12. In an ISDN environment, customer-premises equipment will be classified according to this terminology. Examples of interconnection of various combinations of equipment are shown in Fig. 10-10.

Circuit and Packet Switching in ISDN

ISDN will support both circuit-switched and packet-switched networks. For example, ISDN users will place a circuit-switched telephone call much in the same way they do today, requesting a circuit for the duration of a call. The only difference is that all of the transmission will be digital in ISDN, and extra services will be available to the user.

Existing packet switching networks can continue under ISDN. However, instead of using analog leased lines or dial-up circuits to access packet switching networks, digital lines may be used. ISDN switched circuits will already provide some of a packet switching network's features, such as reliable data transmission and flexible call routing. For

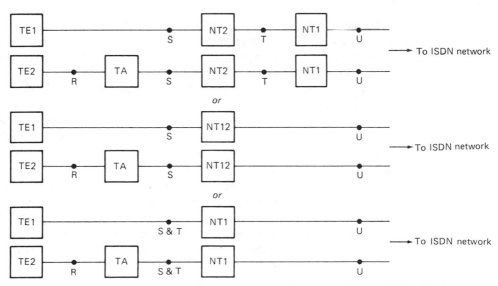

Figure 10-10 Interconnecting ISDN Terminal Equipment and Network Termination Equipment.

users with applications that do not require instant delivery of data, a packet switching network can still prove more economical than an ISDN switched circuit; the patient user can profit from combining data with others on a space-available basis over an ISDN packet switching network.

PBXs, LANs, and ISDN

Though an ISDN public network can provide the features of a PBX, and a bandwidth approaching that of a LAN, both PBXs and LANs are still expected to play an important role in an ISDN world. For example, even though an ISDN central office can provide PBX features like call forwarding and caller identification, it shares the same fundamental inefficiency found in Centrex service. If internal calls must be processed through the central office, a local loop would be required for each desk. The central office charges would be greater than if a PBX were used to minimize the number of central office lines. However, PBXs will be expected to interface to ISDN, typically through the primary-rate interface.

Similarly, some users will require high-bandwidth data transmission. The same ISDN inefficiency discussed above applies here also. Users needing high bandwidth for local data communications may still use a LAN; however, the LAN will probably contain gateways to the ISDN network, so LAN users can access devices located off the LAN when necessary.

ISDN Services

While an integrated digital network is a sound technical concept, there is little reason for users to discard existing analog equipment in the interests of technical purity alone. To motivate users to support a new type of network, special user services are included in addition to digital transmission.

ISDN's signaling capabilities are significantly superior to those of today's public network. The D-channel can carry information about the call's destination, the calling party, billing instructions, and other information. This signaling is passed throughout the ISDN network, so the central office at the destination knows not only who the call is for, but where the call came from. The central office can relay this information on the D-channel to the customer with an ISDN digital phone.

In an ISDN world, when the telephone rings, the phone will display information about the caller, like "(516)-555-1234 John Smith." The user can then choose to answer or ignore the call. In addition, the user could send instructions to the central office to block all calls from John Smith, or forward them to an answering service.

Another example of an often-cited ISDN feature is similar to the PBX camp-on feature. When calling a friend across the country, if we hear a busy signal, we can touch a button on our digital phone that instructs our central office that we really want to reach our friend. Our central office will send special signaling information to our friend's central office, asking it to inform our central office when our friend is off the phone, so that our call can be placed again automatically.

Voice mail systems, currently popular as PBX attachments, are already answering the telephones for thousands of companies. With ISDN, residential users could easily have their messages taken by such a system, be notified of existing messages, forward messages to neighbors, and so on.

Today's digital PBXs already provide many of these features for internal calls, and today's digital central offices could certainly be programmed to accommodate these features. However, until ISDN is implemented universally, there will be no guarantee that the signaling information will be passed to the destination central office. The first users of ISDN may find that the display on their phone is blank most of the time, because the party calling them may not be attached to an ISDN-compatible central office, and the detailed signaling information may not have been sent.

An endless number of features can be provided to the customer with ISDN. The extensive signaling capabilities provided in ISDN will allow new features to be added later simply by modifying the software in existing central office switches.

The Realities of ISDN

ISDN is based on already proven technologies. For example, the basic-rate interface is similar to that used by many PBX manufacturers in their digital phones today. The 23B + D version of the primary-rate interface is similar to the T-1 carrier scheme used in the United States. Almost all the ISDN features are already being used in digital PBXs, so their operation is well understood.

Will ISDN evolve from a set of international standards into a worldwide telecommunications network? Or will ISDN be the next RS-449, a standard that provides for everything, but fails to catch on?

For ISDN to be fully implemented, new customer-premises equipment and transmission equipment will need to be purchased, or existing equipment modified. Existing digital central offices and toll offices can certainly be modified to accommodate ISDN. But who will pay for ISDN?

In some countries, the government strictly regulates the telecommunications industry and sometimes also runs the public network. In these cases, the government could simply insist that all communications equipment in that country conform to ISDN, and the standard could be implemented quickly. The government, and ultimately the citizens, would bear the expense of the conversion.

In the United States, however, it is likely that the FCC and PUCs will require common carriers to continue to offer basic telephone service at reasonable prices. ISDN will initially be made available only as one way to access the public network, in addition to the existing methods.

Simple economics will dictate how fast ISDN is implemented in the United States. For example, the primary-rate interface is almost identical to T-1 carrier; the main difference is that one of the 24 channels is used for signaling instead of data transmission. Assuming that it is priced reasonably close to today's T-1 transmission offerings, the

ISDN primary-rate interface will be a very attractive alternative for today's T-1 customers. By giving up one of the 24 data channels, the customer gains incredible signaling power for the other 23 channels. A customer with PBXs at two locations could tie them together with an ISDN primary-rate circuit; the signaling passed between the two PBXs would make it appear to users that they were on a single PBX.

The basic-rate interface may be only of limited appeal to business users. In Centrex-type installations, where the central office provides the switching function for a customer, the basic-rate interface is a reasonable method of providing digital voice and data service to the desktop.

PBX customers, however, may have already invested in their PBX vendor's own proprietary desktop data interfaces that perform functions similar to the basic-rate interface. These PBXs will likely be compatible with ISDN interfaces to the central office, but may still use their own proprietary digital interface standards internally. Some PBX vendors, however, will also choose the ISDN basic-rate service for transmission between the PBX and the desktop.

Finally, residential telephone users comprise the biggest unknown for ISDN. Will we welcome basic-rate service in our homes? Is there a need for a second channel for data in most residences? Clearly, computer scientists, engineers, doctors, lawyers, and many others can benefit from easy access to computer databases and information. A digital link to the stock exchange computers may eliminate the need for a broker; individuals would have almost instant access to stock quotes, and could execute trades instantly. But do most residential users need a data channel? Only a minority of today's telephone customers take advantage of custom calling services, such as call waiting and call forwarding. Will ISDN's services be any more attractive to residential users?

When home computers were originally introduced over a decade ago, manufacturers touted the computer as an information organizer that would be widely used to store recipes, balance the checkbook, and help manage the household. Over time, many people decided that it was easier to keep recipes in a book or card file, and it was more convenient to carry a checkbook. ISDN advocates believe that we will use the data channel to send instructions from our office computer to our home, turning on the air conditioner, asking our VCR to record that television show we forgot to program, and transferring computer files rather than carrying a briefcase.

Considering the fact that less than half of American bank customers regularly use their automated teller machines, and even a smaller percentage understand how to program their home VCRs, there is certainly some doubt as to who will use all of this ISDN technology. Only time will tell whether users will find a need for, and be willing to pay for, ISDN functions at home.

ISDN will probably have to stand on its own merits in the United States. The FCC and PUC are not likely to let the local exchange carriers use existing telephone service revenues to subsidize ISDN. Either the carrier's shareholders or the initial ISDN customers will have to bear the cost of the ISDN implementation. Ironically, these initial customers will not reap the full benefits of ISDN services, because many of these services depend on both the called and calling party's use of ISDN-compatible equipment.

Clearly, ISDN can provide functional advantages to certain business users at a reasonable cost within existing technology. Portions of ISDN are already being implemented today for business users. However, the real potential of the home market is not yet understood, and a completely digital telephone network may never be realized.

Broadband ISDN

The basic-rate and primary-rate ISDN interfaces were once considered extremely high bandwidth interfaces. However, with improvements in transmission technology and the advent of fiber optic cables, much faster transmission rates are now possible. An even faster class of ISDN interface standards, referred to as *Broadband ISDN*, or *BISDN*, is currently being developed by the CCITT to handle transmission speeds of 150 Mbps and higher. When compared to this new BISDN, the basic-rate and primary-rate ISDN interfaces are sometimes called *Narrowband ISDN*. However, Narrowband ISDN still provides a higher effective bandwidth than that of today's existing analog telephone facilities.

BISDN is expected to transmit data over fiber optic cables to achieve its extremely high data rates. Of course, existing twisted pair wire local loops will need to be replaced with fiber optic cable if BISDN is to be fully implemented.

Though still in the planning stages, BISDN certainly shows promise. In fact, BISDN may be available to some users by the end of the twentieth century. The extremely high bandwidth of BISDN would permit digitized video signals to be transmitted, as well as digitized voice and data. BISDN would integrate our telephone and cable television networks into a single network delivering information to businesses and residences.

The business applications of BISDN would include inexpensive video conferencing. Digital video telephones would cost no more than a small television set today. Residential applications could revolutionize entertainment. Rather than going to the video store to rent a movie, a BISDN user would call the video store's computer, scan a catalog of available movies on the television screen, and make a selection. The rental fee would be automatically deducted from the user's bank account, and the movie would be transmitted to the home from the video store.

With BISDN, many office workers could effectively work at home, and could even attend meetings through video conferencing. Other work could be performed on their home computer and transferred to their boss, who might also be at home. The telephone would still exist for mundane voice conversations.

Compared to today's analog service, Narrowband ISDN simply adds a data channel and signaling, uses digital voice transmission, and provides additional services. BISDN, on the other hand, could actually revolutionize the way we communicate. For this reason, many people believe that BISDN will ''leapfrog'' Narrowband ISDN for residential use. Many feel that Narrowband ISDN will be used mainly by businesses—that most residential users will not be interested. BISDN, however, will provide such clear advantages to residential users that it will be hard to resist. Recognizing this possibility, many local exchange carriers are already wiring new housing developments with fiber optic local loops, to be ready for BISDN.

SUMMARY

As we near the end of the twentieth century, telecommunications and data communications are converging. Both customer premises equipment and transmission facilities are increasingly using digital technology. Digital PBXs are being used to integrate voice and data with digital phones. LANs and PBXs can be connected to packet switching networks, allowing communications among devices attached to any of the three. In addition, transmission of still images, using FAX, or moving images, using video, once performed only by analog transmission methods, can now be done digitally. Digital transmission of voice is possible by using a digitizing method known as pulse code modulation, or PCM. In PCM, an analog signal is typically converted to a 64 Kbps digital signal, using 8000 samples per second and eight bits per sample.

High-bandwidth digital transmission facilities are playing a major role in communications today. The T-1 standard, developed by A.T.&T., provides a 1.544 Mbps digital path now available from almost all of the common carriers. T-1 carrier can provide 24 channels, each able to carry 64 kbps of digitized voice or 56 kbps of data over two twisted pairs; analog transmission of 24 voice channels would require 24 pairs of wires.

Even with the added expense of repeaters and digital transmission equipment, T-1 is an economical alternative for users with high-volume communications traffic. There are several different methods for carrying signaling information using T-1 carrier. The T-1 channels can also be broken down into several lower-speed channels by submultiplexing. In addition, voice and data compression can further increase the effective bandwidth of T-1 circuits. Finally, there are higher-speed digital transmission facilities than T-1, such as T-1C and T-3, providing 48 and 672 channels, respectively.

The Integrated Services Digital Network, or ISDN, is an evolving set of standards for a digital network carrying both voice and data communications. The CCITT is leading the international standards development effort, specifying both interface standards for connecting to the public network and network services. ISDN provides different types of transmission paths, known as channels. The B-channel, or bearer channel, is a 64 kbps digital channel for digitized voice or data. The D-channel is a 16 kbps or 64 kbps digital channel used for signaling information, and sometimes for low-priority data packets. The A-channel is similar to today's analog voice circuits, and the C-channel provides a low-speed 16 kbps data channel for use with low-speed devices.

The basic-rate interface includes 2 B channels and 1 D channel, and is intended for residential or individual business users; this interface provides voice and data communications, as well as extensive signaling capability, for an individual user. The primary-rate interface contains 23 or 30 B channels and 1 D channel, and is aimed primarily at larger business users. The 23 B + D version is intended for use in North America and Japan, where the 1.544 Mbps T-1 carrier is already prevalent, and the 30 B + D version is intended for Europe, where 2.048 Mbps transmission equipment currently exists. The hybrid interface contains both an A-channel and a C-channel, and will provide analog phone users with some of the benefits of ISDN.

Equipment attached to an ISDN network is classified into two basic categories, known either as Terminal Equipment (TE) or Network Termination equipment (NT). In addition, several reference points are defined where various NT and TE devices are interconnected. Terminal equipment compatible with ISDN is known as TE1; terminal equipment not compatible with ISDN is known as TE2, and can be attached to an ISDN network using a Terminal Adapter, or TA. The R reference point is between the TE2 and TA, and the S reference point is between the TE1, or TA, and NT equipment. The NT equipment providing OSI layer 1 services, and terminating the network circuit on the customer's premises, is known as NT1; OSI layer 2 and 3 services, providing concentration and switching if needed, can be provided by NT2. Both the NT1 and NT2 functions can be combined in a single device, known as NT12. The point between the NT1 and NT2 (if an NT2 is used) is known as the T reference point; if no NT2 is used, then the S and T reference points coincide where the NT1 is directly connected to the Terminal Equipment. The U reference point occurs where the NT1 connects to the rest of the ISDN network.

PBXs, LANs, and packet switching networks can all take advantage of an ISDN network's digital transmission facilities. However, to further motivate users to support ISDN, special services are provided. Many of these services are based on the extra signaling information available in the D-channel. ISDN services can include call waiting, call forwarding, calling party identification, camp-on, and message notification.

It is clear that ISDN can provide functional advantages to certain business users at a reasonable cost within existing technology. Portions of ISDN are already being implemented today for business users, though the real potential of the residential market is not yet understood, and a completely digital telephone network may never be realized.

Broadband ISDN, or BISDN, an even faster class of interface standards using fiber optics, is currently being developed. BISDN, which can handle transmission speeds of 150 Mbps and higher, can also carry digitized video transmission, along with digitized voice and data. Because of its extremely high bandwidth and a projected availability to initial users by the end of the century, BISDN may leapfrog Narrowband ISDN for residential users. Many local exchange carriers are currently installing fiber optic local loops in new housing developments, anticipating future BISDN implementation.

TERMS FOR REVIEW

A-channel
Basic-rate interface
B-channel
Bearer channel
BISDN
BRI
Broadband ISDN
C-channel
Channel

Combined Network
  Termination 1 and 2
Common-channel signaling
D-channel
Digital phone
Digitized
DS-1
Facsimile
FAX

Frame
Framing bit
Hybrid interface
In-band signaling
Integrated Services Digital
  Network
Integrated voice/data
  terminal
ISDN

IVDT
Loading coil
Narrowband ISDN
Network Termination
  equipment
Network Termination 1
Network Termination 2
NT
NT1
NT2
NT12
Out-of-band signaling
PCM
PRI
Primary-rate interface

Pulse code modulation
R reference point
Robbed bit signaling
S reference point
Sample
Submultiplexing
Synchronization
T reference point
T-1 carrier
T-1 multiplexer
T-1C
T-1/D1
T-1/D2
T-1/D3
T-1/D4

T-1/D5
T-3
TA
TE
TE1
TE2
Terminal Adapter
Terminal Equipment
Terminal Equipment Type 1
Terminal Equipment Type 2
30 B + D
23 B + D
2B + D
U reference point
Video transmission

EXERCISES

10-1. What are some examples of digital customer premises equipment?

10-2. Explain how pulse code modulation can be used to digitize voice.

10-3. What is the total bandwidth of a T-1 circuit? What portion of this bandwidth is dedicated to framing and synchronization?

10-4. What are the advantages of using a T-1 circuit instead of 24 analog leased lines for PBX-to-PBX communications?

10-5. Why is submultiplexing sometimes used with T-1?

10-6. What are the names, functions, and bandwidths of the major ISDN channels?

10-7. What are the two major digital interfaces specified in the ISDN standards? What combination of channels are used in each? What are their intended functions?

10-8. Compare the different types of ISDN Terminal Equipment and their functions.

10-9. How do the functions of the various types of ISDN Network Termination equipment correspond to the lower layers of the OSI model?

10-10. Why is a service like caller identification possible in ISDN, but not in today's analog public network?

10-11. What is the major difference between Narrowband and Broadband ISDN? Why is fiber optics necessary for BISDN?

The Future of Data Communications

APPENDIX

THE BINARY NUMBER SYSTEM

In the binary number system, all numbers are represented using only zeroes and ones. Computers typically use the binary number system to represent information, because it is easy for computer hardware to represent an off/on, or 0/1 condition.

The binary number system is based on powers of two, while the more familiar decimal number system is based on powers of ten. There are many charts available for converting decimal numbers to binary numbers, and vice versa. However, they are crutches that most people can do without. Like multiplication tables, they are a useful learning tool, but no one wants to have to consult a multiplication table every time they want to multiply.

Fortunately, converting numbers between the binary number system and decimal number system is an easy task. We will first examine the decimal number system, and then the binary number system.

In the decimal number system, the digits 0, 1, 2, 3, 4, 5, 6, 7, 8, and 9 are used to represent all numbers. Each place or position in a number has a value that is a power of ten. The value of the first place is 1 or 10^0, the value of the second is 10 or 10^1, the value of the third is 100 or 10^2, the value of the fourth is 1000 or 10^3, and so on. For example, in the decimal number system, the number 5048 is really 5 times 1000, plus 0 times 100, plus 4 times 10, plus 8 times 1.

In the binary number system, numbers are represented in the same way, but powers of two are used for the places, and only a 0 or a 1 is used for each digit. Each place or position in a number has a value that is a power of two. The value of the first place is 1 or 2^0, the value of the second is 2 or 2^1, the value of the third is 4 or 2^2, the value of the fourth is 8 or 2^3, and so on. For example, in the binary number system, the number 1011 is 1 times 8, plus 0 times 4, plus 1 times 2, plus 1 times 1.

We will only consider binary numbers up to eight bits long to simplify our discussion, though the same principles are applicable for any size number. In an eight-bit binary number, the place values are as follows:

Digits								
Values	*128*	*64*	*32*	*16*	*8*	*4*	*2*	*1*
Powers	2^7	2^6	2^5	2^4	2^3	2^2	2^1	2^0

The eight-bit number 10010110 could be placed in these positions this way:

Digits	1	0	0	1	0	1	1	0
Values	*128*	*64*	*32*	*16*	*8*	*4*	*2*	*1*
Powers	2^7	2^6	2^5	2^4	2^3	2^2	2^1	2^0

This number could be converted to decimal simply by multiplying the digits by the values and adding the results:

$(1 \times 128) + (0 \times 64) + (0 \times 32) + (1 \times 16) + (0 \times 8) + (1 \times 4) + (1 \times 2) + (0 \times 1) =$
128   +   0   +   0   +   16   +   0   +   4   +   2   +   0   = 150

For another example, consider the binary number 11101101:

Digits	1	1	1	0	1	1	0	1
Values	*128*	*64*	*32*	*16*	*8*	*4*	*2*	*1*
Powers	2^7	2^6	2^5	2^4	2^3	2^2	2^1	2^0

This number could be converted to decimal simply by multiplying the digits by the values and adding the results:

$(1 \times 128) + (1 \times 64) + (1 \times 32) + (0 \times 16) + (1 \times 8) + (1 \times 4) + (0 \times 2) + (1 \times 1) =$
128   +   64   +   32   +   0   +   8   +   4   +   0   +   1   = 237

Using eight bits, the binary number system can represent decimal numbers from 0 to 255. 0 in decimal converts to eight zeroes in binary, and 255 converts to eight ones in binary. Anything larger will require more bits. Any binary number can be converted to a decimal number using the addition and multiplication technique shown above.

Converting decimal numbers to binary numbers requires only subtraction, and a simple decision: Is one number greater than or equal to another? For example, to convert the decimal number 185 to binary form, we must start at the left of our binary number form shown below:

Digits								
Values	*128*	*64*	*32*	*16*	*8*	*4*	*2*	*1*
Powers	2^7	2^6	2^5	2^4	2^3	2^2	2^1	2^0

Appendix

We then ask the question, "Is 185 greater than or equal to 128?", the value of the digit on the left of our form. The answer is yes, so we need 128 in the number 185, and we use a 1 for that digit, as shown below:

Digits	1							
Values	*128*	*64*	*32*	*16*	*8*	*4*	*2*	*1*
Powers	2^7	2^6	2^5	2^4	2^3	2^2	2^1	2^0

We then subtract 128 from 185, leaving us with 57. We now ask the question, "Is 57 greater than or equal to 64?", the value of the next digit. The answer is no, so we don't need 64 in the number 185, and we use a 0 for this digit, as shown below:

Digits	1	0						
Values	*128*	*64*	*32*	*16*	*8*	*4*	*2*	*1*
Powers	2^7	2^6	2^5	2^4	2^3	2^2	2^1	2^0

Since we didn't use 64, there is no subtraction necessary. We then ask the question, "Is 57 greater than or equal to 32?", the value of the next digit. The answer is yes, so we need 32 in the number 185, and we use a 1 for that digit, as shown below:

Digits	1	0	1					
Values	*128*	*64*	*32*	*16*	*8*	*4*	*2*	*1*
Powers	2^7	2^6	2^5	2^4	2^3	2^2	2^1	2^0

We then subtract 32 from 57, leaving us with 25. We now ask the question, "Is 25 greater than or equal to 16?", the value of the next digit. The answer is yes, so we need 16 in the number 185, and we use a 1 for this digit, as shown below:

Digits	1	0	1	1				
Values	*128*	*64*	*32*	*16*	*8*	*4*	*2*	*1*
Powers	2^7	2^6	2^5	2^4	2^3	2^2	2^1	2^0

We then subtract 16 from 25, leaving us with 9. We now ask the question, "Is 9 greater than or equal to 8?", the value of the next digit. The answer is yes, so we need 8 in the number 185, and we use a 1 for this digit, as shown below:

Digits	1	0	1	1	1			
Values	*128*	*64*	*32*	*16*	*8*	*4*	*2*	*1*
Powers	2^7	2^6	2^5	2^4	2^3	2^2	2^1	2^0

We then subtract 8 from 9, leaving us with 1. We now ask the question, "Is 1 greater than or equal to 4?", the value of the next digit. The answer is no, so we don't need 4 in the number 185, and we use a 0 for this digit, as shown below:

Digits	1	0	1	1	1	0		
Values	*128*	*64*	*32*	*16*	*8*	*4*	*2*	*1*
Powers	2^7	2^6	2^5	2^4	2^3	2^2	2^1	2^0

Since we didn't use 4, there is no subtraction necessary. We now ask the question, "Is 1 greater than or equal to 2?", the value of the next digit. The answer is no, so we don't need 2 in the number 185, and we use a 0 for this digit, as shown below:

Digits	1	0	1	1	1	0	0	
Values	*128*	*64*	*32*	*16*	*8*	*4*	*2*	*1*
Powers	2^7	2^6	2^5	2^4	2^3	2^2	2^1	2^0

Since we didn't use 2, there is no subtraction necessary. We now ask the question, "Is 1 greater than or equal to 1?", the value of the next digit. The answer is yes, so we need 1 in the number 185, and we use a 1 for this digit, as shown below:

Digits	1	0	1	1	1	0	0	1
Values	*128*	*64*	*32*	*16*	*8*	*4*	*2*	*1*
Powers	2^7	2^6	2^5	2^4	2^3	2^2	2^1	2^0

We then subtract 1 from 1, leaving us with 0, so we know we have accounted for all of the values in the number 185. If our result is not zero at this point, we know that we made an error in our calculation, or the number we chose is too large to be represented in eight bits (greater than the decimal number 255).

Based on our calculations, the binary number 10111001 is the equivalent of the decimal number 185. As a double check, let's convert it back to decimal:

$(1 \times 128) + (0 \times 64) + (1 \times 32) + (1 \times 16) + (1 \times 8) + (0 \times 4) + (0 \times 2) + (1 \times 1) =$
128   +   0   +   32   +   16   +   8   +   0   +   0   +   1   = 185

Converting between the binary and decimal number systems is a matter of following a simple set of rules. It allows us to easily convert between the decimal world we are familiar with, and the binary world of computers.

For those who prefer to use a chart rather than performing the simple calculations, a conversion chart is provided for the decimal numbers from 0 to 255.

Converting Between the Decimal and Binary Number Systems

Binary	Dec.	Binary	Dec.	Binary	Dec.	Binary	Dec.	Binary	Dec.
00000000	0	00110101	53	01101010	106	10011111	159	11010100	212
00000001	1	00110110	54	01101011	107	10100000	160	11010101	213
00000010	2	00110111	55	01101100	108	10100001	161	11010110	214
00000011	3	00111000	56	01101101	109	10100010	162	11010111	215
00000100	4	00111001	57	01101110	110	10100011	163	11011000	216
00000101	5	00111010	58	01101111	111	10100100	164	11011001	217
00000110	6	00111011	59	01110000	112	10100101	165	11011010	218
00000111	7	00111100	60	01110001	113	10100110	166	11011011	219
00001000	8	00111101	61	01110010	114	10100111	167	11011100	220
00001001	9	00111110	62	01110011	115	10101000	168	11011101	221
00001010	10	00111111	63	01110100	116	10101001	169	11011110	222
00001011	11	01000000	64	01110101	117	10101010	170	11011111	223
00001100	12	01000001	65	01110110	118	10101011	171	11100000	224
00001101	13	01000010	66	01110111	119	10101100	172	11100001	225
00001110	14	01000011	67	01111000	120	10101101	173	11100010	226
00001111	15	01000100	68	01111001	121	10101110	174	11100011	227
00010000	16	01000101	69	01111010	122	10101111	175	11100100	228
00010001	17	01000110	70	01111011	123	10110000	176	11100101	229
00010010	18	01000111	71	01111100	124	10110001	177	11100110	230
00010011	19	01001000	72	01111101	125	10110010	178	11100111	231
00010100	20	01001001	73	01111110	126	10110011	179	11101000	232
00010101	21	01001010	74	01111111	127	10110100	180	11101001	233
00010110	22	01001011	75	10000000	128	10110101	181	11101010	234
00010111	23	01001100	76	10000001	129	10110110	182	11101011	235
00011000	24	01001101	77	10000010	130	10110111	183	11101100	236
00011001	25	01001110	78	10000011	131	10111000	184	11101101	237
00011010	26	01001111	79	10000100	132	10111001	185	11101110	238
00011011	27	01010000	80	10000101	133	10111010	186	11101111	239
00011100	28	01010001	81	10000110	134	10111011	187	11110000	240
00011101	29	01010010	82	10000111	135	10111100	188	11110001	241
00011110	30	01010011	83	10001000	136	10111101	189	11110010	242
00011111	31	01010100	84	10001001	137	10111110	190	11110011	243
00100000	32	01010101	85	10001010	138	10111111	191	11110100	244
00100001	33	01010110	86	10001011	139	11000000	192	11110101	245
00100010	34	01010111	87	10001100	140	11000001	193	11110110	246
00100011	35	01011000	88	10001101	141	11000010	194	11110111	247
00100100	36	01011001	89	10001110	142	11000011	195	11111000	248
00100101	37	01011010	90	10001111	143	11000100	196	11111001	249
00100110	38	01011011	91	10010000	144	11000101	197	11111010	250
00100111	39	01011100	92	10010001	145	11000110	198	11111011	251
00101000	40	01011101	93	10010010	146	11000111	199	11111100	252
00101001	41	01011110	94	10010011	147	11001000	200	11111101	253
00101010	42	01011111	95	10010100	148	11001001	201	11111110	254
00101011	43	01100000	96	10010101	149	11001010	202	11111111	255
00101100	44	01100001	97	10010110	150	11001011	203		
00101101	45	01100010	98	10010111	151	11001100	204		
00101110	46	01100011	99	10011000	152	11001101	205		
00101111	47	01100100	100	10011001	153	11001110	206		
00110000	48	01100101	101	10011010	154	11001111	207		
00110001	49	01100110	102	10011011	155	11010000	208		
00110010	50	01100111	103	10011100	156	11010001	209		
00110011	51	01101000	104	10011101	157	11010010	210		
00110100	52	01101001	105	10011110	158	11010011	211		

GLOSSARY

Access method   Means used to allow local area network users to transmit data.

A-channel   The analog voice channel in ISDN.

Acknowledgment   Typically used in protocols, it is sent by the receiving device to the transmitter to confirm successful receipt of data.

ACK0   In BSC, the control character indicating an acknowledgment.

Active monitor   The station on a token ring network responsible for watching for the token, and for generating a new token if the token is lost.

ADCCP   *See* Advanced Data Communications Control Procedures.

Address   Typically used to identify different devices, either in a polling/selecting environment or in a local area network.

Address Field   The part of an SDLC frame containing the eight-bits representing the identity of the Secondary station.

Advanced Data Communications Control Procedures (ADCCP)   A bit-oriented ANSI protocol.

Algorithm   A set of instructions for performing a task.

AM   *See* Amplitude Modulation.

American National Standard Code for Information Interchange (ASCII) The ANSI seven-bit character code, with an eighth bit for parity checking.

American National Standards Institute (ANSI) An umbrella organization for all standards organizations in the United States. These organizations can submit standards to ANSI for acceptance as a national standard.

American Telephone & Telegraph (A.T.&T.) Now a long-distance company, researcher, and equipment manufacturer; formerly, the parent company of the Bell System, which also included many local phone companies.

Amplitude The strength of an electronic signal (in volts), or the volume of a tone (in decibels).

Amplitude modulation (AM) Transmission of information by varying the volume of a tone (the amplitude of a sine wave).

Amplitude shift keying (ASK) Another name for amplitude modulation.

Analog A signal that can vary infinitely over a given range, like voice.

Analog test equipment Devices used to diagnose voice-grade telephone circuits.

ANSI *See* American National Standards Institute.

Answer-only modem A type of modem that can only receive calls.

Application Layer Layer 7, the highest layer of the OSI model; it provides access to the network to the end user.

Application Program In SNA, a software program running on a Host Processor that communicates through an SNA network.

Applications software User programs running on a host computer, such as word processing programs, spreadsheets, and accounting programs.

Area code Three-digit code used in the public network to route calls to a particular geographical area.

ARPANET The packet switching network used to connect U.S. government computing facilities.

ARQ *See* Automatic Repeat Request.

ASCII *See* American National Standard Code for Information Interchange.

ASK Amplitude shift keying. *See* Amplitude modulation.

Asserted state The state of an RS-232-C control signal when it is ON, raised, or true.

Asymmetric keys An encryption technique where a different key is used to encrypt a message than is used to decrypt the message.

Asynchronous transmission   Method of data transmission requiring start and stop bits.

A.T.&T   *See* American Telephone & Telegraph.

A.T.&T. Premises Distribution System   A.T.&T's method for wiring office buildings with standard cable.

Attendant   Operator of a PBX console.

Automatic repeat request (ARQ)   An error control method where the receiving device detects an error in data transmission and asks for a retransmission of the block of data.

Availability   The ratio of uptime to the total of uptime and downtime.

Backoff   The length of time a device waits after a collision occurs before attempting retransmission.

Balanced transmission   A method of sending data requiring two wires, as in RS-422-A.

Bandwidth   The carrying capacity of a circuit, usually measured in bits per second for digital circuits, or Hertz for analog circuits.

Baseband transmission   Transmission of a data signal directly on a wire.

Basic service element (BSE)   A feature or service provided by the local exchange carrier to the public, as part of Open Network Architecture.

Basic-rate interface (BRI)   The preferred method for attachment to ISDN by individual users; it includes 2 B-channels, one for digitized voice and one for data, and 1 D-channel for signaling.

Baud rate   The number of possible signal changes in a second; sometimes equivalent to the bit per second rate, but not always.

Baudot code   One of the first character codes, it uses five bits to represent characters.

BCC   In BSC, a block check character used for error detection.

BCD   *See* Binary Coded Decimal.

B-channel   The bearer channel in ISDN, it carries 64 kbps of digitized voice or data.

Bearer channel   *See* B-channel.

Bell 103/113   A.T.&T.'s 300 bps frequency modulation method, now widely accepted as an industry standard.

Bell 212A   A.T.&T.'s 1200 bps dibit phase shift keying method, now widely accepted as an industry standard; it falls back to the Bell 103/113 300 bps frequency modulation method when communicating with Bell 103/113 modems.

Bell Communications Research   The research arm of the RBOCs formed after divestiture, also known as Bellcore.

Bell Labs   The research arm of A.T.& T.

Bell Operating Company (BOC)   Individual local exchange carrier, previously owned by A.T.& T. before divestiture.

Bell System   The name used to designate the combination of the Bell Operating Companies and A.T.&T.'s long-distance business before they were broken up by divestiture.

Bellcore   *See* Bell Communications Research.

BERT   *See* Bit error rate test.

Binary Coded Decimal (BCD)   An early character code used internally by computers to represent information.

Binary number system   A numeric system based on powers of two; therefore, all numbers are represented using only the digits 0 and 1.

Binary Synchronous Communications (BSC)   IBM's character or byte-oriented, half duplex, stop-and-wait ARQ protocol.

BISDN   *See* Broadband ISDN.

Bisync   *See* Binary Synchronous Communications.

Bit   A binary digit, either a 1 or a 0.

Bit error   A transmission error in which a 1 is received as a 0, or vice versa.

Bit error rate test (BERT)   An industry standard measure of reliability, it is the ratio of the number of bit errors detected to the total number of bits received.

Bit interleaving   A time division multiplexing method where each time slot contains a bit from each channel.

Bit-oriented protocol   A protocol using single bits for communicating control information.

Bits per second (bps)   A typical measurement of data speed, it is the number of bits transmitted (or received) in a second.

BLERT   *See* Block error rate test.

Block   A group of characters or bytes.

Block error rate test (BLERT)   An industry standard measure of reliability, it is the ratio of the number of block errors detected to the total number of blocks received.

BOC *See* Bell Operating Company.

Bps *See* Bits per second.

Branch port The low-speed port of a multiplexer, usually attached to the terminal or front end processor.

Breakout box Test equipment used to monitor the interface status, determine if a device is a DTE or DCE, modify interfaces, and test cables.

Break-up The divestiture of the Bell Operating Companies from A.T.& T.

BRI *See* Basic-rate interface.

Bridge A device used to connect two separate networks that use the same communications method.

Broadband ISDN (BISDN) A set of interface standards being developed by the CCITT for transmission of 150 (or more) Mbps.

Broadband transmission A transmission method where data is modulated on a carrier signal, such as a sine wave.

Broadcast message Data intended for multiple users, as on a multidrop circuit.

BSC *See* Binary Synchronous Communications.

BSE *See* Basic Service Elements.

Buffering Holding data temporarily, usually until it is properly sequenced, as in packet switching networks, or until another device is ready to receive it, as in front-end processors.

Bus network A network topology where all devices are connected to a single cable.

Busy signal A signal provided by the central office to the user indicating that the called party is already using the phone.

Busy token A pattern of bits used to indicate that another station is already using the token passing network.

Byte A group of bits, usually eight.

Byte interleaving A time division multiplexing method where each time slot contains a byte from each channel.

Byte-oriented protocol A protocol using entire bytes for communicating control information.

Call-back device Data security equipment used with dial-up modems, which calls back users to verify their location.

Carriage return A special character used to send a terminal's cursor or printer's head to the left margin.

Carrier Detect (CD) *See* Data Carrier Detect.

Carrier sense multiple access (CSMA) A collision avoidance contention method often used with local area networks, it requires the transmitting device to check if the network is free before transmitting.

Carrier sense multiple access/collision detection (CSMA/CD) A contention method often used with local area networks, it requires the transmitter to check if the network is free before transmitting, and continue monitoring to determine if there is a collision during transmission.

Carrier signal An electronic signal used to modulate data in broadband transmission; usually a sine wave.

Category I The RS-449 signals that require two wires, allowing for RS-422-A transmission.

Category II The RS-449 signals that require only a single wire and a common return, and use RS-423-A transmission.

Cathode ray tube (CRT) Another name for a terminal.

CC *See* Control codes.

C-channel The low-speed data channel in ISDN, carrying up to 16 kbps.

CCITT *See* Consultative Committee on International Telephone and Telegraph.

CD Carrier Detect. *See* Data Carrier Detect.

Central office The local exchange carrier's office, where the central office switch is located, which provides power, routing, and signaling functions for the user.

Central office switch The device in the central office that provides the power, routing, and signaling functions for the user.

Central office trunk A local loop between the central office and a PBX.

Central processing unit (CPU) Often used as another name for a host computer, it actually refers only to the heart of the host computer.

Centralized control A control method in which a single device runs a network.

Centrex Service with which the local exchange carrier handles both external and internal calls for a customer.

Channel Transmission path used in ISDN, available in various sizes.

Channel interface The high-speed port of a front end processor that connects directly to the host computer's high-speed input/output channel.

Channel service unit (CSU) The device terminating the common carrier's digital circuit on the customer's premises.

Character   A letter of the alphabet, number, punctuation mark, or a special key used by different terminals; also includes special codes used by devices to communicate.

Character code   Methods of representing characters, typically with ones and zeroes.

Character interleaving   Another name for byte interleaving.

Character-oriented protocol   Another name for byte-oriented protocol.

Chassis ground   The RS-232-C pin used to connect cable shields to the electrical ground.

Checksum   An error checking method where bits are added before and after transmission, and compared.

Cipher text   Data that has been encrypted for transmission.

Clear text   Data that is not encrypted.

Clear to Send (CTS)   The RS-232-C control signal generated by the DCE indicating that the DTE can transmit data.

Closed user group (CUG)   A security measure often used in packet switching networks, it restricts access to a certain set of users.

Cluster Controller   Device used in SNA to allow several Workstations a single point of access to the network.

CNM   *See* Communications Network Management.

Coax   *See* Coaxial cable.

Coaxial cable   A transmission medium consisting of a single wire in the center, surrounded by a core of insulating material with an outer conductive wrapping, covered by an insulating sheath.

Code conversion   To translate from one character code to another, thereby allowing certain incompatible devices to communicate.

Collect calls   A packet switching and public network service where call costs are billed to the called party.

Collision   The result of two devices transmitting at the same time, usually causing data to be lost.

Collision avoidance   A contention technique in which devices check if the network is free before transmitting.

Collision detection   A contention technique in which devices check whether collisions occur during transmission.

Combined Network Termination 1 and 2 (NT12)   ISDN equipment combining the Network Termination 1 and Network Termination 2 functions.

Common carrier Company providing voice and/or data communications transmission services to the general public.

Common return A single wire serving as a shared path for returning electrical signals, as in RS-423-A transmission.

Common-channel signaling A method in which a separate channel is used for signaling bits.

Communications architecture A manufacturer's strategy for connecting its host computers, terminals, and communications equipment; it defines the elements necessary for data communications between devices.

Communications Controller In SNA, a device responsible for routing data through a network and controlling the communications links.

Communications Controller Node An SNA node containing a Communications Controller.

Communications line control Rules for sharing a communications path.

Communications Network Management (CNM) A series of IBM tools for managing networks.

Communications server A device that provides local area network users access to resources located off the network, and vice versa, through modems or other communications circuits.

Concentrator Another name for a port sharing device.

Conditioned line A type of leased line suitable for high-speed data transmission, requiring extra hardware and available at an added cost.

Consultative Committee on International Telephone and Telegraph (CCITT) An international telecommunications standards organization, whose members include regulating bodies from member countries, representatives from leading companies, and representatives from other organizations.

Contention Method used to share a communications path.

Continuous ARQ An automatic repeat request method in which the transmitter continues sending data blocks without waiting for acknowledgment messages, until a set number of unacknowledged blocks have been sent, or a negative acknowledgment is received.

Control character Character used in character codes to perform special functions.

Control codes (CC) ASCII characters used to convey control information in protocols.

Control Field The part of an SDLC frame containing control information.

Control information In a protocol, the data sent to perform polling, selecting, ARQ, and error checking, as well as to convey status information to devices.

Control key A specific key on a terminal that will cause a special character to be generated, when struck in conjunction with another key on the terminal.

Control signal In RS-232-C and RS-449, the pins indicating the status of a given connection.

Control station In BSC, the single station that can communicate with all the other (Tributary) stations.

Corporation for Open Systems (COS) A non profit corporation consisting of major host computer manufacturers, whose purpose is to facilitate the implementation of OSI.

COS *See* Corporation for Open Systems.

CPE *See* Customer-premises equipment.

CPU *See* Central processing unit.

CRC *See* Cyclical redundancy check.

Crossover Function performed by DCEs in a communications circuit, taking the transmitted data from one DTE and delivering it to the other DTE for reception.

CRT *See* Cathode ray tube.

CSMA *See* Carrier sense multiple access.

CSMA/CD *See* Carrier sense multiple access/collision detection.

CSU *See* Channel service unit.

CTS *See* Clear to Send.

CUG *See* Closed user group.

Customer-premises equipment (CPE) Devices used at the customer site, either leased or owned.

CX *See* Data Carrier Detect.

Cycle A full repetition of a sine wave, including one peak and one valley.

Cycles per second A measure of frequency, the number of cycles of a sine wave in a second.

Cyclical parity A parity checking method designed to detect two sequential bit errors in a byte.

Cyclical redundancy check (CRC) A sophisticated version of a checksum, it uses a complex mathematical formula combining division and addition to detect errors.

Dash In Morse code, a long beep used to send characters.

Data Carrier Detect (DCD) The RS-232-C control signal generated by the DCE indicating that the DTE should expect to receive data at any time.

Data circuit-terminating equipment (DCE) The type of interface typically found on modems and some multiplexers.

Data communications The exchange of digital information between two devices using an electronic transmission system.

Data compression devices Equipment that allows more data to be transmitted per second than the speed of the link would normally allow.

Data conversion Protocol and/or code conversion.

Data Encryption Algorithm (DEA) The name used by ANSI for the Data Encryption Standard.

Data Encryption Standard (DES) A standard, general-purpose encryption algorithm using secret keys developed by IBM and later adopted by the National Bureau of Standards.

Data Link Layer Layer 2 of the OSI model, it is responsible for ensuring error-free, reliable transmission of data.

Data rate The speed at which bits are transmitted and received, usually measured in bits per second, or bps.

Data Rate Select (DRS) The RS-232-C control signal used by devices to change each other's speed.

Data Set Ready (DSR) The RS-232-C control signal generated by the DCE to indicate it is powered on and is ready to begin communications.

Data terminal equipment (DTE) The type of interface usually found on terminals, host computers, and printers.

Data Terminal Ready (DTR) The RS-232-C control signal generated by the DTE to indicate it is powered on, on-line, and ready to begin communications.

Data transport network A general term describing a system that carries data communications, like local area networks and packet switching networks.

Dataphone Digital Service (DDS) A.T.&T.'s four-wire, digital data communications service operating at speeds ranging from 2400 bps to 64 kbps.

Datascope A type of data communications test equipment that provides all the functions of a breakout box, and also provides a display screen for monitoring data and analyzing protocols; it can also trap events and sound alarms, and can be programmed for complex simulations.

DB9 A 9-pin connector, available in male and female versions, defined in ISO standard 4902 and in the RS-449 standard, and used with the secondary channel of the RS-449 interface.

DB25 A 25-pin connector, available in male and female versions, defined in ISO standard 2110, and often used with the RS-232-C interface.

DB37 A 37-pin connector, available in male and female versions, defined in ISO standard 4902 and in the RS-449 standard, and used with the primary channel of the RS-449 interface.

DCD *See* Data Carrier Detect.

DCE *See* Data circuit-terminating equipment.

D-channel In ISDN, the signaling channel, carrying 16 kbps or 64 kbps, depending on circuit type.

DDD network *See* Direct distance dial network.

DDS *See* Dataphone Digital Service.

DEA *See* Data Encryption Algorithm.

Decoder circuit The part of a modem's circuitry that translates incoming square waves to an internal representation of ones and zeroes.

Decryption The decoding, or descrambling, of received data.

Default A term often used to describe a customer's standard long-distance carrier.

Demodulation Converting analog signals back to digital form.

Demodulator circuit The part of a modem's circuitry that converts analog signals back to digital form.

DES *See* Data Encryption Standard.

Destination node In the OSI model, the host computers at each end of a connection, often used to describe the transmitting and receiving computers that implement the higher layers; in a packet switching network, the node attached to the DTE that is receiving the data.

Dial tone A signal provided by the central office to the user indicating it is ready to accept digits.

Dial-up A telephone circuit connection that requires the user to place a new call each time, allowing destination flexibility.

Dibit modulation A technique for modulating two bits for every baud or signal change.

DID trunk *See* Direct inward dial trunk.

Digital A way of representing information using ones and zeroes.

Digital circuit   Special lines provided by the common carriers that are suitable for transmitting data directly in square wave form without modulation.

Digital PBX   Computer that treats telephones and trunks as specialized input and output devices; voice is either digitized in the phone or at the PBX, and voice as well as data communications can be switched.

Digital phone   A device that digitizes voice, and is attached to either a digital PBX or an ISDN-type public network.

Digital service unit (DSU)   A device connected between the user's DTE and the common carrier's digital circuits, which are typically terminated by a channel service unit.

Digital signature   A method of verifying message authenticity or sender identification by encrypting with a secret key and decrypting with a public key.

Digital transmission   Sending data in square-wave form rather than by using modulation over analog circuits.

Digitize   To convert voice to ones and zeroes, or digital form.

Direct distance dial (DDD) network   Another name for the public network.

Direct inward dial (DID) trunk   A local loop between the central office and a PBX allowing for automatic call routing, where the central office signals the PBX to indicate the called party's extension.

Display station   Another name for a terminal.

Distributed control   A design for spreading the responsibility of running a network throughout the attached devices, as in some local area networks.

Distributed Processor   In SNA, a device similar to a Host Processor, though more limited in function.

Divestiture   The breakup of the Bell System, whereby A.T.&T. lost its local phone companies, but kept its long-distance business, Bell Labs, and Western Electric.

Domain   In SNA, a System Services Control Point and all the devices it controls.

Dot   In Morse code, a short beep used to send characters.

Double encrypted   When a message is encrypted with the sender's secret key and the receiver's public key, and is decrypted with the sender's public key and the receiver's secret key, to provide both data confidentiality and authenticity.

Downlink   The satellite dish receiving information from the satellite.

Downtime   The time when a system or network is unavailable.

Driver circuit The part of a modem's circuitry that translates the modem's internal representation of ones and zeroes to square waves at the appropriate voltage levels.

DRS *See* Data Rate Select.

DS-1 The standard specifying the electrical characteristics for 1.544-Mbps transmission over four wires, as in T-1 transmission.

DSR *See* Data Set Ready.

DSU *See* Digital service unit.

DTE *See* Data terminal equipment.

DTMF *See* Dual-tone multifrequency dialing.

DTMF register Equipment that can recognize DTMF digits.

DTR *See* Data Terminal Ready.

Dual-tone multifrequency (DTMF) dialing Also known as touch-tone, a dialing method using two simultaneous tones of different pitches to represent digits.

Dumb modem Modem that performs only modulation and demodulation, but is not able to dial calls; the user needs a separate phone to dial the calls, or a PBX can automate the process.

Dumb terminal A terminal that receives data from a host computer and displays it on its screen, but is unable to change or modify the data; similarly, any data typed into the keyboard is sent directly to the host computer without major modifications.

EBCD *See* Extended Binary Coded Decimal.

EBCDIC *See* Extended Binary Coded Decimal Interchange Code.

Echo canceller Device used to remove echoes from conversations on voice-grade lines by actually subtracting the echo before it reaches the user.

Echo checking An error detection method in which the receiver repeats everything received to the transmitting device.

Echo suppressor Device used on voice-grade lines to prevent echoes by allowing transmission in only one direction at a time, in a half duplex fashion.

Echo testing Another name for loopback testing.

ECSA *See* Exchange Carriers Standards Association.

EIA *See* Electronic Industries Association.

800 number Another name for a toll free number.

Electronic Industries Association (EIA)   A standards organization representing many manufacturers in the U.S. electronics industry.

Encryption   Scrambling or coding data for transmission.

Encryption device   Equipment that scrambles or codes data for transmission.

End office   Another name for a central office.

End User   In SNA, the parties on the end of each LU-LU session, including Application Programs and people at Workstations.

Enhanced service provider (ESP)   In Open Network Architecture, a company that delivers a special function or service to the customer through the public network.

ENQ   In BSC, the control character used as an enquiry.

Enquiry   In a protocol, when a device asks permission to send data.

EOT   In BSC, the control character signifying the End of Transmission.

Equal access   Ability to choose a default long-distance carrier and still access all other long-distance carriers by using a simple dialing method.

Error detection   Determining that one or more bits changed from a 1 to a 0, or vice versa, during transmission.

Error detection and correction   Determining which bits changed from a 1 to a 0, or vice versa, during transmission, and changing the bits back to their original form.

Error detection with flagging   Determining that one or more bits changed from a 1 to a 0, or vice versa, during transmission, and notifying the user of the error.

Error detection with a request for retransmission   Determining that one or more bits changed from a 1 to a 0, or vice versa, during transmission, and asking that the block of data be repeated.

ESP   *See* Enhanced service provider.

Ethernet   The CSMA/CD bus local area network originally used by Xerox, DEC, and Intel, and now by many other vendors as well.

ETX   In BSC, the control character signifying the end of actual user data.

Even parity   An error detection method requiring an even number of ones in each byte.

Exchange Carriers Standards Association (ECSA)   A standards organization consisting of telephone equipment manufacturing companies, formed after the A.T.& T. divestiture to continue work on standards previously developed by the Bell System.

Expert system   A type of artificial intelligence computer software tool often used in network management to help isolate and diagnose problems.

Extended ASCII   A version of the ASCII character code providing eight data bits, allowing for graphics or foreign language characters, but at the expense of the parity bit.

Extended Binary Coded Decimal (EBCD)   The predecessor of the Extended Binary Coded Decimal Interchange Code.

Extended Binary Coded Decimal Interchange Code (EBCDIC)   An eight-bit character code developed by IBM.

External PAD   A PAD located on the user's premises, outside a packet switching network.

External Transmit Clock (XTC)   The RS-232-C Timing Signal generated by a DTE that times its own data transmission.

Facsimile (FAX)   A method of sending still images, like a printed page, over telephone lines.

False state   The state of an RS-232-C control signal when it is OFF or lowered.

FAX   *See* Facsimile.

FCC   *See* Federal Communications Commission.

FCS   *See* Frame Check Sequence Field.

FDDI   *See* Fiber Distributed Data Interface.

FDM   *See* Frequency division multiplexing.

FE   *See* Format effectors.

FEC   *See* Forward error correction.

Federal Communications Commission (FCC)   The body regulating all interstate communications in the United States.

Federal Information Processing Standards (FIPS)   A set of specifications that must be met to supply the U.S. government with computing and data communications equipment.

FEP   *See* Front end processor.

Fiber Distributed Data Interface (FDDI)   A high-speed local area network, using fiber optic cable to form an inner and outer token ring suitable for mainframe computer communications and other applications.

Fiber optic cable   A high-bandwidth transmission medium allowing data to be transmitted by shining a light through a special glass fiber.

Figures   A special character in the Baudot character code indicating that future transmission will be from the Upper Case set of characters.

File server A shared storage device for local area network users, typically in the form of a personal computer with a high-volume disk, attached to the network.

FIPS *See* Federal Information Processing Standards.

Firmware encryption An encryption method in which software containing the algorithm, or the keys, can be stored on preprogrammed chips in an encryption device.

Flag In SDLC, the pattern of eight bits beginning each frame.

Flow control negotiation A packet switching service allowing DTEs to specify the size of the packet and other parameters.

FM *See* Frequency modulation.

Foreign exchange A voice communications service offered by common carriers for business users that want phone numbers in areas other than their actual location.

Format effectors (FE) The ASCII control characters that perform special functions on printers and terminals.

Forward error correction (FEC) Another name for error detection and correction.

Four-wire communications Communicating over two pairs of wires; this term is often incorrectly used as a synonym for full duplex; full duplex communications no longer require four wires.

Frame A block of data sent using a protocol, like BSC or SDLC, or a group of bits representing data from many channels, as in T-1 transmission.

Frame Check Sequence (FCS) field In SDLC, the part of the frame containing the CRC error checking bits.

Frame ground Ahother name for chassis ground.

Frame Level The second level of the CCITT X.25 standard, it conforms to the CCITT LAP-B Protocol.

Framing bit In T-1 transmission, a bit used for synchronization, and sometimes for error checking.

Free token A pattern of bits on a token passing network, indicating that the network is available for use.

Frequency The pitch of a tone, or the number of cycles per second of a sine wave.

Frequency division A local area network contention method based on the frequency division multiplexing technique.

Frequency division multiplexing (FDM)   A multiplexing method in which devices continually share the bandwidth of the link by dividing the communications circuit into many separate frequencies or channels.

Frequency modulation (FM)   Transmission of information by varying the pitch of a tone (the frequency of a sine wave).

Frequency shift keying (FSK)   Another name for frequency modulation.

Front end   Another name for a front end processor.

Front end port   Another name for the line interfaces of a front end processor.

Front end processor (FEP)   A device acting as a communications assistant for the host computer, handling all communications with terminals and other devices, allowing the host computer to concentrate on calculations.

FSK   Frequency shift keying. *See* Frequency modulation.

Full duplex communications   A simultaneous, two-way communications path.

Gateway   A device used to connect two separate networks that use different communications methods.

GND   Ground. *See* Chassis ground.

Go-back-N continuous ARQ   A type of automatic repeat request where transmission continues until too many frames are unacknowledged, or until a negative acknowledgment is received; the frame in error, and all succeeding frames, must be retransmitted.

Half duplex communications   An alternating transmission path, two ways, but only one direction at a time.

Hamming code   A method devised by Richard Hamming for detecting a single bit error in a byte and correcting it with 100% accuracy.

Handshaking   The interaction of control signals between devices.

Hardware encryption   Encryption and decryption of data using a separate device; the algorithm is changed by purchasing a new device.

HDLC   *See* High-level Data Link Control.

Header   In BSC, the information in a user data frame required for addressing purposes.

Hertz   Another name for cycles per second.

High-usage intertoll trunk   Trunk connecting toll offices that can carry many conversations simultaneously.

Higher layers   Layers 4 though 7 of the OSI model (Transport, Session, Presentation, and Application Layers).

High-level Data Link Control (HDLC)   The ISO bit-oriented protocol, similar to SDLC, but with some additional features.

Historical logging   A security method providing a complete recording of all data passed through a particular device.

Hop   Intermediary step in terrestrial microwave transmission that requires repeaters because of distance limitations or blockages in the line of sight.

Host computer   The heart of a data communications network, it can perform numerical calculations, store and retrieve data, and perform a variety of tasks known as applications.

Host Node   In SNA, a node containing a Host Processor.

Host Processor   The SNA term for a host computer.

Howler signal   The signal sent by the central office to the user to indicate the phone has been left off the hook.

Hybrid interface   An ISDN interface which combines the A-channel and C-channel, providing a user with analog voice and low-speed data, along with access to some of the ISDN services.

Hz   Hertz. *See* Cycles per second.

IBM   International Business Machines Corporation.

IBM Cabling System   IBM's method for wiring office buildings with standard cable.

IBM PC Network   An IBM local area network available in baseband and broadband CSMA/CD versions.

IBM Token Ring Network   An IBM local area network using token passing on a baseband, star-wired ring, similar to the IEEE 802.5 standard.

IEC   *See* Interexchange carrier.

IEEE   *See* Institute of Electrical and Electronics Engineers.

IEEE 802   An IEEE local area network standards committee, made up of several subcommittees.

IEEE 802.1   A standard providing an overview of local area networks, methods for connecting networks, and systems management.

IEEE 802.2   A Logical Link Control standard for local area networks.

IEEE 802.3   A CSMA/CD bus Medium Access Control standard for local area networks.

IEEE 802.4   A token bus Medium Access Control standard for local area networks.

IEEE 802.5   A token ring Medium Access Control standard for local area networks.

IEEE 802.6   A metropolitan area network Medium Access Control standard for local area networks.

IEEE 802.7   An advisory subcommittee on using broadband transmission in local area networks.

IEEE 802.8   An advisory subcommittee on using fiber optics in local area networks.

IEEE 802.9   An advisory subcommittee on integrating voice and data in local area networks.

I-Frame   *See* Information Format Frame.

In-band signaling   Interspersing signaling bits with user data, instead of transmission of signaling on a separate channel.

Incoming calls only   A packet switching network service allowing DTEs to accept calls, but not place them.

Independent Telephone Company (ITC)   Local exchange carriers not formerly controlled by A.T.&T. before divestiture.

Information Field   In SDLC, the part of the Information Frame containing user data.

Information Format Frame (I-Frame)   In SDLC, the type of frame used to send and receive user data.

Information separators (IS)   In ASCII, the control characters used by host computers in storing and retrieving data.

Information Systems Network (ISN)   A.T.&T.'s combination of local area network and packet switching network transmission methods to provide connections to a wide variety of devices.

Input/output channel   The high-speed port of a host computer, usually connected to a front end processor.

Institute of Electrical and Electronics Engineers (IEEE)   A professional organization of engineers, consisting of specialized societies whose committees prepare standards in their area of specialty.

Integrated Services Digital Network (ISDN)   An evolving set of standards for a digital network carrying both voice and data communications.

Integrated voice/data terminal (IVDT)   A device, usually attached to a PBX, combining the capabilities of a digital phone with those of a terminal.

Intelligent terminal   A programmable smart terminal.

Interexchange carrier (IEC)   Long distance companies.

Interexchange circuit (IXC)   Another name for an intertoll trunk, as well as the link connecting nodes in a packet switching network.

Interface   The point at which one device connects to another.

Inter-LATA call   A call between two local access transport areas, also known as a long-distance call.

Intermediate node   The device between two communicating host computers which implements the lower layers of the OSI model.

Internal PAD   A PAD located inside a packet switching node.

International Baudot   A version of the Baudot code with a sixth bit added for parity checking.

International Standards Organization (ISO)   A standards organization in which each member country is represented by its own national standards organization.

Internetworking   Connecting two or more separate networks.

Interoffice trunk (IOT)   A communications circuit connecting two central offices in a local area.

Intertoll trunk   A communications circuit connecting two toll offices.

Inverse multiplexer   A device used to combine the bandwidth of two or more communications circuits to meet high-bandwidth requirements.

Inward WATS trunk   Another name for a toll-free number.

IOT   *See* Interoffice trunk.

IS   *See* Information separators.

ISDN   *See* Integrated Services Digital Network.

ISN   *See* Information Systems Network.

ISO   *See* International Standards Organization.

ISO Standard 2110   A standard describing the DB25 connectors.

ISO Standard 4902   A standard describing the DB37 and DB9 connectors.

ITC   *See* Independent Telephone Company.

IVDT   *See* Integrated voice/data terminal.

IXC   *See* Interexchange circuit.

Key   A specific set of codes used by an encryption algorithm to encode data, and by a decryption algorithm to decode data.

Key system A customer-premises equipment solution to small business tele-communications needs; it eliminates the inefficiencies of Centrex, but is smaller and less sophisticated than a PBX.

Keyboard The part of a terminal where data is entered by the user.

LAN *See* Local area network.

LAP-B *See* Link Access Procedure—Balanced.

LATA *See* Local access and transport area.

Layer Division according to function as found in the OSI model; *see* also Application Layer, Presentation Layer, Session Layer, Transport Layer, Network Layer, Data Link Layer, and Physical Layer.

Leased line Circuit rented from the common carriers for a flat monthly fee, with no usage charge per call.

Least-cost routing A PBX system feature that chooses the least expensive trunk for a given call at a particular time of day.

LEC *See* Local exchange carrier.

LED *See* Light-emitting diode.

Letters A special character in the Baudot character code indicating that future transmission will be from the Lower Case set of characters.

Light-emitting diode (LED) A small light bulb, about an eighth of an inch in diameter, typically found on a breakout box.

Limited-distance modem Another name for a short-haul modem.

Line discipline Another name for a protocol.

Line feed A special character used to send a terminal's cursor or printer's head to the next line.

Line interface The low-speed port on a front end processor that is typically attached to terminals.

Line of sight The requirement that in terrestrial microwave transmission, there be no obstructions between two dish antennas.

Line splitter A device that allows many terminals to share one front end port, and is located remotely from the front end processor.

Link In SNA, the communications circuit connecting Nodes.

Link Access Procedure—Balanced (LAP-B) The CCITT bit-oriented protocol similar to SDLC.

Link level protocol A set of rules precisely defining methods for communicating over a communications circuit, or link.

LLC *See* Logical Link Control.

Loading coil Device used in some analog telephone circuits to improve voice quality at longer distances.

Local access and transport area (LATA) A geographical region where the local phone company provides the user with entry, or access, to the public network, and carries or transports calls.

Local analog loopback test A modem diagnostic technique that can be performed with a modem, a cable, and a terminal.

Local area network (LAN) A privately owned data communications system that provides reliable high-speed, switched connections between devices in a single building, campus, or complex.

Local exchange Another name for the central office.

Local exchange carrier (LEC) Another name for the local phone company that provides service inside the LATA.

Local loop The pair of wires that runs from the central office into our home or business.

Logical Link Control (LLC) The IEEE 802.2 subcommittee standard relating to local area network functions like error checking and reliability.

Logical Unit (LU) In SNA, the Network Addressable Unit that is the End User's access point to the network.

Long-distance call Another name for an inter-LATA call.

Loopback plug A special connector used to perform echo testing with an asynchronous dumb terminal.

Loopback testing A diagnostic technique where transmitted data is returned to the sender for comparison with the original message.

Low The state of an RS-232-C control signal when it is off or false.

Lower Case The portion of the Baudot character code used for the letters of the alphabet.

Lower layers Layers 1 through 3 of the OSI model (Physical, Data Link, and Network Layers).

LU *See* Logical Unit.

MAC *See* Medium Access Control.

Mainframe Host computer usually serving a large organization.

MAN *See* Metropolitan area network.

Manufacturing Automation Protocol (MAP) A user-defined networking standard originally developed by General Motors.

MAP   *See* Manufacturing Automation Protocol.

Mark   In RS-232-C, transmission of a 1, using an electrical signal between -3 and -15 volts.

Mark parity   An error detection method where the parity bit is always a 1.

Mbps   Millions of bits per second.

Mean time between failures (MTBF)   The average time between network failures, or uptime.

Mean time to repair (MTTR)   The average time required to diagnose and correct a problem, or downtime.

Medium Access Control (MAC)   A group of IEEE standards relating to local area network access methods, describing how devices share time on a network.

Mesh network   A network topology where each device is connected by a cable to every other device in the network.

Metropolitan area network (MAN)   The IEEE 802.6 standard describing Medium Access Control for networks spanning a city.

MFJ   *See* Modified Final Judgment.

Microcomputer   Host computer usually serving only a single user.

MI/MIC lead   *See* Mode indicator leads.

Minicomputer   Host computer usually serving a group of users, such as a department or a division.

Mode indicator (MI/MIC) lead   A pair of wires connected to a dumb modem; when closed by a PBX, they cause the modem to begin communicating with a remote modem.

Modem   A device that performs modulation and demodulation, allowing data communications to occur in analog form over telephone circuits.

Modified Final Judgment (MFJ)   The edict requiring A.T.&T. to divest itself of the Bell Operating Companies.

Modulation   Converting digital signals to analog form for transmission.

Modulator circuit   The part of a modem's circuitry that performs modulation.

Morse code   A character code used in telegraph transmission, where long and short tones are used to represent characters.

MTBF   *See* Mean time between failures.

MTTR   *See* Mean time to repair.

Multidrop   A configuration where several terminals are directly attached to, and share, a single communications line leading to a single front end or host computer port.

Multiplexer (Mux)   A device used to allow a single communications circuit to take the place of several parallel ones; often used to allow several remotely located terminals to communicate with several front end processor ports over a single circuit.

Multispeed   A capability found in many modems allowing them to communicate at different speeds.

Mux   *See* Multiplexer.

NAK   In BSC, the control character signifying a negative acknowledgment.

Narrowband ISDN   The ISDN standard currently being implemented, including the basic-rate, primary-rate, and hybrid interfaces; *See* Integrated Services Digital Network.

National Bureau of Standards (NBS)   The federal standards organization in the United States, it produces the Federal Information Processing Standards.

National Electrical Code   A widely used standard for electric wiring and safety practices.

National Security Agency (NSA)   A federal agency that has adopted the Data Encryption Standard for protecting sensitive, but not classified, information.

NAU   *See* Network Addressable Unit.

NBS   *See* National Bureau of Standards.

Netview   IBM's host computer-based network management software.

Netview/PC   IBM's personal-computer based network management software that allows any device conforming to IBM's standard set of protocols to transmit network management information to Netview.

Network   A group of interconnected, communicating devices.

Network Addressable Unit (NAU)   In SNA, device with unique address to which data is routed.

Network control   The network management function, acting as the network "boss", allowing for the activation and deactivation of network components and features.

Network Layer   Layer 3 of the OSI model, it is responsible for setting up the appropriate routing of messages throughout a network.

Network management   Ensuring consistent reliability and availability of a network, as well as timely transmission and routing of data; it can be performed by dedicated devices, by host computers, by people, or by some combination of all of these.

Network monitoring   The network management function, acting as the network "watchdog," that constantly checks on the network, and reports on any problems.

Network statistical reporting   The network management function, acting as the network "statistician", that pinpoints which parts of a network are being utilized, and how often.

Network Termination (NT) equipment   In ISDN, equipment providing functions similar to those found in the lower layers of the OSI model.

Network Termination 1 (NT1)   In ISDN, the equipment providing only OSI Layer 1 (Physical Layer) functions, including the electrical and physical termination of the network on the customer's premises.

Network Termination 2 (NT2)   In ISDN, the equipment providing OSI Layers 2 and 3 (Data Link and Network Layer) functions, including concentration and switching, if needed.

Network troubleshooting   The network management function, acting as the network "diagnostician," that assists in isolating and diagnosing problems.

Node   In SNA, the component or device interconnected by the SNA network; in a packet switching network, the device that switches and routes calls at each location.

NSA   *See* National Security Agency.

NT   *See* Network Termination equipment.

NT1   *See* Network Termination 1.

NT2   *See* Network Termination 2.

NT12   *See* Combined Network Termination 1 and 2.

Numbering   In a packet switching network, the method of tracking the proper sequence of packets.

Odd parity   An error detection method requiring an odd number of ones in each byte.

OFF   The state of an RS-232-C control signal when it is false or low.

Off-hook   The status of a phone that has been picked up; also the signal sent by the user to the central office when the phone is picked up.

Office code   The three-digit prefix that designates the destination central office.

ON   The state of an RS-232-C control signal when it is asserted, raised, or true.

On-hook The status of a phone that has been hung up; also the signal sent by the user to the central office when the phone is hung up.

ONA *See* Open Network Architecture.

Open Network Architecture (ONA) The post-divestiture FCC requirement that all network services be divided into basic service elements, and be made available separately to enhanced service providers.

Open Systems Interconnection (OSI) model The International Standards Organization's set of standards that breaks down the task of computer communications into seven independent layers, each with its own tasks; *see* Lower layers, Higher layers.

Operator The person running the console of a PBX.

Originate-only modem A type of modem that can only place calls.

Originate/answer modem A type of modem that can place calls and answer calls.

OSI model *See* Open Systems Interconnection model.

Outgoing calls only A term used to describe a packet switching network service that allows DTEs to place calls, but not accept them.

Out-of-band signaling A method of sending signaling bits on a separate channel, rather than interspersed with the data.

Outward WATS trunk A type of PBX trunk that connects to a discounted long-distance service.

Overhead Non-data bits or characters necessary for transmission, error detection, or for use by protocols.

Packet Block of data, including addressing, routing, and numbering information.

Packet assembler disassembler (PAD) A device used to connect a packet switching network with equipment that does not perform packet formatting.

Packet Level In packet switching networks, the X.25 level providing for network level addressing and call connection.

Packet switching network (PSN) Network providing a switched service, where data is sent in packets through nodes over various routes, and is recombined at its destination in the proper sequence.

Packetized Describing data which is divided into packets.

PAD *See* Packet assembler disassembler.

Parallel transmission A method of transmission where all the bits in a byte are sent at once on separate wires.

Parallel/serial conversion Changing data from parallel to serial form, and vice versa.

Parallel/serial converter A device that changes data from parallel to serial form, and vice versa.

Parity bit A bit reserved for error detection in the parity checking method.

Parity checking A method of error detection in which a single bit is added by the transmitter, and checked by the receiver, to determine if errors occurred; *see* Even parity, Mark parity, Odd parity, and Space parity.

Password The most common form of security, it requires the user to enter a secret set of characters to access information or systems.

PBX *See* Private branch exchange.

PCM *See* Pulse code modulation.

Peer level In the OSI model, the corresponding layers on two communicating host computers; for example, the Network Layers on each computer.

Period The length of time of a complete cycle of a sine wave.

Peripheral Node In SNA, a single Workstation, or a Cluster Controller with several Workstations.

Personal computer Host computer usually serving only a single user.

Personal identification number (PIN) The password used with an automated teller machine.

P/F bit The bit in the SDLC control frame that can be used for polling by the Primary station, or to indicate the final frame of transmission by the Secondary station.

Phase modulation (PM) Transmission of information by varying the phase of a sine wave.

Phase shift keying (PSK) Another name for phase modulation.

Physical Layer Layer 1 (the lowest layer) of the OSI model, it is responsible for the transmission of bits, and is always implemented in hardware.

Physical Level The lowest level of X.25, it describes the actual interface, which conforms to the CCITT V.24/V.28 standard, and is similar to RS-232-C.

Physical Unit (PU) In SNA, the Network Addressable Unit that manages and monitors a node's resources.

PIN *See* Personal identification number.

Plain text Another name for clear text.

PM *See* Phase modulation.

Point of presence (POP)   The point where a long-distance call is handed from the local exchange carrier to the interexchange carrier.

Polling   The method used by a host computer or front end processor to ask a terminal if it has data to send.

POP   *See* Point of presence.

Port sharing device   A device that allows many terminals to share a single front end port, and is located near the front end processor; often called a concentrator.

Postal, telephone, and telegraph (PTT) administration   Government agencies in many countries that regulate and often also operate the public network.

Prefix   Another name for an office code.

Presentation Layer   Layer 6 of the OSI model, it provides format and code conversion services.

Presubscription   The method by which a customer selects a default long-distance carrier.

PRI   *See* Primary-rate interface.

Primary station   In SDLC, the single device or station that communicates with all of the other (secondary) stations.

Primary-rate interface (PRI)   The preferred method for attachment to ISDN by PBXs and LANs, it consists of 23 or 30 B-channels for user data and digitized voice, and 1 D-channel for signaling.

Print server   A shared printing device for local area network users, typically in the form of a personal computer with a high-speed printer, attached to the network.

Priority backoff   A backoff method in which each device on a network has a different backoff time, providing those with lower times a higher priority in using the network.

Private branch exchange (PBX)   A telecommunications switching system owned by the customer, it acts as an in-house central office with advanced features and capabilities.

Processing unit   The intelligent part of a front-end processor, it is actually a special-purpose computer programmed for communications functions.

Protective ground   Another name for chassis ground.

Protocol   A set of rules precisely defining the methods used to communicate.

Protocol analyzer   Another name for a datascope.

Protocol conversion   Translating data from one protocol to another.

Protocol converter A device that performs protocol conversion.

PSK Phase shift keying. *See* Phase modulation.

PSN *See* Packet switching network.

PTT *See* Postal, telephone, and telegraph administration.

PU *See* Physical Unit.

Public key An asymmetric key published in a directory; typically used for encryption, in conjunction with a secret key used for decryption.

Public network The telephone network, also called the direct distance dial network, accessed when using a home telephone.

Public packet switching network A packet switching network owned and operated for customers by service providers.

Public utilities commission (PUC) The regulating body of each state responsible for regulating intra-state phone service.

PUC *See* Public utilities commission.

Pulse code modulation (PCM) A method of digitizing normal telephone conversation.

Pulse dialing A dialing method in which a switch is opened and closed at the end of the local loop at a fixed rate of speed; also known as rotary dialing.

Pure time division multiplexing A time division multiplexing method in which the transmission speed of the trunk port is at least as great as the sum of the speeds of the branch ports, guaranteeing enough bandwidth to handle the attached devices' maximum transmission.

Quadrature amplitude modulation A modulation method used in the CCITT V.22 bis standard, that combines changes in phase and amplitude to send four bits with each baud.

R reference point In ISDN, the point between the TE2 and the TA.

Raised state The state of an RS-232-C control signal when it is on, asserted, or true.

Random access A contention method allowing devices to transmit whenever they please.

Random backoff A backoff method in which each device picks a random amount of time to wait before retransmitting after a collision.

RBOC *See* Regional Bell Operating Company.

RC *See* Receive Clock.

RD *See* Received Data.

Receive Clock (RC) The RS-232-C timing signal generated by the DCE to time synchronous data transmission from the DCE to the DTE.

Receive Common One of the RS-423-A signal returns.

Received Data (RD) The RS-232-C data signal received by the DTE from the DCE.

Receiver Not Ready (RNR) In SDLC, the Control Field message indicating a temporary busy condition.

Receiver Ready (RR) In SDLC, the Control Field message indicating data has been successfully received, and that more data can be sent.

Recommended Standards *See* RS-232-C, RS-422-A, RS-423-A, and RS-449.

Regional Bell Operating Company (RBOC) Any of seven holding companies, each a collection of local Bell Operating Companies, formed after divestiture to permit the new BOCs to remain efficient and achieve economies of scale.

Regional Holding Company (RHC) Another name for a Regional Bell Operating Company.

REJ *See* Reject.

Reject (REJ) In SDLC, the Control Field message indicating that a retransmission of data is necessary.

Reliability The ability of a network to pass data without errors, often measured using a bit or block error rate test.

Remote digital loopback test A modem diagnostic technique that can test the phone line itself as well as parts of the modem; it requires two modems, a terminal, a phone line, and a cable.

Remote intelligent controller A device, similar to a line splitter, which can also perform some front end processor functions.

Repeater Device used to keep a digital signal strong and recognizable over long distances.

Request to Send (RTS) The RS-232-C control signal generated by the DTE to ask permission to transmit data.

Resequencing A function performed by destination packet switching nodes to arrange received packets in their proper order before transmitting them to the DTE.

Response time Though its definition varies with each application, it often refers to the total amount of time it takes a message to travel from the terminal to the host computer, plus the processing time at the host computer, plus the travel time of the reply.

Reverse charging   Another name for collect calls.

RHC   Regional Holding Company. *See* Regional Bell Operating Company.

RI   *See* Ring Indicator.

Ring Indicator (RI)   The RS-232-C control signal generated by the DCE to alert the DTE that a remote device wants to initiate communications.

Ring network   A network topology where all devices are connected in a continuous loop.

Ringback signal   A signal provided by the central office to the caller to indicate that the called party's phone is being rung.

Ringing signal   A signal provided by the central office to the called party to cause the telephone to ring.

RNR   *See* Receiver Not Ready.

Robbed bit signaling   A common T-1 signaling method in which a bit is occasionally stolen from a channel to carry signaling information.

Rotary dialing   Another name for pulse dialing.

Rotary register   A device in the central office that can detect the opening and closing of a switch at the end of the local loop used in rotary or pulse dialing.

Route optimization   Another name for least-cost routing.

RR   *See* Receiver Ready.

RS-232-C   One of the most common interface standards for data communications in use today, it is an EIA standard defining exactly how ones and zeroes will be transmitted, including voltage levels needed, and other electronic signals necessary for communication.

RS-422-A   An EIA standard describing a method of balanced transmission that can be used for RS-449 Category I signals.

RS-423-A   An EIA standard describing a method of unbalanced transmission used for RS-449 Category II signals.

RS-449   An EIA standard describing the mechanical and functional characteristics of the DTE/DCE interface, and specifying the RS-422-A and RS-423-A standards for transmission.

RTS   *See* Request to Send.

S reference point   In ISDN, the point between the Network Termination equipment and the TE1 or TA.

Sample   A snapshot of a signal at a given moment, as used to digitize voice in pulse code modulation.

Satellite   An orbiting vehicle often used for communications.

Satellite dish A special antenna used to transmit signals to, or receive signals from, a satellite.

Satellite transmission Use of an orbiting satellite to repeat signals to all antennas in view of the satellite.

Screen The part of a terminal where received data is displayed.

SCTS *See* Secondary Clear to Send.

SDCD *See* Secondary Data Carrier Detect.

SDLC *See* Synchronous Data Link Control.

Sealed message A type of message that cannot be modified by an unauthorized party.

Secondary Clear to Send (SCTS) The RS-232-C Clear to Send signal for the secondary channel.

Secondary Data Carrier Detect (SDCD) The RS-232-C Data Carrier Detect signal for the secondary channel.

Secondary Received Data (SRD) The RS-232-C Received Data signal for the secondary channel.

Secondary Request to Send (SRTS) The RS-232-C Request to Send signal for the secondary channel.

Secondary station In SDLC, a device or station that communicates with the primary station; there may be several secondary stations.

Secondary Transmitted Data (STD) The RS-232-C Transmitted Data signal for the secondary channel.

Secret key A type of encryption code that is not publicly known.

Secret message A secure message that cannot be understood by an unauthorized party, and is encrypted.

Secure channel A communications link that is known to be safe from intrusion or eavesdropping.

Selecting Method used by a host computer or front end processor to ask a terminal if it is ready to receive data.

Selective repeat continuous ARQ A type of automatic repeat request whereby transmission continues until a negative acknowledgment is received, and only the frame with the error is repeated.

Send Common One of the RS-423-A signal returns.

Sequenced message A message protected against undetected loss or repetition by numbering.

Serial transmission   A method of transmission where the bits in a byte are sent one after the other on the same wire.

Service level   The criterion for acceptable network performance.

Session   In SNA, a communications path through a network.

Session Layer   Layer 5 of the OSI model, it requests that a logical connection be established or terminated, and handles logon and password procedures.

SFDM   *See* Statistical frequency division multiplexing.

S-Frame   *See* Supervisory Format Frame.

SG   See Signal Ground.

Short-haul modem   A modem that transmits data over twisted pair wire over a limited distance on a customer's premises, but not through telephone company central offices.

Signal Ground (SG)   The RS-232-C ground that acts as a zero volt reference for all other signals.

Signal Quality Detect (SQ)   The RS-232-C control signal asserted by the DCE when it perceives that transmission is of a high quality, and no errors are occurring.

Signaling   In the telephone network, information sent between devices, or between devices and users, to convey status and information, like dialed digits, busy signals, and ringing.

Signed message   A message that includes proof of the sender's identity.

Simplex communications   A one-direction communications path.

Sine wave   An electronic representation of a pure tone, it is a signal that repeats indefinitely its pattern of equal height peaks and equal depth valleys.

Smart modem   A modem that can accept dialing instructions from the user and dial the call, as well as perform the necessary modulation and demodulation.

Smart terminal   A terminal that sends extra information to a host computer, beyond what the user types, typically using a protocol containing error checking and addressing information.

SNA   *See* Systems Network Architecture.

Software encryption   A method of programming the encryption algorithm and keys into a host computer or intelligent terminal, without the use of separate encryption devices.

SOH   In BSC, the character indicating the start of the header.

Space   In RS-232-C, sending a 0, using an electrical signal between 3 and 15 volts.

Space parity   An error detection method where the parity bit is always a 0.

SQ   *See* Signal Quality Detect.

Square wave   A signal that alternates between two voltage levels almost instantaneously.

SRD   *See* Secondary Received Data.

SRTS   *See* Secondary Request to Send.

SSCP   *See* System Services Control Point.

Stamped message   A message whose receipt by the correct party is guaranteed.

Standards organization   Group or committee which devises specifications or standards for a particular industry or country.

Standby monitor   In a token ring network, station that is ready to take over the monitoring function for the active monitor, if necessary.

Star network   A network topology where each user is connected to a center point, and all data is routed through that point.

Starlan Network   A.T.&T.'s star network for connecting personal computers in an office environment.

Start bit   In asynchronous transmission, the bit sent before each character (always a 0).

Start-stop transmission   Another name for asynchronous transmission.

Star-wired ring network   A network topology where data flows in a continuous loop through each device, but the physical wiring returns to a center point between each device.

Stat mux   A device that performs multiplexing using statistical methods like statistical time division multiplexing.

Station   Another name for a device in the BSC and SDLC protocols.

Station feature   PBX function controlled by and performed for the individual user.

Station line   The circuit between a PBX and individual user's phones.

Statistical frequency division multiplexing (SFDM)   A multiplexing method continually changing the allocation of channels to accommodate the demands and needs of the attached devices.

Statistical logging   A security method providing a record of which users accessed particular ports and at what times.

Statistical time division multiplexing (STDM) A multiplexing method continually changing the allocation of time slots to accommodate the demands and needs of the attached devices.

STD *See* Secondary Transmitted Data.

STDM *See* Statistical time division multiplexing.

Stop bit In asynchronous transmission, the bit or bits sent after each character (always a 1).

Stop-and-wait ARQ A type of automatic repeat request in which transmission halts after each block, until an acknowledgment is received.

STX In BSC, the character indicating the start of user data.

Subarea In SNA, a Subarea Node and the resources that node controls.

Subarea Node In SNA, a Host Node or Communications Controller with its attached Workstations.

Submultiplexing A method of dividing an already multiplexed channel into smaller channels.

Supercomputer An extremely fast host computer dedicated to extensive mathematical calculations.

Supervisory Format Frame (S-Frame) In SDLC, the type of frame used to transfer control information, including acknowledging the accurate receipt of data.

Switch A device that routes calls to different locations, such as a PBX or central office.

Switched service A type of service requiring that a connection be made to different locations each time, as in the public telephone network, or a packet switching network.

Switching node In a packet switching network, the device that routes communications.

Symmetric keys An encryption technique using the same key to encrypt and decrypt a message.

SYN In BSC, the sync characters transmitted before the start of actual data.

Sync character In synchronous transmission, special character sent at the beginning of a block to allow the receiver to adjust to the speed of the transmitting device.

Synchronization In T-1 transmission, the timing function provided by the framing bit.

Synchronous Data Link Control (SDLC) IBM's bit-oriented, full duplex, go-back-N continuous ARQ protocol.

Synchronous transmission   A transmission method using special characters and clock signals for timing.

System feature   PBX functions performed and controlled for the entire system.

System Services Control Point (SSCP)   In SNA, the Network Addressable Unit that monitors and controls a network's resources.

Systems Network Architecture (SNA)   IBM's communications architecture that connects a wide variety of devices, it is highly flexible and versatile.

T reference point   In ISDN, the point between the NT1 and NT2.

T-1 carrier   A.T.&T.'s standard for 1.544 Mbps digital transmission over two twisted pairs.

T-1 multiplexer   A device that divides the 1.544 Mbps of T-1 bandwidth into 24 separate channels of digitized voice or data.

T-1C   A 3.152 Mbps digital transmission standard offering 48 channels.

T-3   A 44.736 Mbps digital transmission standard offering 672 channels.

TA   *See* Terminal Adapter.

Tandem office   A switch used by the local exchange carrier to route calls between central offices in the same LATA.

Tandem trunk   A circuit connecting a central office to a tandem office.

Tap   The point at which devices connect to a bus network.

Tariff   A complete description of a common carrier's service, including the rate charged for that service.

TASI   *See* Time assignment speech interpolation.

TC   *See* Transmit Clock.

TCT   *See* Toll connecting trunk.

TD   *See* Transmitted Data.

TDM   *See* Time division multiplexing.

TE   *See* Terminal Equipment.

TE1   *See* Terminal Equipment Type 1.

TE2   *See* Terminal Equipment Type 2.

Technical and Office Products (TOP)   A user-defined local area network standard developed by Boeing Computer Services, using a CSMA/CD bus network.

Telecommunications   The exchange of information, usually over a significant distance and using electronic equipment for transmission.

Telenet   A public packet switching network operated by GTE.

Terminal   A device permitting users to communicate with a computer, it typically contains a screen and a keyboard; more generally, any device at the end of a communications circuit is sometimes considered a terminal, as in ISDN.

Terminal Adapter (TA)   In ISDN, a device connected between the Terminal Equipment Type 2 and the Network Termination equipment.

Terminal Equipment (TE)   In ISDN, customer-premises equipment attached to the ISDN network that transmits or receives voice, data, or other information. Examples are digital telephones, host computers, dumb terminals, and smart terminals.

Terminal Equipment Type 1 (TE1)   In ISDN, Terminal Equipment that is compatible with the ISDN network.

Terminal Equipment Type 2 (TE2)   In ISDN, Terminal Equipment that is not compatible with the ISDN network, and can only be connected to the network through a Terminal Adapter.

Terminal handler   Another name for an external PAD.

Terrestrial microwave   A medium for transmission of data using radio waves over relatively short distances, using dish antennas with a clear line of sight between them.

30 B + D   The European version of the ISDN primary-rate interface.

Throughput   A measure of effective network transmission speed, it is the net bandwidth of a network.

Throughput class negotiation   A packet switching network service allowing DTEs to negotiate for a certain bandwidth on a virtual circuit.

Tie trunk   A telephone circuit connecting two PBXs.

Time assignment speech interpolation (TASI)   A method of sharing an intertoll trunk, in which a communications path is allocated a few milliseconds after sound is detected; this is suitable for voice communications, but can damage data transmission.

Time division   A local area network contention method based on the time division multiplexing technique.

Time division multiplexing (TDM)   A method of allowing lower-speed channels to share time on a high-speed communications circuit, by allocating separate time slots to each channel.

Time slot   The time reserved for a particular channel's communications in time division multiplexing.

Token   A pattern of ones and zeroes with a special meaning in token passing networks, typically used to control access to the networks.

Token bus A local area network using a bus topology and token passing, as in the IEEE 802.4 standard for Medium Access Control.

Token passing Using a token, typically either a free token or a busy token, to regulate access to a network.

Token ring network A local area network using a ring topology and token passing, as in the IEEE 802.5 standard for Medium Access Control, or the IBM Token Ring Network.

Toll call Another name for a long distance, or inter-LATA call.

Toll connecting trunk (TCT) A telephone circuit between the toll office and the central office.

Toll-free number A service where the called party agrees to pay the charges for all calls, also known as inward WATS.

Toll office The switching office of a long-distance carrier.

TOP *See* Technical and Office Products.

Topology The form, or physical shape, of a network.

Touch-tone dialing Another name for dual tone multifrequency dialing.

Transfer rate of information bits (TRIB) The ANSI formula for calculating throughput, it is the average rate at which users can expect the network to transport actual information bits to their destination.

Transmission Group In SNA, the communications Links between Subarea Nodes.

Transmission medium The physical path for carrying information, such as twisted pair wires, coaxial cable, fiber optic cable, terrestrial microwave, and satellite transmission methods.

Transmit Clock (TC) The RS-232-C timing signal generated by the DCE to time synchronous data transmission from the DTE to the DCE.

Transmitted Data (TD) The RS-232-C data signal sent by the DTE to the DCE.

Transparent A term often used to describe pure time division multiplexing, because its functions are not visible to the user.

Transparent data mode In BSC, a method used to send control characters as data.

Transponder The device on a satellite that receives signals from uplink stations and transmits them to downlink stations.

Transport Layer Layer 4 of the OSI model, it is responsible for isolating the function of the lower layers from the higher layers.

Tree network   A network topology similar to a bus network, but sometimes with many different branches off the main bus.

Trellis coded modulation   A modulation technique used for high speeds, usually 9600 bps and above, relying on a special error correction process.

TRIB   *See* Transfer rate of information bits.

Tributary station   In BSC, a device or station that communicates with the single Control station.

True state   The state of an RS-232-C control signal when it is asserted, ON, or raised.

Trunk   A line or circuit connecting two switches.

Trunk port   The high-speed port of a multiplexer, usually attached to the communications circuit.

23 B + D   The North American and Japanese version of the ISDN primary-rate interface.

Twinax   *See* Twinaxial Cable.

Twinaxial cable   A cable similar to coaxial cable, but with two inner conducting wires.

Twisted pair   Typically used in a local loop, it consists of two wires continuously twisted throughout its entire length.

2B + D   The ISDN basic-rate interface.

Two-wire communications   Communicating over a single pair of wires, this term is often incorrectly used as a synonym for half duplex; both half duplex and full duplex transmission can now occur over two wires.

Tymnet   A public packet switching network operated by McDonnell-Douglas.

U reference point   In ISDN, the point between the NT1 and the rest of the ISDN network.

U-Frame   *See* Unnumbered Format Frame.

Unbalanced transmission   A method of sending data requiring one wire for data, and a common return wire or reference that can be shared with other signals, as in RS-423-A.

Unified Network Management Architecture (UNMA)   A.T.&T.'s network management structure that allows for network management at a customer site or at an A.T.&T. control center.

UNMA   *See* Unified Network Management Architecture.

Unnumbered Format Frame (U-Frame)   In SDLC, the type of frame used for special functions, including establishing connections, reporting procedural problems, and special cases of data transfer.

Uplink   The satellite dish transmitting data to the satellite.

Upper Case   The portion of the Baudot character code used for the numbers and punctuation marks.

Upper layers   Another name for the higher layers of the OSI model.

Uptime   The time when a system or network is available.

V.10   The CCITT equivalent of the ANSI RS-423-A standard.

V.11   The CCITT equivalent of the ANSI RS-422-A standard.

V.21   The CCITT standard for 300 bps modulation, similar to the Bell 103/113 standard popular in the United States.

V.22   The CCITT standard for 1200 bps modulation, similar to the Bell 212A standard popular in the United States.

V.22 Bis   The CCITT standard for 2400 bps modulation, it is widely used throughout the world.

V.24   The CCITT equivalent of the signals in the ANSI RS-232-C standard.

V.28   The CCITT equivalent of the voltage levels in the ANSI RS-232-C standard.

VDT   *See* Video display terminal.

Video display terminal (VDT)   Another name for a terminal.

Video transmission   The transmission of moving images, it can be performed using analog or digital techniques.

Virtual circuit   A circuit that appears to the user like a permanent connection, it simply ensures that data is appropriately routed, using the network's resources only when data is transmitted.

Voice call multiplexing   A method of sharing an intertoll trunk where there is no additional risk of losing voice or data.

Voice grade circuit   A standard telecommunications circuit.

WACK   In BSC, the control character indicating that the device is temporarily busy, but will be ready soon.

WAN   *See* Wide area network.

WATS   *See* Wide-area telecommunications services.

Western Electric   A.T.&T.'s equipment manufacturing organization.

Wide area network (WAN) A network covering a large geographical area, such as a packet switching network.

Wide-area telecommunications services (WATS) A bulk rate, long-distance service for business users with high call volume.

Workstation The SNA term for a terminal.

X.3 The CCITT standard for the functions and parameters of an internal PAD.

X.25 The CCITT standard for connecting a DTE to a packet switching network.

X.28 The CCITT standard for connecting a DTE to an internal PAD in a packet switching network.

X.29 The CCITT standard for communications between an internal PAD and the remote host computer.

XON/XOFF ASCII control characters that can be used to start and stop host computer transmission.

XTC *See* External Transmit Clock.

BIBLIOGRAPHY

A general listing of data communications books is provided first, followed by a suggested reading list of books and articles for each chapter in this book.

GENERAL DATA COMMUNICATIONS BOOKS

Abrams, Marshall, and Ira. W. Cotton, eds., *Computer Networks: A Tutorial* (4th ed.). New York: IEEE Computer Society Press, 1984.

Benedetto, Sergio, Ezio Biglieri, and Valentino Castellani, *Digital Transmission Theory.* Englewood Cliffs, N.J.: Prentice-Hall, Inc., 1987.

Black, Uyless D., *Computer Networks: Protocols, Standards, and Interfaces.* Englewood Cliffs, N.J.: Prentice-Hall, Inc., 1987.

Black, Uyless D., *Data Communications and Distributed Networks* (2nd ed.). Englewood Cliffs, N.J.: Prentice-Hall, Inc., 1987.

The Executive Guide to Data Communications (Vol. 8). New York: McGraw-Hill Book Company, 1987.

Fitzgerald, Jerry, *Business Data Communications: Basic Concepts, Security, and Design.* New York: John Wiley & Sons, Inc., 1984.

Folts, Harold C., ed., *McGraw-Hill's Compilation of Data Communications Standards,* (3rd ed.). New York: McGraw-Hill Book Company, 1986.

Freeman, Harvey A., and Kenneth J. Thurber, eds., *Local Network Equipment*. New York: IEEE Computer Society Press, 1985.

Hamming, Richard W., *Coding and Information Theory* (2nd ed.). Englewood Cliffs, N.J.: Prentice-Hall, Inc., 1986.

Housley, Trevor, *Data Communications and Teleprocessing Systems* (2nd ed.). Englewood Cliffs, N.J.: Prentice-Hall, Inc., 1987.

Lam, Simon S., ed., *Tutorial: Principles of Communication and Networking Protocols*. New York: IEEE Computer Society Press, 1984.

Sherman, Ken, *Data Communications: A Users Guide* (2nd ed.), Englewood Cliffs, N.J.: Prentice-Hall, Inc., 1985.

Stallings, William, *Data and Computer Communications*. New York: Macmillan Publishing Company, 1985.

Stallings, William, ed., *Tutorial: Computer Communications: Architectures, Protocols, and Standards*. New York: IEEE Computer Society Press, 1985.

Stallings, William, ed., *Tutorial: Local Network Technology*. New York: IEEE Computer Society Press, 1985.

Tanenbaum, Andrew S., *Computer Networks*. Englewood Cliffs, N.J.: Prentice-Hall, Inc., 1981.

Williams, Richard A., *Communication Systems Analysis Design: A Systems Approach*. Englewood Cliffs, N.J.: Prentice-Hall, Inc., 1987.

CHAPTER 2:
UNDERSTANDING TELECOMMUNICATIONS

Borsook, Paulina, "Specter of incompatibility raised about ONA offerings," *Data Communications*, November 1987.

Divestiture Speak. Santa Clara, Calif.: ROLM, An IBM Company, 1985.

Graham, John, *The Facts on File Dictionary of Telecommunications*. New York: Facts on File, Inc., 1983.

Green, James Harry, *The Dow Jones-Irwin Handbook of Telecommunications*. Homewood, Ill.: Dow Jones-Irwin, 1986.

Moffett, R. H., "Echo and delay problems in some digital communications systems," *IEEE Communications*, August 1987.

Rey, R. F., ed., *Engineering and Operations in the Bell System* (2nd ed.). Murray Hill, N.J. : A.T. & T. Bell Laboratories, 1983.

Telecommunications and You (2nd ed.). White Plains, N.Y.: International Business Machines Corporation, 1987.

Wolfson, Joel R., "Computer III: the beginning or the beginning of the end for enhanced services competition," *IEEE Communications*, August 1987.

CHAPTER 3:
BASIC DATA COMMUNICATIONS CONCEPTS

Data Communications Concepts (2nd ed.). White Plains, N.Y.: International Business Machines Corporation, 1987.

Touring Datacomm, A Data Communications Primer. Cupertino, Calif.: Hewlett-Packard Company, 1983.

CHAPTER 4:
DATA INTERFACES AND TRANSMISSION

Connecting to Your Computer. Cupertino, Calif.: Hewlett-Packard Company, 1984.

Ferguson, David D., "New digital network service capabilities," *Proceedings of the IEEE International Conference on Communications*, 1987.

Folts, Harold C., "A powerful standard replaces the old interface standby," *Data Communications*, May 1980.

Hansen, Richard C., "A.T.& T.'s digital network evolution," *Proceedings of the IEEE International Conference on Communications*, 1987.

Kaiser, Peter, John Midwinter, and Sadakuni Shimada, "Status and future trends in terrestrial optical fiber systems in North America, Europe, and Japan," *IEEE Communications*, October 1987.

Nagel, Suzanne R., "Optical fiber—the expanding medium," *IEEE Communications*, April 1987.

Pahlavan, Kaveh and Jerry L. Holsinger, "Voice-band communication modems—a historical review: 1919–1988," *IEEE Communications*, January 1988.

Pruitt, James B., "The real case for microwave," *Computer and Communications Decisions*, August 1987.

Wilkens, William B., "Standards for communications," *IEEE Communications*, July 1987.

CHAPTER 5:
IMPROVING DATA COMMUNICATIONS EFFICIENCY

Boyd, Joseph A., "Communications cost-containment through high technology," *Journal of Telecommunications Networks*, Summer 1982.

Hoffman, Darlane, "Squeezing line costs via data compression," *Data Communications*, August 1987.

CHAPTER 6:
DATA INTEGRITY AND SECURITY

Abrams, Marshall D., and Albert B. Jeng, "Network security: protocol reference model and the trusted computer system evaluation criteria," *IEEE Network*, April 1987.

Branstad, Dennis K., "Considerations for security in the OSI architecture," *IEEE Network*, April 1987.

Folts, Hal, "Open systems standards," *IEEE Network*, April 1987.

Hellman, Martin E., "Commercial encryption," *IEEE Network*, April 1987.

Newman, David B., Jr., Jim K. Omura, and Raymond L. Pickholtz, "Public key management for network security," *IEEE Network*, April 1987.

Zorpette, Glenn, "Breaking the enemy's code," *IEEE Spectrum*, September 1987.

CHAPTER 7:
ARCHITECTURES AND PROTOCOLS

Bass, Charlie, "Data networks' endangered and protected species," *Data Communications*, October 1987.

Bonnet, Luther, *SNA Fundamentals*. Chicago: Science Research Associates, An IBM Company, 1987.

Carlson, David E., "Bit-oriented data link control procedures," *IEEE Transactions on Communications*, April 1980.

Communicating with IBM. Cupertino, Calif.: Hewlett-Packard Company, 1984.

Conrad, James W., "Character-oriented data link control protocols," *IEEE Transactions on Communications*, April 1980.

General Information: Binary Synchronous Communications (3rd ed.). White Plains, N.Y.: International Business Machines Corporation, 1970.

Lam, Simon S., "Data Link Control Procedures," in *Computer Communications, Vol. 1: Principles*, W. Chou, ed.: Englewood Cliffs, N.J.: Prentice-Hall, Inc., 1983.

Martin, James, with Kathleen Kavanagh Chapman, *SNA: IBM's Networking Solution*. Englewood Cliffs, N.J.: Prentice-Hall, Inc., 1987.

Rothberg, Michael, "The architecture battle," *Computer and Communications Decisions*, January 1988.

Stix, Gary, "Special report: heeding a call to distribute," *Computer Decisions*, January 1987.

Stix, Gary, "Special report: peer pressure," *Computer and Communications Decisions*, January 1988.

Systems Network Architecture, Concepts and Products (4th ed.). White Plains, N.Y.: International Business Machines Corporation, 1986.

Systems Network Architecture, Formats (9th ed.). White Plains, N.Y.: International Business Machines Corporation, 1987.

Systems Network Architecture, Technical Overview (3rd ed.). White Plains, N.Y.: International Business Machines Corporation, 1986.

Synchronous Data Link Control Concepts (4th ed.). White Plains, N.Y.: International Business Machines Corporation, 1986.

Weissberger, Alan J., "Bit oriented data link controls," *Computer Design*, March 1983.

CHAPTER 8:
DATA TRANSPORT NETWORKS

Cooper, Edward, *Broadband Network Technology: An Overview for the Data and Telecommunications Industries*. Englewood Cliffs, N.J.: Prentice-Hall, Inc., 1986.

Cotton, Ira W., "Technologies for local area computer networks," *Computer Networks*, November 1980.

Dixon, Roy C., "Lore of the token ring," *IEEE Network*, January 1987.

Farowich, Steven, "Communicating in the technical office," *IEEE Spectrum*, April 1986.

Folts, Hal, "Open systems standards," *IEEE Network*, January 1987.

Francett, Barbara, "MAP confronts the real world," *Computer and Communications Decisions*, November 1987.

Goldberg, Glenn, "Unshielded twisted-pair wiring can overcome Ethernet cabling woes," *Computer Technology Review*, Fall 1987.

Kaminski, Michael A., Jr., "Protocols for communicating in the factory," *IEEE Spectrum*, April 1986.

Kummerle, K., and M. Reiser, "Local-area communication networks—an overview," *Journal of Telecommunication Networks*, Winter 1982.

Langdal, James, "Systems integrators' MAP to the promised LAN," *Systems and Software*, October 1985.

Making the LAN Connection. Cupertino, Calif.: Hewlett-Packard Company, 1984.

Markov, J. D. and N. C. Strole, "Token-ring local area networks: a perspective," *Proceedings of COMPCON F82*, 1982.

Metcalfe, Robert M., and David R. Boggs, "Ethernet: distributed packet switching for local computer networks," *Communications of the ACM*, July 1976.

Networking with X.25. Cupertino, Calif.: Hewlett-Packard Company, 1985.

Pitt, Daniel, "Standards for the token ring," *IEEE Network*, January 1987.

Reiss, Leszek, *Introduction to Local Area Networks with Microcomputer Experiments*. Englewood Cliffs, N.J.: Prentice-Hall, Inc., 1987.

Ross, Floyd E., "Rings are 'round for good!" *IEEE Network*, January 1987.

Rybczybski, Antony, "X.25 interface and end-to-end virtual circuit service characteristics," *IEEE Transactions on Communications*, April 1980.

Saltzer, Jerome H., David D. Clark, and Kenneth T. Pogran, "Why a ring," *Proceedings of the 7th Data Communications Symposium*, 1981.

Stallings, William, "Beyond local networks," *Datamation*, August 1983.

Strole, Norman C., "The IBM token-ring network—a functional overview," *IEEE Network*, January 1987.

Weissberger, Alan J., "Bit oriented data link controls," *Computer Design*, March 1983.

Willett, Michael, "Token-ring local area networks—An Introduction," *IEEE Network*, January 1987.

CHAPTER 9:
NETWORK MANAGEMENT

Boyd, Richard C., Alan R. Johnston, "Network operations and management in a multi-vendor environment," *IEEE Communications*, July 1987.

Cameron, W. H., C. LaCerte, and J. F. Noyes, "Integrated network operations architecture and its application to network maintenance," *IEEE Communications*, August 1987.

Data Communications Testing. Colorado Springs, Colo.: Hewlett-Packard Company, 1980.

Rosenberg, Robert, "Are users up in the air over network management?" *Data Communications*, December 1987.

Salazar, A. C., P. J. Scarfo and R. J. Horn III, "Network management systems for data communications," *IEEE Communications*, August 1987.

Taylor, Floyd, "Data comm testing," *Computer/Electronic Service News*, October 1982.

Terplan, Kornel, *Communications Network Management*. Englewood Cliffs, N.J.: Prentice-Hall, Inc., 1987.

CHAPTER 10:
THE FUTURE OF DATA COMMUNICATIONS

Armbruster, Heinrich, and Gerhard Arndt, "Broadband communication and its realization with broadband ISDN," *IEEE Communications*, November 1987.

Borsook, Paulina, " 'U' marks the critical spot for user interface to ISDN," *Data Communications*, October 1987.

Chen, Po, "How to make the most of ISDN's new LAPD protocol," *Data Communications*, August 1987.

Chester, Jeffrey A., "The price is right for T1 communications," *Infosystems*, April 1987.

Chu, N. N. Y., and P. B. Deleski, "ISDN readiness assessment," *Proceedings of the IEEE International Conference on Communications*, 1987.

Falek, James I., and Mary A. Johnston, "Standards makers cementing ISDN subnetwork layers," *Data Communications*, October 1987.

Guinn, Donald E., "ISDN: is the technology on target?" *IEEE Communications*, December 1987.

Herman, James G., and Mary A. Johnston, "ISDN when? What your firm can do in the interim," *Data Communications*, October 1987.

Kemezis, Paul, "What price ISDN? First cost details bared," *Data Communications*, August 1987.

Mier, Edwin E., "Are analog local loops too 'dirty' for ISDN?" *Data Communications*, July 1987.

Pandhi, Sushil N., "The universal data connection," *IEEE Spectrum*, July 1987.

Pruitt, James B., "Stepping up to T-3," *Computer and Communications Decisions*, November 1987.

Russotto, Thomas V., "The integration of voice and data communications," *IEEE Network*, October 1987.

Sazegari, Steven A., "Network architects plan broadening of future ISDN," *Data Communications*, July 1987.

Skrzypczak, Casimir S., "The intelligent home of 2010," *IEEE Communications*, December 1987.

Stallings, William, ed., *Tutorial: Integrated Services Digital Networks (ISDN)*. New York: IEEE Computer Society Press, 1985.

Strauss, Paul R., "Small is beautiful: new T1 muxes stress savings," *Data Communications*, January 1988.

Strauss, Paul R., "Squeeze play: carriers quietly trying compressed voice; users could soon squeeze big savings," *Data Communications*, July 1987.

Tang, W. Victor, "ISDN—new vistas in information processing," *IEEE Communications*, November 1986.

Watanabe, Hitoshi, "Integrated office systems: 1995 and beyond," *IEEE Communications*, December 1987.

Weinstein, Stephen B., "Telecommunications in the coming decades," *IEEE Spectrum*, November 1987.

INDEX

INDEX

RS-232-C, *(cont.)*
    data signals, 55–56, 62–63
    ground signals, 56–57, 62–63
    handshaking, 59–61
    secondary signals, 59, 62–63
    timing signals, 57, 62–63
RS-422-A, 61–64
RS-423-A, 61–64
RS-449, 61–64
RTS. *See* Request to Send

S reference point, 193–95
Sample, 185–86
Satellite, 72
    dish, 72–73
    transmission, 72–75
Screen, 30
SCTS. *See* Secondary Clear To Send
SDCD. *See* Secondary Data Carrier Detect
SDLC. *See* Synchronous Data Link Control
Sealed message, 112
Secondary Clear To Send (SCTS), 56, 59, 62–63
Secondary Data Carrier Detect (SDCD), 56, 59, 62–63
Secondary Received Data (SRD), 56, 59, 62–63
Secondary Request To Send (SRTS), 56, 59, 62–63
Secondary station, 141–43
Secondary Transmitted Data (STD), 56, 59, 62–63
Secret key, 115–19
Secret message, 112
Secure channel, 116
Secure transmission facilities, 113
Security, 111–19
    concerns, 112
    goals, 112
    importance of, 111
    measures, 112–13
Selecting, 89, 136, 156–57
Selective repeat continuous ARQ, 136–37
Send Common, 62–64
Sequenced message, 112
Serial/parallel conversion, 89
Serial transmission, 40–41
Servers, 153–54
Service level, 168–72
Session, 131–32
Session Layer, 125–27
SFDM. *See* Statistical frequency division multiplexing
S-Frame. *See* Supervisory Format Frame
SG. *See* Signal Ground
Short-haul modem, 81–82
Signal:
    busy, 8–9
    clock, 43–44, 57, 62–63
    dial tone, 8–9
    howler, 8–9
    off-hook, 8–9
    on-hook, 8–9
    ringback, 8–9
    ringing, 8–9
    RS-232-C control, 56–63
    RS-232-C data, 55–56, 62–63
    RS-232-C ground, 55–57, 62–63
    RS-232-C secondary, 59, 62–63
    RS-232-C timing, 57, 62–63
Signal Ground (SG), 56–57, 62–63
Signal Quality Detect (SQ), 56, 59, 62–63
Signaling, 7–10, 188–89, 191–93

    common-channel, 191–93
    in-band, 190–93
    out-of-band, 191–93
    robbed bit, 188–89
Signature, digital, 117–18
Signed message, 112
Simplex communications, 45–48
Sine wave, 68–69
Smart modem, 76
Smart terminal, 30
SNA. *See* Systems Network Architecture
Software, applications, 29–30
Software encryption, 119
SOH, 140
Sources of errors, 105–7
Space, 53
Space parity, 107–9
SQ. *See* Signal Quality Detect
Square wave, 64–66
SRD. *See* Secondary Received Data
SRTS. *See* Secondary Request To Send
SSCP. *See* System Services Control Point
Stamped message, 112
Standards, digital interface, 51–64
Standards organizations, 51–52
Standby monitor, 160–61
Star network, 6, 8, 154–56, 162
Starlan Network, 162
Start bit, 41–45
Start-stop transmission, 41–45
Star-wired ring network, 154–56
Stat Mux. *See* Statistical time division multiplexing.
Station:
    Control, 137–40
    downlink, 72–73
    Primary, 141–43
    Secondary, 141–43
    Tributary, 137–40
    uplink, 72–73
Station feature, 23–25
Station line, 22
Statistical frequency division multiplexing (SFDM), 98–99
Statistical logging, 89, 113–14
Statistical time division multiplexing (STDM), 96–98
STD. *See* Secondary Transmitted Data
STDM. *See* Statistical time division multiplexing
Stop bit, 41–45
Stop-and-wait ARQ, 136–37
STX, 140
Subarea, 132–35
Subarea Node, 132–35
Submultiplexing, 187–89
Supercomputer, 30
Supervisory Format Frame (S-frame), 141–43
Suppressor, echo, 18–19
Switch, central office, 7
Switched service, 75–76, 147–53
Switching node, 148–53
Symmetric keys, 117
SYN, 139–40
Sync character, 43–45, 139–40
Synchronization, 187–89
Synchronous Data Link Control (SDLC), 141–43
Synchronous transmission, 41–45
Synchronous transmission efficiency, 44–45
System feature, 23–26
System Services Control Point (SSCP), 130–35
Systems Network Architecture (SNA), 128–35

Index   267